PELICAN BOOKS

A911

THE PSYCHOLOGY OF CHILDHOOD
AND ADOLESCENCE

C. I. SANDSTRÖM

The Psychology of Childhood and Adolescence

TRANSLATED BY
ALBERT READ

PENGUIN BOOKS

Penguin Books Ltd, Harmondsworth, Middlesex, England
Penguin Books Inc., 7110 Ambassador Road, Baltimore, Maryland 21207, U.S.A.
Penguin Books Australia Ltd, Ringwood, Victoria, Australia
—
Original Swedish edition entitled
Barn- och ungdompsykologi
first published by Almqvist & Wiksell/Gebers Förlag AB, Stockholm
English translation published by Methuen 1966
Published in Pelican Books 1968
Reprinted 1969
Copyright © Almqvist & Wiksell/Gebers Förlag AB, 1961
Translation copyright © Penguin Books Ltd, 1966
—
Made and printed in Great Britain
by Hazell Watson & Viney Ltd
Aylesbury, Bucks
Set in Monotype Times Roman

CONTENTS

Contents

Contents

EDITORIAL FOREWORD

This book differs in some important ways from most of the texts in Methuen's Manuals of Modern Psychology. Volumes in this series are addressed in the main to students or to specialists in some fields of theoretical or applied psychology. They are intermediate texts – intermediate in several ways. They are intermediate in scope, something between general texts and monographs. They are intermediate in level, half-way between the books for beginners and those for advanced students, and as such generally presuppose some prior studies in psychology.

This book is rather different. Though very successful as a text for university students and teachers in training colleges in Sweden it has also been something of a 'best seller' to the general reader and to young parents who take an intelligent interest in the development of their children.

Its author writes with authority as a psychologist. A pupil of, and assistant to, Professor David Katz of Stockholm (the latter known to readers of these Manuals as the author of the volume on Gestalt Psychology), he made an original contribution to the psychology of space-perception in a Ph.D. dissertation. Soon after he was appointed Assistant Professor of Education and Educational Psychology at the University of Uppsala. He was one of the founders of the *Scandinavian Journal of Psychology* and has been its Editor since its foundation in 1960. He is also the Swedish editor of *Acta Psychologica*. He is known in England through his lectures in 1957 at Oxford, Cambridge and London.

Among the features of this book likely to be of special interest to parents and teachers are the fairly detailed 'norms of development' it contains. It may not be necessary, but it can do no harm, to draw attention to the ambiguities in this tricky concept of 'a norm'.

'A norm' can be a standard to be aimed at. 'Normal health' is, roughly, the condition of freedom from disease or disability. Normal development can be defined in a series of stages which a child can be desired to attain in each year of its life. On the other hand norms can be defined in terms of *averages* or other representative measures. Normal intelligence is defined in terms of levels of intelligence which the *average* child attains, as measured by intelligence tests, in a given population. Some confusion arises from the fact that norms, as averages, can be taken to be certain *minimum* standards to be aimed at. But published norms must be treated with caution. They are relative to the population from which they are obtained. Many of them are subject to variations in rates of development. Some 'late developers' overtake the more precocious. So anxious parents need not be unduly anxious if their child is below the norm. Nor for that matter should proud parents be unduly proud if their child is in advance of the norm. After all, good parenthood and good education does count for something. So parents can be advised to take their child to a clinic only when deviations from 'the norm' are very marked. The author of this book is anxious to avoid moralizing or sermonizing, but these reflections are explicit in the text, and need have only to be underlined.

The Editor as well as the Author owes much to Vida Carver for her assistance in preparing the English edition of this book.

C. A. MACE

PREFACE

This book was written to satisfy a demand for an introductory text-book in the psychology of childhood and adolescence for Swedish teachers' training colleges and elementary courses in psychology and education at university level. The aim was to write a survey, not exceeding about 250 pages, of the more important problems.

I considered it best to base the discussion on experimental studies, and to avoid speculation and sermonizing. Experiments concerned with perception psychology have perhaps been considered and adapted to developmental psychology more than is usual in a work of this kind. But there must always be different opinions about what should be included in a textbook and how much space should be allotted to the various problems.

An English reader may perhaps find it somewhat surprising that reference is made to so few Swedish studies. It has not been my ambition to cite as many Swedish sources as possible, and more-over discussion and references concerned with specifically Swedish conditions have been excluded from this edition. The last chapter in particular, *Children at School*, which dealt with Swedish prob-lems, has been revised to suit British conditions, for which revision, and for many other valuable suggestions, I am much indebted to Mrs Vida Carver.

C. I. SANDSTRÖM

Chapter I

INTRODUCTION

The capacity to react to stimuli is characteristic of all living creatures. The nature and extent of this ability varies from one species to another; and it takes time for it to become fully developed. Lower organisms reach full development more quickly than higher ones. A newly hatched chicken remains close to the hen for protection, but it can find its own food immediately. It learns the technique of pecking very early, but (as shown in Fig. I.1) training and maturation are of great importance to the perfection of the technique. More primitive animals show still more rapid adjustment to their surroundings. Among mammals, on the other hand, the time the young need the care of their mothers is increased in proportion to the prenatal period. The more complicated an organism is, the longer the time it takes to adjust itself to its surroundings.

THE ADJUSTMENT OF MAN

There is no organism that requires a longer period of adjustment than man. For nine months the child is in its mother's womb. After birth it can continue to grow independently, but this independence is restricted for some time. The infant is helpless even in such essential things as the satisfaction of hunger and thirst, and is unable alone to find shelter from cold and heat. The chicken can immediately move about, and its actions are goal-directed. A child, on the other hand, during the greater part of its first year simply lies where it is put, and if it is to survive it must be helped in many ways.

The maturation of a human being does not only mean the physiological process but also – and this is even more important – incorporation into the society man has created. This prolongs considerably the time required for human beings to attain maturity. Boys and girls become capable of reproduction during puberty, but are not often ready at this age to raise families of their own.

Fig. I.1. Newly hatched chickens can peck grain very skilfully, but the curves (from a study by Cruze) show that both practice and maturation contribute to improve the rèsults. The different experimental groups were kept in a dark room, and their degree of hunger was controlled by feeding each chicken with the same amount of food from the experimenter's hand. Only at trials were the chickens allowed to peck grains of corn (25, one at a time, each miss being noted) under good lighting conditions. The first trial with group A was made the same day as the chickens were hatched, that with group B the day after hatching and so on.

The ability to cope with all the responsibilities of family and occupational life is seldom attained before the twenties. The more complicated a society is, the greater are the demands on this ability. The knowledge and skill that the individual needs to deal with even simple social problems are acquired only by long and purposeful training. The role of the school has never been more significant than it is today.

It is essential to learn *how* to learn. To understand this we must know something about the principles underlying the behaviour of an organism. Many branches of psychology can throw light on these principles.

DEFINITION AND SCOPE OF DEVELOPMENTAL PSYCHOLOGY

Psychology is the science of behaviour. The aspects of psychology to be dealt with in this book are concerned with the development of behaviour in human beings from their earliest stages of life to the age at which their most important functions have become mature.

'Developmental psychology' is the term used for this kind of study of behaviour. Child psychology and the psychology of adolescence are its main branches.

The concept of development

From the very beginning of life up to old age and death, human beings are subjected to innumerable internal and external influences. Two terms often used in this context are 'heredity' and 'environment'. The way a human being functions in a given situation is a product of the influences emanating from these two factors.

The word used to describe these processes is 'development'. Applied to the whole life cycle of an organism, this term covers not only growth and maturation, but also stagnation and decline. Usually, however, we mean by development the processes that lead to greater strength and stability, and it is in this meaning the term is used here.

In biology there is a distinction between *phylogenesis* and *ontogenesis*. By 'phylogenesis' we mean the evolution of a species of animal (e.g. man) through innumerable centuries. By 'ontogenesis' we mean the evolution and development of the individual organism. In this book we shall be mainly concerned with ontogenetics, that is to say, with problems connected with the normal development of the behaviour of individuals.

The starting point for a study of behaviour is before birth. The prenatal stage in the development of an organism is of considerable interest to the psychologist.

Sequential development

Both physical and mental development seem to be subject to definite sequences. Every stage of development is dependent on the previous stage. A child crawls before it walks and prattles before it talks. It grips an object with the whole of its hand before it can press its thumb against its fingers and use its hand as an effective gripping tool.

It also seems possible to distinguish separate rhythmic periods, characterized by mental balance or its absence. Thus at one stage of development a child is comparatively difficult to handle, at another it is more accessible. The ages of two, five, ten and sixteen years are considered to be stages at which behaviour is characterized by good mental balance.

It is an axiom of developmental psychology that the time of appearance of a characteristic feature, and its prominence, vary widely from one individual to another. But the sequences and periods still seem to be present, though it is very difficult to say how late in life the idea of sequences and periods is applicable. Anthropological studies of simpler and more harmonious societies have produced different results to those of our culture.

Growth, maturation and learning

Growth refers primarily to physical development: the stabilization of the skeleton, increase in height and weight, changes in the internal organs and so on. Growth and the development of behaviour are intimately related to each other. The body and its organs must develop in order to make possible the changes in behaviour that are a characteristic of different ages.

By *maturation* is meant the attainment of a particular level of functional ability which makes possible the achievement of a certain pattern of behaviour. Maturation must always be regarded as relative.

Learning is generally considered to mean modification of behaviour. Education implies modifications that are the results of the conscious and goal-directed influence of other individuals, in the first place parents and teachers. Social training, which includes the adjustment of human beings to their environment, is especially important. Learning has to do with almost all aspects of behaviour.

The integration of behaviour

It is difficult, but very necessary to decide which are important and which unimportant among the multitude of behavioural traits. This book deals only with the most central aspects of the general psychological development of human beings. The problems chosen are those to which most attention has been paid and which may therefore be assumed to be the most vital ones.

A human being is a unit. He functions as an integral whole. The division of this book into chapters, each dealing with a separate aspect of behaviour, is for convenience only. The fact that emotional development is treated in one chapter and social development in another, for example, does not mean that these two aspects have no connection with each other.

A survey of physical development may seem out of place in a book on psychology but we have already pointed out that growth exerts immediate influence on behaviour. Physical disturbances cause disturbances in the development of behaviour. We will meet with many examples of this later. The functioning of the endocrine glands is a clear case in point.

Thus we cannot separate behaviour (function) from the physical conditions (structure) or, as it has often been expressed, the 'soul' from the 'body'. They are essential to each other. Each human being, like any other organism, forms a unified system of action. In its behaviour, this system reflects the biological governing mechanisms (heredity) which, within certain limits, are characteristic of the species. It also reflects the results of the external influences (environment) to which these governing mechanisms are exposed.

PRACTICAL APPLICATIONS OF DEVELOPMENTAL PSYCHOLOGY

It should now be apparent that developmental psychology is a wide field of research, with complicated problems. Few of these problems are simple ones, and few have been solved completely. As is only natural, both teachers and parents show great interest in the study of child and adolescent psychology. Sometimes, however, this has been a disadvantage. The findings which are taken as the basis of applied psychology are not always fully valid, and are seldom wholly unambiguous.

The picture of the perplexed mother with a child over her knee, a cane in one hand and a book on psychology in the other, pokes fun not only at the poor mother, but also at child psychology. Psychology can contribute towards a generally intelligent attitude to problems of bringing up children, but it cannot replace common sense. Teachers who accept uncritically the results of intelligence tests probably allow them to have too much influence on their opinion of a pupil's abilities. The results of such testings or of standard achievement tests must not be allowed to give a teacher the impression that he is incompetent to form his own personal opinions about his pupils.

Psychology has no use for simple faith. A single incision is not enough to reveal all the physiological mechanisms that make up a growing person, and the shortcomings and idiosyncrasies of human beings cannot be confined in a formula or figure. One characteristic of successful parents and teachers has always been the will to understand the individuality of the child. Patience is a happy gift for those responsible for assisting the development of individuals.

SURVEY OF CONTENTS

Many aspects of developmental psychology are dealt with in general textbooks of psychology. This book does not presuppose acquaintance with general psychology, but such acquaintance may be helpful.

The first section of Chapter II, which gives a *historical survey*, indicates, among other things, how developmental psychology is connected with other aspects of psychology. Many workers in other branches have contributed greatly to child and adolescent psychology. The remainder of Chapter II deals with *research methods*.

Chapters III and IV *outline the development of a child up to the age of ten years*. The prenatal period is described, and it is shown that elementary learning can be observed towards the end of the

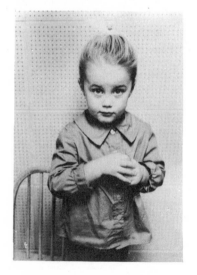

Fig. I.2. A child once asked, 'Do grown-ups know all about children?' Many teachers and parents seem to think so. A Swedish author wrote that there are things one must be expert in not to understand.

foetal stage. The account of the development of behaviour contained in these two chapters is necessarily sketchy and could be misleading to a reader who failed to bear in mind the immense variety in behaviour displayed by 'normal' human beings. This survey of development is continued in Chapters XIII and XIV which deal with puberty.

Physical growth is the subject of Chapter V and is also discussed in the first chapter on puberty (Chapter XIII). The decisive influence of the endocrine glands on both physical and mental development is stressed.

Chapters VI and VII are concerned with the concept of *learning*. In the first of these chapters it is related to *perception*. An important problem is how the interaction between them is generated and developed. In Chapter VII learning is considered in connection with *motivation* – a concept sometimes defined as the energy-creating and guiding processes behind the activities of an organism. There can be no learning without such processes. A number of general learning problems are also treated in these two chapters from the aspect of developmental psychology. Part of Chapter XI is devoted to social learning. Its importance to the development of human behaviour is discussed on several occasions.

The development of *language* is closely connected with that of *thought* (Chapter VIII). Language may be regarded as a prerequisite of development of human thought. Language and thought are also the objects of fundamental learning actions, and are therefore dealt with immediately after the chapters on learning. Chapter IX is concerned with the *development of intelligence*, and also gives specimens of different so-called 'factor' tests for different ages.

Three chapters (X, XI and XII) are devoted to *emotional* and *social development* and the *development of personality*. The greater part of Chapter XII deals with methods of investigation.

Chapters XIII and XIV are devoted to *problems of adolescence*. The account of the development of behaviour closes with the period of puberty and its transition into adolescence proper.

The last chapter (XV) is mainly practical. It deals with some problems concerning *the child at school*. Side by side with the home, the school is the most important organ in society for the social incorporation of the individual. The school is today especially responsible for social education, and questions connected with this aspect of education are discussed in that chapter.

Chapter II

SURVEY OF HISTORY
AND METHODS

There has never before been such keen interest in why children behave as they do, why they are obstinate and disobedient, why young people pass through puberty crises, and why it is so difficult for them to adjust themselves to the world of adults. Yet the fact that such questions are difficult to answer is not a discovery of our time. The history of education shows that such problems have always existed.

The study of child and adolescent psychology has arisen out of educational needs and problems. The history of modern psychology shows, too, how closely education and psychology are related.

A SHORT HISTORY

Many educational-psychological problems of development that are still of current interest were discussed in ancient times. Both Socrates and Plato showed great interest in education, but from the point of view of developmental psychology Quintilianus, a Roman rhetorician, is particularly interesting. His views on the bad effects of corporal punishment and on the value of comradeship in school life, in contrast to the private instruction that was then the rule in Rome, are relevant today.

Like many ancient writers, Quintilianus was rediscovered at the beginning of modern times. His views stimulated educational thought, which had been rather neglected during the Middle Ages. The most influential of the sixteenth-century humanists, Erasmus of Rotterdam, agreed with Quintilianus' views on corporal punishment, and denied categorically its moral significance in education. He also stressed the part played by interest in learning.

During the seventeenth century Comenius, one of the most prominent figures in the history of education, stressed the necessity of taking the individuality of the child into consideration. Locke, towards the end of the same century, expressed the view that a child has natural inclinations and interests, but that they should be curbed on account of the sinful nature of man. Such views dominated the debate well into the eighteenth century.

Rousseau's gospel

Rousseau, with his gospel of the natural goodness of man, opposed the view that man is vile. His educational novel, *Émile*, published in 1762, was probably, more than any other work, the cause of the lively discussion that has been going on ever since then, and has been an important contributory factor in the rise of modern child psychology. In Rousseau's sermon on a return to nature, the education of the child was naturally a central theme. Adults should not force their opinions and behaviour on children. The child's own gifts and interests should be the guiding principles, and consideration should be paid to the wishes and impulses of the child.

The decades following the publication of *Émile* saw the beginnings of systematic studies of the development of children. The best-known work is Tiedemann's biographical account of the physical and mental development of his children (1787). Pestalozzi, whose theories of education had enormous influence on nineteenth-century thought, wrote a similar account. The following quotation from one of his main works shows how much he was influenced by Rousseau: *Man is good, and strives to attain goodness, and if he is evil it is because the path to goodness has been closed to him.*

Fröbel, the founder of the kindergarten system, was greatly inspired by Pestalozzi. He was a pioneer of education during the years before formal schooling began. His views on the continuity of development have been generally accepted in modern developmental psychology.

Darwin and the theory of evolution

Doubts about the validity of the biological views contained in the theory of preformation were expressed during the nineteenth century. According to this theory, all parts of a perfect organism exist in the germ, which is nothing but a miniature model. Growth simply implies an enlargement of the model. The theory was finally abandoned after Darwin's theory of evolution had been generally acknowledged.

Darwin brings us to the beginnings of modern psychology. Child psychology was naturally the first branch of general psychology to appear, because of its close relationship to the theory of evolution. Darwin made a direct contribution to child psychology by the publication in 1877 of *A Biographical Sketch of an Infant*. It was an old manuscript, begun early in 1840 when his first son was a few days old.

'My first child was born on December 27, 1839, and I at once commenced to make notes on the first dawn of the various experiences which he exhibited, for I felt convinced, even at this early period, that the most complex and fine shades of expression must all have a gradual and natural origin,' wrote Darwin.

Darwin's main interest, however, was phylogenetic, that is to say, it was aimed at illustrating the origin of species by comparative studies of human beings and animals. In order to gain as broad a basis as possible for this study, he kept up a lively correspondence with physiologists, physicians and missionaries. In a comparative work with a psychological outlook, *The Expression of the Emotions in Man and Animals*, intended originally to be a section of *The Descent of Man and Selection in Relation to Sex*, it is maintained that discontented anthropoid apes protrude their lips to a great degree, that Europeans do so to a smaller extent, while infants all over the world express dissatisfaction by pouting.

The emergence of modern child psychology

The ontogenetic approach has characterized recent child psychology, and Darwin, therefore, is no longer regarded as its pioneer. It was a German physiologist, Wilhelm Preyer, whose book *The Mind of the Child*, was published in 1882, who came to be looked on as the father of modern child psychology. His work is a systematic report of the development of the child, and in particular of the evolution of consciousness, intelligence and will.

Preyer had many followers, and a number of biographical accounts of children – still based on observations of their authors' own children – were published later. One well-known account was written by Clara and William Stern, dealing with the development of language. In 1914 William Stern published *The Psychology of Early Childhood*, the first handbook of child psychology.

Shortly after Preyer came Stanley Hall, a pioneer of modern psychology in America. He introduced new methods of obtaining information about children. He began the systematic use of the questionnaire, now so widely employed. Parents were asked for information about their children at various ages, and teachers, particularly those at elementary schools, were asked to report their observations on their pupils. One of his most important contributions was in the psychology of adolescence, a branch of psychology for which his great work *Adolescence* (1904) laid the foundations.

John Dewey, at the turn of the century, exercised great influence with his theories of active education. His ideas were discussed all over the world, and were applied in various ways in teaching. Developmental-psychological research found a natural anchorage in schools. Associations for child psychology were founded in America and Europe, and lay interest, so stimulating to research of this sort, was aroused. In 1900, Ellen Key published a book with the prophetic title *The Child's Century*, which became an internationally famous Swedish contribution to the discussion.

Child psychology and other branches of psychology

Child psychology, and developmental psychology as a whole, have by no means been isolated from other fields of psychology; and it is hard to make a clear distinction between what are usually called the 'differential' and 'educational' branches of psychology.

L. M. Terman, the best-known contemporary test constructor, is one of the authors most quoted in modern textbooks on child psychology, as are the founder of intelligence testing, Alfred Binet, and a large number of other students of intelligence, and test constructors. E. L. Thorndike, the experimental learning psychologist, is another, and Kurt Lewin, who inclined toward Gestalt psychology, has also had much influence on child psychology. The founder of behaviourism, John B. Watson, must not be forgotten in this connection.

Psychoanalysis has provided practical child psychology with many insights, and probably no single person has stimulated the psychological debate more than Sigmund Freud. No one else has emphasized as strongly the importance of the first years of life to later development, and their influence on adult personality.

Gesell, Piaget and Bühler

None of those mentioned in the previous section were child psychologists pure and simple. In 1911, however, studies were begun at

Yale University that have made an important contribution to knowledge of the mental development of human beings. New methods were also introduced and developed. The most prominent figure in this work was Arnold Gesell, who died in 1961. He and his coworkers devoted themselves especially to the interaction between physical and mental development. They considered that this takes place in definite sequences.

Jean Piaget became well known in the early 1930's by his studies of children's thinking, and their social and moral development. He has been mainly attached to the famous Jean-Jacques Rousseau Institute in Geneva.

Karl Bühler and his wife Charlotte founded a research centre for child psychology in Vienna during the 1920's, where Charlotte Bühler in particular was very active. She has devoted her energies to a number of different problems and has endeavoured to discriminate between different stages of development.

These workers are child psychologists in the strict sense of the term. The child has been the main object of their research, and the development of the child their chief interest. There will be occasion to mention others later. Here we should note the prominent part played by women in child psychology. Of course, children are a natural subject of study for women, but the work of women scientists has by no means been restricted to bare observation, but has also been concerned with important systematic studies of development, and the formulation of fruitful theories.

METHODS

When we call psychology a new science we mean that the methods of approaching psychological problems are new. Psychology became a science in the modern sense of the term about the middle of the nineteenth century, when scientific methods were first applied, and exact results demanded. This is true of general psychology and of its branches. Developmental psychology is no exception.

General Methods

A characteristic feature of all scientific method is experimentation. Trials are arranged according to exactly defined conditions, the findings are checked by repeated experiments and only one condition is changed at a time. The change made by the experimenter, i.e.

the factor in the experimental situation that is excluded, included or modified, is usually called the *independent variable*. This factor must be kept under careful observation by the experimenter, and it implies a conscious and systematic modification of the experimental conditions on his part. The result of the modification of the conditions, i.e. the factor that appears, disappears or varies as the experimenter introduces, excludes or modifies the independent variable, is called the *dependent variable*.

This approach is nearly always subject to great difficulties in sciences dealing with organic processes, for an organism cannot be kept in a constant condition. The processes of life change an organism and we cannot keep the stimuli to which it is subjected under complete control. The more complicated an organism is, the greater are the possibilities of variations in its behaviour, and the more difficult is the experimental work. Thus the study of the behaviour of human beings is the most difficult of all. The manipulation of dependent variables seldom gives unambiguous results.

One way of overcoming at least some of these difficulties is to use large groups of subjects and assume that the mean values reflect a levelling-off of the various influences. *Control groups* are also examined side by side with the *experimental* groups. The control group must perform the test without the inclusion of any independent variable – this is reserved for the experimental group. Naturally the composition of the two groups must be as similar as possible, which may demand a great deal of work in matching them.

An experimental set-up of the kind described above is applicable, for instance, to the study of the effects of different educational and teaching methods, e.g. how punishment or reward may affect performances (Fig. II.1). Punishment and reward are the independent variables.

If the results obtained by the control group are on the whole unchanged, while the performances of the experimental group vary in a definite direction, it is reasonable to presume that the difference is due to the experimental changes made.

There are, however, many problems that cannot be studied by purely experimental methods. It is of great value to learn the effects of such influences as, for example, undernourishment, lack of love, and insecurity on children, but it cannot be done according to the methods outlined above. We cannot take two groups of children and

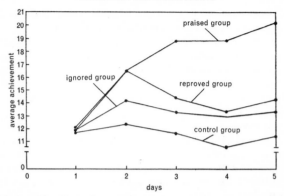

Fig. II.1. The effects of various forms of educational motivation. A class
was divided into three equal parts on the basis of marks in mathematics,
and given mathematical problems to solve. All the members of one group
were praised regardless of results, the second group was reproved, and the
third ignored completely. The control group was outside the experiment.
The curves illustrate the results. Three different types of *independent variable* can be distinguished: reward, punishment and indifference. The
variations in achievement are the *dependent variables*. One of the most
important independent variables in developmental psychology is *time*.
Fig. I.1 is an example of this, and the importance of the time and age
variables must always be taken into account in studies concerned with
achievement-level. (After Hurlock.)

deliberately expose one of them to unfavourable influences. In many
cases we must refrain from laboratory-controlled experiments and
make use of other methods, often quite simple ones.

One fundamental aim of science is to make methods more exact
and reliable. In addition to the general conditions that must be
observed, and which have been described above, distinction is usually
made between two practicable possibilities.

Information on behaviour at different stages may be obtained
either by studying a large number of individuals of the same age –
the so-called *cross-sectional method* with groups composed of quite
different individuals – or the *longitudinal* method, following the
development of one and the same group by making observations and
measurements at certain intervals of time. Investigations of the latter
type are among the most valuable in modern child psychology and in
adolescent psychology. Accounts will be given later of several such
investigations (cf. e.g. Fig. IX.1).

The longitudinal method makes it possible to study the development and growth of a single individual, and to investigate changes both individually and in groups. It also makes possible an analysis of conditions between different growth processes. These investigations are also called follow-up-studies.

Special methods

There are many methods available to developmental psychology. In addition to general psychological methods, all of which are used as far as is practicable, special methods have been developed. Different methods are required for various age levels and stages of development. When a child has begun to talk and understand, the available methods increase in number, and there is even further scope when the child can write.

Observation techniques are very important in child psychology. Attempts at systematic observation are very common among parents, who make notes on the development of their children. Some observations can be made with a high degree of exactness and regularity. The weight of the child for instance is a common object of systematic recording, and parents are often models of exactitude.

It is far more difficult to give, for instance, the time for the cutting of the 'first tooth'. Such psychological phenomena as the first smile and the 'first word' are extremely difficult to define. It is hard for parents – even those with scientific training – to be objective.

Much biographical data on the development of children has been collected at homes for children and different kinds of day nurseries. Linguistic, social and emotional development have been charted in this way. Partly standardized observation methods have been evolved for these studies. The most famous is that introduced by Arnold Gesell, intended primarily for the study of development. A description of his arrangement is of interest.

Openings are made in the walls of the observation room, and specially constructed looking-glasses are built in. From the room they look like ordinary looking-glasses, but from the other side they are transparent and allow clear observation of the child's behaviour without the child being disturbed. This method has been combined with filming and, using cameras able to take up to 3000 pictures a second, it has been possible to make minute analyses of the movements of infants. This arrangement is called a 'one-way screen', and the observation method 'one-way vision' (Fig. II.2). The observations are systematic, but the stimuli causing the response are usually uncontrolled (cf. also Fig. XII.3).

Such things as children's letters and drawings, paper work and models in plasticine form concrete material that can be used in various ways. Both subject-matter and execution provide interesting

Fig. II.2. An early type of Gesell's observation dome. It is a special form of his one-way-screen, and has facilities for filming (cf. p. 194).

information. Such material is used not only to study the level of development but also, sometimes, for therapeutic purposes. The choice of subject-matter may often give valuable information on interests, and the treatment may provide evidence of various emotional disturbances.

Autobiographical data of the diary type have thrown much light on the emotional life of early adolescence. This study was pursued by Charlotte Bühler and the Vienna School. Documents of this kind seem to have played a less prominent role in America.

These and other methods will be further discussed later in the book. The chapter on development of personality (XII) in particular will describe special methods.

Statistical methods fall outside the scope of this book, but frequent use is made of 'correlation coefficients'. This is a measure of the degree of agreement between two sets of compared variables such as the marks of a class of children in an arithmetic and a language test. The value of the correlation coefficient can vary between $+1$ and -1. $+1$ implies that all the children were placed in the same rank order in both tests. -1 would mean that the order was completely reversed, i.e. the top child in arithmetic came bottom in language and vice versa. A coefficient of ±0 would mean no kind of agreement, positive or negative, between the two sets of results.

Chapter III

SURVEY OF DEVELOPMENT

When historians divide history into periods limited by dates, they do so for practical reasons. Sometimes the dates may be exact, but frequently they give only a very approximate estimate. For example, the year 1500 is said to mark the end of the Middle Ages. The main features implied in the concept of 'modern history' appear at different points during a long transitional period. It may even be impossible to date the most important events.

We can give more or less exact dates for when discoveries were made, or for events of political importance. But we cannot indicate alterations in ways of life, social customs and religious thought in the same way.

AGE LEVELS

It is equally difficult to divide human development into different stages, but divisions are necessary for practical purposes. We must choose events that we consider important in development and let them form the boundaries. However, classification calls for a degree of uniformity, and we find that some valuable criteria cannot be taken into account. The following classification is convenient but in some respects arbitrary.

Newborn (neonate)	0–4 weeks
Early infancy	4 weeks–1 year
Infancy	1–6 years
Middle childhood	6–10 years
Late childhood or early puberty	10–13½ years
Puberty (rough average)	Girls 13 years / Boys 14 years
Early adolescence	13½–16 years
Late adolescence	16–20 years

An extremely important stage of growth has not been mentioned at all, namely the prenatal period. It is possible to make a less arbitrary division of this stage, as follows:

Egg or germ stage	0–2 weeks
Embryo stage	2–7 or 8 weeks
Foetal stage	7 or 8–40 weeks
Birth (average)	40 weeks

Space does not allow a detailed treatment of the prenatal stage, but it cannot be ignored altogether.

THE PRENATAL PERIOD

The fertilized egg is not a new organism in the strict biological sense, for it exists already in the parent organisms, and contains a biological inheritance going back for countless generations.

Cell mechanisms, probably of a biochemical nature, begin a strictly regulated course of development. According to the accepted view, the material units of heredity, the genes, are enzymes, the functions of which are to stimulate the chemical processes inside and outside the cells in a definite direction, but without suffering any change themselves. The cells divide and form a round mass. Some cells grow faster than others, and are driven to the upper part of the mass. At the same time, a cavity, the 'blastula', is formed inside the cell mass, where the organism develops.

Three distinct layers of germs, from which different cell structures develop, can be observed quite early. The outer layer, the ectoderm, forms the organs of sense and other nerve mechanisms; the central layers, the 'mesoderm', become the skeleton, muscles and circulatory organs, and the inner layer, the 'endoderm', produces some of the internal glands (Fig. III.1).

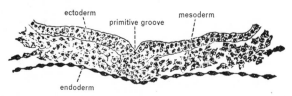

Fig. III.1. A human foetus a few weeks old (embryonic stage), schematic section. The three layers of cells mentioned in the text and the primitive groove, from which the spinal cord develops, can be distinguished.

This course of development takes places from the very beginning in an environment whose chemical and other conditions must be adequate in relation to the continual changes in the egg. Disturbances in this environment, the mother's body, influence the development of the embryo.

During its second week of life, the new organism becomes attached to the uterus and the embryo stage begins. Signs of activity have been observed very early in this period. Heart-beats are the first, and they have been observed during the third week, when the embryo is only a couple of millimetres long. These heart-beats are purely muscular, however, and the nerve control mechanism of the heart cells develops later.

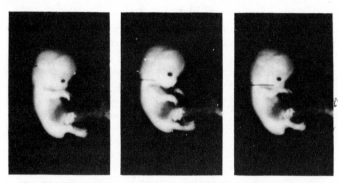

Fig. III.2. The most important source of knowledge we have of the early behaviour of a human foetus consists of studies made after the removal of a foetus by means of a caesarean section performed to save the mother's life. Davenport Hooker, who has collected a great deal of this material, from which these pictures are taken, has found that a human foetus does not, before the middle of its seventh week, show any signs of reflex activity. The pictures show the reaction of a foetus (8½ weeks old) whose cheek has been touched gently. The depression of the hand is produced by the extension (backward movement) of the entire upper extremity at the shoulder and is emphasized by the fact that the trunk of the foetus was flexed or bent away from the stimulus. These illustrations, which show the actual size of the foetus, are reproduced from *Preliminary Atlas of Early Human Foetal Activity* by Davenport Hooker, by permission of the author.

The genesis of behaviour

All the elements of the nerves required for simple reflexes are formed by the sixth week, but they are not able to function until the beginning of the foetal period. Reactions to stimulation of skin nerves have been observed at this time.

It has been shown that touching the region round the mouth results in the head bending away from the stimulus. This reaction by a foetus $7\frac{1}{2}$ weeks old is the first recorded sign of behaviour as a result of direct stimulation applied to a human organism (cf. Fig. III.2).

Here we can speak of the zero point of human behaviour. It presumes that communication has been established between nerve elements leading inwards and outwards. This process takes place in the spinal cord: the cortex does not function at all during the foetal period. It is not until a month after birth that this occurs.

The law of anticipatory morphological maturation

Signs of the grip reflex can be discerned at eleven weeks. A stimulus applied to the palm at this stage causes a brief but incomplete closing of the hand. The grip reflex is more complete in the fifteenth week, when the hand can close and hold an object. By then reflexes and movements are more fully developed and the foetus has the same response patterns, except for breathing movements and voice, as can be observed in a newborn child. But it will be some time before they can function satisfactorily.

A principle can be traced in this early development of the organs, however, which makes possible the survival of a foetus, even if parturition occurs before the normal time. A child born three months too early has good prospects of survival. This principle, which is usually called the law of anticipatory morphological maturation, may be formulated as follows: ability to function can often be demonstrated experimentally in the growing organism long before the time when the functions will normally be called upon to play an active and meaningful role in the life of the organism.

Spontaneous foetal movements

So-called spontaneous movements occur from the fourteenth week of the foetal stage, but as a rule they are not felt by the mother until the seventeenth week – the beginning of the fifth month – when a great increase in the activity of the foetus begins.

This behaviour is called spontaneous because nothing definite is known about the stimuli that cause the movements. They are assumed

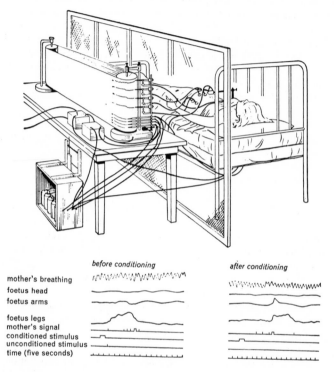

before conditioning *after conditioning*

mother's breathing
foetus head
foetus arms

foetus legs
mother's signal
conditioned stimulus
unconditioned stimulus
time (five seconds)

Fig. III.3. The picture illustrates the device used by Spelt for the observation of simple learning through conditioning by a foetus. The curves show the records before and after the experimental measures. The rubber tambours were placed so that the movements of the head, arms and legs of the foetus could be recorded separately. The mother's breathing was unchanged, and no head movements of the foetus were observed, but arm and leg movements were recorded. By pressing a button the mother communicated when she felt movements of the foetus. The unconditioned stimulus (sound) caused a marked response. When only the conditioned stimulus (vibration) was applied, the foetus responded with arm and leg movements although, as can be seen from the curve, they came somewhat later than the unconditioned response.

to be due to changes in the internal environment or to still unknown stimuli acting on the receptive organs in muscles, sinews and joints.

Learning during the foetal period

An extremely interesting question is whether the behaviour of the foetus can be modified by learning. There is no conclusive proof that this is the case. Nevertheless, some critical and competent judges are of the opinion that an investigation made by Spelt in 1948 answers the question in the affirmative.

It is known that acoustic stimuli normally increase movements during the last two months of the prenatal period. Mothers often observe that a visit to a concert, for instance, causes an increased activity of the foetus. Spelt used a loud wooden clapper that was made to sound close to the mother's stomach. This provoked a kind of quivering response in the foetus. To this stimulus was added another consisting of a vibrator placed on the mother's stomach. It was found that at first the foetus did not react to the vibrations by increased movement. Thus the vibrations served as stimuli leading up to the conditioned, i.e. 'learned' response reactions. The vibrations were given first and then, 5 seconds later, came the sound of the wooden clapper. After a series of such coupled stimuli, it was found that the vibrations alone provoked the response reactions. Thus learning had occurred. The apparatus and recording equipment are shown in Fig. III.3.

DEVELOPMENT AFTER BIRTH

At birth, which means the bursting of the foetal membranes and transition from the protecting womb to a new and difficult environment, the child is normally about 280 days old. Its average weight is $7\frac{1}{2}$ lb.; boys are 4 oz. heavier on average, girls about 4 oz. lighter. Its length is about 20 inches. Further the child has all the nerve cells it will have during its life. It has been calculated that there are between 12 and 15 milliards of them. This number will not increase, but the cells continue to increase greatly in size until the child is about sixteen years of age. Thus, unlike other cells in the organism, nerve cells are never renewed or replaced.

The newborn child cannot imbibe nourishment in the same passive way as before birth. To consume food it must perform sucking and swallowing actions. The mechanisms of these reflex movements are well developed. The fat in the fleshy suction cushions in the cheeks is so composed that it is not absorbed into the body until much later. This means that these tissues can function efficiently even in very emaciated children. The sucking and swallowing actions are closely co-ordinated. As soon as the child loosens its hold on its mother's breast, the milk it has not swallowed runs out of its mouth.

Just as important as nourishment is the absorption of oxygen. Formerly oxygen was led direct into the blood through the umbilical cord, but after birth the child must ensure a supply of oxygen by breathing with its lungs.

Side by side with these direct physiological conditions of dependence on the outside world, other types of contact are established which influence the way the organism reacts. Several of these may be regarded as psychological. The newborn baby cannot consciously effect changes in its surroundings, but it still manages to do so in various ways.

The arrival of a new member of the family often causes a radical change in the habits and interests in the rest of the family. The mother, especially, must change her way of life, and at first it is her influence that determines the child's behaviour. If she is a normal mother she will wish to create a friendly atmosphere round her child. She will make it comfortable while she is feeding it, she will do her best to make it feel cosy and safe in its cot, she will prattle with it, and keep all her senses tuned in to its reactions. No one in the family can understand better than she can the different sounds the baby makes.

All this care means that the child is exposed to influences that lead it into a course of development the aim of which is to make it a social being.

Description of the development of behaviour

For a short survey of the development of behaviour, we can select a few important aspects of the process. This will enable us to compare stages of development at different ages, and to combine cross-sectional and longitudinal descriptions. This section is based mainly on the work of Arnold Gesell, who studied development up to the age of sixteen years, and broke it down into distinguishable sequences.

Gesell chose four aspects of development for his accounts, and adhered to this division strictly up to the age of ten years. The later stages, with their greater differentiation of behaviour, have made other divisions necessary. The four aspects are as follows:

(1) *Motor behaviour*, which refers to posture, ability to grasp, movement, general co-ordination of the different parts of the body and more specific motor co-ordination.

(2) *Adaptive behaviour* refers to adjustment actions that reflect the ability to begin new activities and take advantage of earlier experience. It is closely related to intelligence.

(3) *Language behaviour* implies all ways of communicating with other people.

(4) *Personal-social behaviour* includes the child's reactions to other people and to cultural influences, adjustments to home life, to 'mine and thine', to social groups and social conventions.

Gesell's division may seem unwieldy and diffuse, and it is obvious that the various stages must overlap, but such drawbacks cannot be avoided. Development cannot be compared to a ladder with rungs at regular intervals, but rather to a slope, sometimes steep and uneven, sometimes flat, and at times even seeming to slope in the opposite direction.

The summaries are intended to be normative, i.e. to give the characteristic pattern for a certain degree of maturity, but every child has its own individuality. There is always considerable variation, not only in the time when the different features appear, but also in their distinctness.

THE FIRST FOUR WEEKS

The whole of the first month after birth is characterized by unstable adjustment to the new environment. The functioning of the organs, even of such primary organs as the heart, and blood pressure, is irregular because the organization of the autonomic nerve system is incomplete. There are no definite boundaries between sleep and wakefulness. It is not until the end of a month that more distinct patterns of behaviour can be discerned.

Motor behaviour in a waking state is dominated by the so-called tonic neck reflex, to which Gesell attributes great significance in the development of the whole action system. When the child is lying on its back it usually has its head turned to one side, with the arm at that side stretched out, while the other arm is bent with the hand

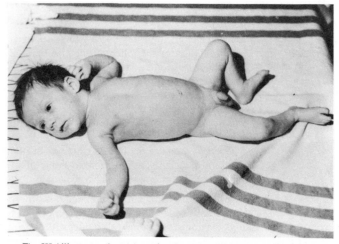

Fig. III.4 illustrates the tonic neck reflex. The child is five weeks old and
shows a right tonic neck reflex. See text.

resting near the upper part of the breast. This asymmetric pattern is
not transformed into a symmetric one until the child is about
sixteen weeks old. Occasionally the head is turned forwards, usually
in combination with starting movements (Fig. III.4).

Adaptive behaviour is mostly concerned with the mouth. Tickling
the corners of the child's mouth causes it to close it and purse its
lips. The ability to control the eye muscles has increased, and the
gaze can be kept fixed for quite a long time. The angle of vision is
restricted, however, by the tonic neck reflex.

A four-week-old baby takes no notice of an object hanging immediately above it, but if the object is moved while in the line of
sight, the child follows it by head and eye movements within a
limited sector. (A child sixteen weeks old can catch sight of an
object and follow it more easily with its gaze, without moving its
head.) The hands are kept closed, and they are not stretched out to
grasp the object. Thus a child can notice objects with its eyes long
before it can take them with its hands.

In *language behaviour* screaming is still the dominant means of
vocal expression. Certain sounds occur that may be interpreted as

'pre-prattle'. The child also reacts to sounds. It pauses in its move-ments when it hears a bell, for instance, and behaves as if it were listening.

Socially the child seems more wide-awake. If it is upset and is picked up, it shows signs of becoming calm. It behaves as if it has a feeling of security when it is well cared for.

SIXTEEN WEEKS

The initial position of being an alien in a strange new world has been overcome after four weeks. The process of socialization begins, and by sixteen weeks this has progressed quite a long way. The periods of wakefulness are more distinctly separated from sleep, and individual features of personality appear more clearly. The great improvement of central nervous, particularly cortical, organization which appears is very important. Among other things co-ordination of eye and hand can be achieved.

The *motor behaviour pattern* is changed. The tonic neck reflex shows signs of disappearing – on an average it disappears at 20 weeks – and is replaced by a symmetrical movement pattern. The head is mostly turned forward, and the arms can be moved symmetrically. The organization of leg and trunk muscles commences. The child enjoys sitting up for a time propped up by cushions, and it can keep its head upright without support. It sometimes stretches its arms towards an object, but the movement is not isolated; other parts of the body are engaged. The nervous impulses from visual stimuli do not yet control the response system, but there are clear signs that the process has begun.

Progress in *adaptive behaviour* is connected with increased ability to co-ordinate. The primitive gazing at light surfaces or large moving objects, typical of the four-week stage, has disappeared, and per-ception of surroundings is more selective. The child observes its own movements, looks at its hand or a cube that is held in front of it. It follows an object moved within a field of vision over an arc of up to 180°.

Language behaviour becomes more versatile by the appearance of several new sounds, and the child's reactions to human voices are more meaningful. The organs of speech cannot yet produce articulate sounds, but the greater diversity of prattle implies a big step forward towards real speech.

Social behaviour has developed significantly, and the child can distinguish its mother's face, hands and voice. The child has clearly acquired a feeling of familiarity with her, and with other members of the family, from their behaviour while it is being fed, bathed and dressed, and the way they express their affection. It can smile and laugh, and respond to smiles, but can also purse its mouth uneasily at the sight of a strange face. Uneasiness in the presence of strangers is not general until the age of about six months (cf. p. 94 f.). When the child can sit up, physical activity is increased, the eyes open wider, the pulse becomes stronger and respiration is more rapid. By sitting up the child also commands a larger social space, which is further enlarged when the child can crawl, and still further when, at the age of rather more than one year, it learns to walk.

TWENTY-EIGHT WEEKS

By this age the child has become a sitting human being. It can manage well in its chair with only a little support, and it shows clear signs of preferring a sitting position. The nervous system is now so well developed and functionally co-ordinated that the child can actively handle various objects like wooden cubes.

Motor behaviour becomes more diversified as a consequence of this improved sitting balance. The child can, sitting at a table, experience the thrill of grasping things in different ways; it can hold an object in its hand and move it to its mouth to examine it. The technique of

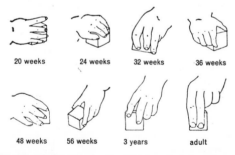

20 weeks 24 weeks 32 weeks 36 weeks

48 weeks 56 weeks 3 years adult

Fig. III.5. The ability to press the thumb against the other fingers is characteristic of human beings. (Cf. Fig. III.6.) This phenomenon, so important for grasping, is illustrated by the way a cube is grasped at different stages. From an investigation by Halverson.

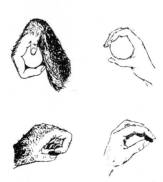

Fig. III.6. The way human beings and chimpanzees grasp an object represents different stages of development. The chimpanzee cannot achieve thumb–finger opposition. (After Kellogg & Kellogg.)

grasping is improved by the use of the thumb (Fig. III.5). The hand is now an efficient grasping tool (Fig. III.6). The child can also transfer an object from one hand to the other.

Adaptive behaviour has become more active. To be able to hold an object in one hand at a time is a great advance. The child begins to explore its surroundings on its own initiative. If it is given a wooden cube, it will turn it round and round, study it from different angles, carry it to the mouth and study it again. Such activities may be continued for long periods at a time. 'If you like', says Gesell, 'it is intelligence.'

Language behaviour: Vocalizations and the beginnings of word formations such as 'ma' and 'da' can be distinguished. Such combinations of sounds are now observed to occur time after time in definite situations. But the child is still more occupied in trying out its newly gained motor ability.

Socially this results in a high degree of self-sufficiency. The child has not much time to spare for the people around it. Another such period occurs at the age of eighteen months. At 28 weeks it can sit, at eighteen months it can walk, but during both periods it is busily engaged on its own exploratory activities. This seems wise, for the experience gained in this way is a necessary condition of more versatile social relationships.

FORTY WEEKS

Now the child is no longer satisfied to lie awake on its back. By rolling over on its side it can sit up by itself. It can even pull itself up and stand unsteadily by holding on to the ribs of its play-pen, or some other support. It makes social contacts, and is included in the family circle on more equal terms than before. Between 28 and 40 weeks there often occurs a period, rather troublesome for the rest of the family, of lack of balance before the child has fully attained this new motor ability and is able to open up socially.

Motor behaviour: The child has greater control of the peripheral

28 weeks   28 weeks

29 weeks   30 weeks   32 weeks

34 weeks   36 weeks   36 weeks

36 weeks   36 weeks   40 weeks

42 weeks   45 weeks   49 weeks

FIG. *III.7.* Phases in the development of a child's way of moving. The time when a child reaches a certain phase varies considerably. The ages given refer to the average of the 20 children on which the study was made. (After Louise B. Ames.)

parts of its body, due to continued development of the nervous system. The legs are strong enough to support the body, but balance is very unsatisfactory. The child can sit firmly, turn its body and lean to the side without falling. It can raise itself from a prone into a sitting position. It can move by dragging itself along the floor or by crawling (Fig. III.7).

Many changes occur in the *adaptive behaviour* as a consequence of increased neuro-motor control. The lips fit better round the rim of the mug when the child is drinking. The tongue is more effective when eating. It can help to spit out unsuitable food more efficiently. A crumb of bread can be picked up between the thumb and index finger. The habit of carrying objects to the mouth gets weaker, and instead the child studies them visually, or feels them with its sensitive finger tips. It is better able to fix its attention, and it can regard two objects alternatively, which seems to imply some kind of primitive conception of the number two.

Language behaviour is favoured by the open social attitude and better control of the tongue and pharynx. The 'first word' – sometimes a child has two words at this age – can now be recorded. The child reacts to its name and to such exclamations as 'No, no!', but at this stage there is hardly any understanding of language in its general symbolic function.

Socially the child is interested in the people around it, and enjoys games of the type 'Pat-a-cake, pat-a-cake baker's man' (cf. p. 157 ff.). The child smiles at its reflection in a looking-glass but it shows hesitation and fear when confronted with strangers, particularly if they are exaggeratedly inquisitive.

TWELVE MONTHS

A year-old child shows hardly any new, clearly defined behaviour pattern. It is eagerly engaged in learning to walk, and it is acquiring fine motor co-ordination. But generally these things are not fully achieved until a few months later.

Motor behaviour: Crawling is the typical means of locomotion. The child can creep on hands and knees, but also – and for preference perhaps – on hands and the soles of its feet. This is the last stage before the child learns to walk upright (Figs. III.7 and 8). There is a clearly expressed desire to walk upright, and the child can stand for brief moments before it falls. It can even move upright if it has something to hold on to. Grasping is approaching an adult level of skill and there are signs that the child is beginning to release objects in a muscularly correct manner.

Adaptive behaviour is characterized by an increased understanding of shape and number. Round objects are a source of great interest, and signs of a better conception of space can be observed.

A one-year-old child shows great interest in *language*. It repeats the words it knows, and learns one or two new ones. It shows signs of obeying orders by, for instance, stretching out its hand with a ball in reply to the words 'Give it me'.

Socially the child is the focal point in the family circle. It happily repeats actions and does things that arouse amusement and attention. Such situations seem to reflect an awakening ego in the child. It appreciates 'Peep-bo' games very much.

The emotional register is widened and the behaviour patterns expressing fear and uneasiness, anger and jealousy, affection and sympathy become clearer. The child also shows a better understanding of other people's emotions, and greater sensitivity towards emotional adjustment and influence. The child is beginning to use its fingers as an aid to eating. Bowel movements become more regular as a rule, and the child tries to help when it is being dressed.

EIGHTEEN MONTHS

A child usually begins to walk without support between the ages of twelve and eighteen months. By then he can build a tower with two bricks, and he is also learning to put on simple articles of clothing. He is now in a period when general muscle control is improving rapidly. This is accompanied by progress in the adaptive and social spheres, although these improvements are less marked.

The upright posture of the child dominates the picture so strongly during this period that the psychological consequences are easily overlooked. The child is now leaving the helpless baby stage and entering the more independent and mature early childhood stage.

The range of behaviour has now been extended so much, that it is hard to give an account of it that has uniform validity. There are no units of measurement available, and the interpretation of the forms of behaviour that appear must be made and judged by comparisons drawn from extensive observation material.

The most important aspect of *motor behaviour* is, of course, upright locomotion (Fig. III.8). The balance of the body is on quite a different level, although the ability to balance on one leg does not appear until after another eighteen months. As already mentioned, the child can build a tower with two cubes, but it must practice before it can build one with three. The ability to drop the cubes in the right position at the right moment is still imperfect. A one-year-old child can roll a ball, a child of eighteen months tries to throw it.

In *adaptive* behaviour the one-year-old showed signs of distinguishing certain shapes, and was particularly interested in round objects. A child eighteen months old can take in many space relations in his surroundings. He knows where many objects are to be found and

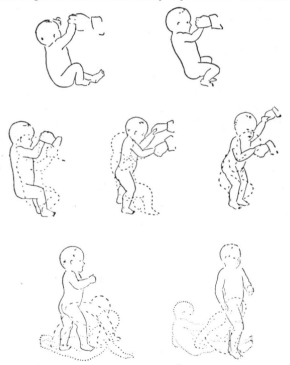

Fig. III.8. There are numerous phases in the development of upright locomotion; a few of them are illustrated here. (After Myrtle B. McGraw.)

can point to them. He recognizes pictures of different things, and it is clear that the environment he is aware of has become more differentiated and richer in many ways.

The vertical conception, which precedes the horizontal, has become stabilized. Scribbling consists mainly of vertical lines, while horizontal ones are not drawn until the child is about two years of age, when 'tower-building' is superseded by 'wall-building', with the cubes placed one after another. The way of handling the cubes is also different. The older child likes to pile them up and then spread them out again, while at the age of one year it takes the cubes one by one and places them on the table in a stereotyped manner.

Linguistic ability has developed, both as regards understanding and communication with others. The vocabulary has increased – ten or so words can often be distinguished – and is used more effectively. Gestures are accompanied by words, and words begin gradually to replace gestures.

Socially the child is less accessible, as he was at the age of 28 weeks. The child is better able to distinguish between himself and others, and is beginning to understand the idea of 'mine and thine'. But he is impatient and wants what he asks for immediately, and he often does exactly the opposite of what he is asked to do. This is not mainly due, Gesell maintains, to an inclination to be rebellious, but because he has so few and insufficient concepts and associations at his disposal that he anxiously holds fast to them in the same way that he clings to his mother or an object he has in his hand. Sudden changes seem dangerous, and the child therefore avoids them. He is defiant and disobedient out of self-preservation rather than aggression.

Chapter IV

SURVEY OF DEVELOPMENT
(Continued)

TWO YEARS

A mother is always inclined to regard her child as a 'charmer' and she usually has excellent reasons for doing so when he is two years of age. This birthday, more than the first one, seems to mark a definite stage of development, characterized by a harmonious rounding off of advances already made. Control of the body is much more efficient, and the child can walk without any great difficulty.

Linguistically the child has improved enormously, and socially he can, at least occasionally, disregard his own interests to devote himself to other people. The improvement in language (cf. p. 111 ff.) and the perfection of upright locomotion are reasons for regarding the child's second birthday as the beginning of a new phase. We find developmental periods with similarly high levels of integration later at the ages of five and ten years.

A two-year-old child is very lively. He can walk upstairs and downstairs without help, although he must take one foot at a time, resting with both feet on each stair. He likes to jump from the bottom stair, though not with his feet together, but with one foot at a time. Jumping and dancing and clapping hands are typical ways of expressing joy. The finger muscles obey impulses much better – earlier the child turned several pages at a time when looking through a book, now he can turn one. The spoon is held in the right way and carried to the mouth more expertly.

The dependence of *adaptive behaviour* on motor development is clearly seen at this age. There is marked interaction between observation and conduct, and this interaction is now more closely connected with language. Attention increases, and the duration of memory, measured by so-called delayed reaction experiments (see p. 101 ff.), is usually rather more than a quarter of an hour, as compared with eight minutes at eighteen months and only one minute or so at twelve months old.

The child goes on building towers, now up to six cubes high. But it is becoming more common for him to build horizontally also,

Fig. IV.1. A two-year-old has usually a well-balanced and harmonious personality.

putting the cubes in a row. However, a combination of horizontal and vertical building – a train, for example, made of three cubes in a line with a fourth cube on the top of the first one to represent a funnel – cannot be achieved for some time to come.

Language has improved considerably. The vocabulary has become at least ten times as great during the past six months, and usually consists of up to 200 words or more (cf. table p. 113). Unintelligible speech has almost completely disappeared, and a considerable understanding of language has been gained. Language is now an effective means of communication, although phrases of one word only are still most common. Two-word and sometimes three-word phrases may be used, but only seldom.

A two-year-old child is still much occupied with itself. At the same time, however, other people are becoming more interesting. Personal pronouns usually appear in the order of *my, me, you, I,* and have, at this age, a certain definite meaning. *We* is seldom used before the child is three years of age.

Games are still mainly restricted to the child himself, but consciousness of other members of the family is expressed in various ways. Sometimes a child may hide toys to be certain of having them later. He obeys commands willingly, and looks happy when he is praised. The child is progressing from a pre-social to a social phase, a change of which there is evidence in his alternation between a reserved uncommunicativeness and a socially extrospective openness.

THREE YEARS

Before the third birthday, a child passes through a phase of development – a rather trying one for the family – that culminates at about $2\frac{1}{2}$ years. This period may be called the 'rebellious age', and its duration and intensity vary greatly from one child to another. The child is domineering and exacting, and wants to try out all possible courses of action: will – will not, want – don't want, go out – stay indoors. He is bound up in his wishes, and lacking in consistency, because he wants to try all the alternatives at one and the same time. The lack of ability to choose, and the pull of mutually opposed actions, make it almost impossible for the child to adjust his behaviour.

These difficulties have usually been overcome by the third birthday, when negativism generally gives way to positivism. The earlier need for doing everything in a definite, almost ritual way, for hearing the same stories over and over again – preferably told in the same words – is less marked. The will to co-operate is more developed, this being reflected in the use of the pronoun *we*. The year between the third and fourth birthdays is, in many respects, decisive for growth and maturation.

The *motor behaviour* of the three-year-old is much more assured. The child can go upstairs and downstairs without having to rest with both feet on every stair. He can run much more gracefully, take corners sharply and increase and decrease his speed much more efficiently than before. This ability to slow down and restrict movements is also evident in drawing; the lines are controlled better and are more varied. A three-year-old cannot normally draw a man;

that will take another year or so. He can fold a piece of paper across and lengthwise, but not diagonally, not even when he is shown how it is done.

The development of *adaptive behaviour* is striking too. The ability to distinguish within the field of perception increases both in extent and keenness. Circular, square and triangular pieces of wood can be fitted into equivalent holes in a board quite easily (Fig. IV.2). There is other evidence of the improvement of mental organization. Ability to combine increases. This makes possible more reliable measurement of intelligence, because tests can be varied. This is specially true of the development of language.

Language behaviour is characterized by a deeper understanding of words, a necessary condition for what might be called intellectual liberation. The child now can classify, identify and compare. Questions about what things are and what they are called bear witness to a burning desire to bring order and system into the surrounding world. The two-year-old learned words, the three-year-old uses them. He can fit words to actions, and actions to words. This ability to use

Fig. IV.2. A child three years old can easily place the pieces of wood in the right holes.

words as symbols puts him surely on his way into the world of grown-ups.

It is obvious that this is very important *socially*. A child three years old likes to make new friends, and he may be willing to surrender something -- a toy, for instance – to gain a person's appreciation. But this level of maturity is also attended with a greater wealth of experiences. Outbursts of anger are often aimed directly at objects. A child may strike a chair for being 'silly', or say 'naughty floor' when he has fallen down and hurt himself. Fear may also be associated with particular objects and become fixated for a long time to come, but the increased power of imagination also causes fear to extend beyond reality. Fear of noises and strange objects diminishes but instead fear of darkness and solitude increases. Bad dreams are not uncommon.

FOUR YEARS

Between the ages of three and four years comes another period of uneasiness and lack of confidence, which may seem to be a time of regression. Behaviour is less harmonious, and the efficiency of motor regulation is variable. Wendell Johnson has confirmed that stammering most often begins at this age. There is also a high frequency of stammering at $2\frac{1}{2}$ years of age, and when school life begins. It seems clear that emotional stress, due not least to unnecessary anxiety on the part of parents, is a fundamental cause of stammering. (Stammering is dealt with in greater detail on p. 117 ff.)

The child changes rapidly from shyness to frankness, which makes him socially unstable. This phase is usually over by the time he is four. His behaviour is now characterized by great confidence, and the go-ahead linguistic spirit – not only polite words are used – sometimes gives the impression of a degree of maturity that has not really been attained.

Now the child is more and more accepted as an independent social being. His age usually guarantees some kind of social collaboration on his part, and he can more or less fend for himself. But this does not mean that he is particularly easy to handle. Liveliness and resoluteness are, on the contrary, marked features of his behaviour, as are boastfulness and an enormous degree of inquisitiveness. It is also common for the child to show much uncertainty, expressed in, among other things, sudden and unreasoning fears about various objects.

The *motor behaviour* of the four-year-old has become finer. The skeletal and other muscles are getting more and more independent. The ability to perform isolated movements of the body gives an impression of greater suppleness of the joints. The four-year-old can balance on one leg much longer than before – but he cannot yet hop, at least not for another six months. He can button his clothes and put on his shoes, but he will not be able to tie his laces for some time yet. He is still unable to fold a piece of paper diagonally.

The *adaptive behaviour* of a four-year-old seems advanced, but his great inquisitiveness is apparently due not so much to a craving for knowledge as to a need to learn attributes for the many things in the physical and social world around him. A four-year-old collects and names impressions like a three-year-old, but he has also an urge to order and systematize his experiences. His ideas of past and future are vague and he is not much interested in the plots of stories. His drawings of human beings consist of a head and two lines representing legs. Sometimes the head is given two eyes, but it will be a year or two before a body is added (Fig. IV.3).

A four-year-old's liveliness may easily make us overestimate his knowledge. We frequently regard him as being profound when he is merely industrious.

In *language* the four-year-old is extremely active, and 'how' and 'why' questions are at their most insistent. The explanations do not seem to be of prime interest to him; he seems more to notice how the answers fit his own thoughts. The pronoun *I* plays a very important part in his language.

Fig. IV.3. These drawings of a man were made by the same girl at different ages. It is not unusual for the figure to be upside down (as at 4 years). It is a common phenomenon both in drawing and looking at pictures up to that age; William Stern has called it *Raumverlagerung*. The drawings are from a study by Gesell.

Social ability is well developed, but the desire to apply it is often expressed defiantly. The child frequently refuses to obey – and he sometimes has an exaggerated need of stubborn independence, which is also reflected in his games. His social advances increase in number, and he devotes more time to group games. He will lend his toys, but he may suddenly turn cantankerous and do nasty things on purpose. These should not necessarily be regarded as anti-social impulses. They seem rather to arouse some kind of response that may be made use of socially. Thus four-year-old children are often eager to command others.

FIVE YEARS

There are good reasons why a child should begin school, as in England, when he is five years of age, for he has then reached a level of maturity that differentiates him clearly from children at earlier stages. A new period of integration begins, during which the various processes of development combine in the creation of the whole personality. But not until the age of seven years (when Swedish children begin school) has the early childhood phase been passed. Before then the child usually passes through a period of disorganization and anxiety.

In *motor behaviour* the five-year-old acts more like an adult. Locomotion and carriage have become more stable, and balance is practically perfect. The child is often attracted by rhythmical and other movements in groups, and fine motor co-ordination allows him to begin using things like combs and toothbrushes.

A period of equilibrium also occurs in *adaptive behaviour*. The child has become calmer, and does not rush into new adventures and unknown situations with the same fearless enthusiasm. Now a square or triangle can be copied, but the slanting sides of a diamond still cause difficulty. Drawing has also a more definite and purposeful content. A five-year-old knows what he is going to draw before he begins, while the four-year-old made up his mind what it was when he had finished.

The conception of number was usually limited to *one, two* and *many* in the four-year-old; now the child can count up to ten, and also add up within that range of numbers. He can also say how old he is. He is able to criticize himself, too, this being one expression of his more realistic orientation. He is now less amused by fantastic fairy-tales, and demands more reality. The questions asked are prompted by an urge to learn something, and they are often of a practical nature.

A five-year-old child is better fitted to complete a task. He can return to a piece of work day after day until it is finished.

Language is practically free from childish sounds. It can be used graphically to describe experiences, and sentences follow each other correctly. The form and structure of the language are more or less perfect, rules of grammar are applied and sentences completed.

Five years is also a happy age *socially*. A five-year-old child likes to help about the house, and is protective towards weaker playmates and younger brothers and sisters. He no longer has the four-year-old's need to stand his ground at all costs, although he likes to impress his playmates; his behaviour is slightly similar to the endeavours of grown-ups to make a good impression socially. A five-year-old child has self-confidence combined with trust in others, and his social adaptivity is often striking. He is more balanced emotionally.

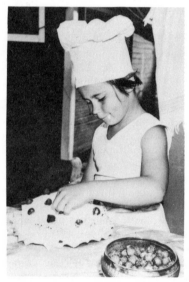

Fig. IV.4. The five-year-old, like the two-year-old, is in a period when the various processes of development have fused into a harmonious whole. Children of this age are better able to finish a task they have begun.

He is not stricken with fear as often and seriously as formerly, or as may happen again when he is six.

The school-mistress is a new source of authority, and may compete seriously with the parents for the child's confidence. The reception the teacher gives her new pupils is not without importance, for she is their first real 'employer', at the same time as she is the first representative of the community they have met in their lives. The child is very receptive to friendly contacts. The wise teacher knows how to deal adequately with his desire for them. She does not stay at her desk, but moves about the classroom so that she will be able to make personal contact with all the children, and has a kind word for each of them. This will not by any means prevent necessary firmness in her conduct. Gentleness and affability need not interfere with discipline.

We will discuss the important problem of 'school readiness' in another connection (p. 238 ff.).

SIX YEARS

The five-year-old gets top marks for behaviour, as the two-year-old does. But just as a child of $2\frac{1}{2}$ years may pass through a rebellious phase, the well-adjusted behaviour of the five-year-old usually disintegrates when he is approaching his sixth birthday. 'I can't understand what's come over the child', is often the disappointed mother's complaint. The openness and gentleness so often a feature of the five-year-old's attitude to his surroundings will not return until the child is about ten years old. The six-year-old feels once again the difficulties of making up his mind experienced by the child $2\frac{1}{2}$ years old. He will change rapidly from one alternative to another.

Gesell speaks of marked bipolarity, a kind of double motivation in the child's actions. The child loves his mother at one moment, and hates and wishes to kill her the next. He has physical troubles, too, and infectious illnesses are most common during this period.

The *motor behaviour* of the six-year-old is very lively, but rather restless. He plays indoors and outside, but never really knows where he wants to be. Boys try their strength in many ways, and like to fight with their brothers and father, but such fights often end unhappily for they cannot stop in time.

A six-year-old develops a kind of 'tool consciousness'. He discovers his hand in this connection and experiments with it, but seems little interested in the results of his experiments. He gives up his tricycle for a bicycle, which gives him training for his legs and sense of balance.

Girls dress and undress their dolls over and over again.

In *language behaviour* the six-year-old is aggressive and boastful. Stammering often appears at this age, more frequently among boys than girls. Answering the telephone becomes a source of amusement, and sometimes children of six can put through a call.

Adaptive behaviour becomes more comprehensive. The 'here' and 'now', to which the child was formerly bound, extend into the surrounding world and make room for space relationships between the home and different places in the neighbourhood. Duration is beginning to be comprehensible, and the child has a rough idea of intervals of time. He shows spontaneous interest in what things were like when mother was a child, and also wants to hear about his babyhood.

Often the child can distinguish between right and left from his own point of view, but if he is asked to point to another person's right or left arm he usually finds it difficult. Drawings are more realistic. The 'man's' legs are drawn with two lines each instead of one, which seems to bear witness to better conception of dimension. The child likes colouring pictures in books, but he holds the crayons clumsily and changes his hold often; he seems to be working with his whole body. He can print a number of letters, and he can also recognize figures.

Social behaviour is characterized by brusqueness. Just as he cannot control his motor impulses, he cannot manage social and personal relations. He wants to be first and best, which often leads to conflicts with his playmates and brothers and sisters. But in spite of his demonstrations of self-sufficiency he is sensitive to his surroundings. If his mother is ill or he finds her weeping, he is a pattern of kindness and comfort. He is interested in her well-being for he needs her help in many situations in which, at the same time, he often refuses to accept it.

SEVEN YEARS

Compared with six, seven is a tranquil age, usually with fewer conflicts. A seven-year-old is generally a good listener, and ability to concentrate attention has improved. These are very important factors for the methods of work used at school.

The seven-year-old is lively, but he is usually more careful than a six-year-old and more conscious of danger. He will not climb too high up a tree. Often he will calculate its height before he begins to climb, and test the strength of the branches carefully.

His improved sense of balance makes it possible for him to begin playing football and shooting successfully with bow and arrows. These occupations require asymmetrical balance. Girls enjoy hop-scotch and skipping.

A favourite position is lying full length on the floor with the head resting on one hand, in which positions boys (in particular) read, write and play for hours.

Great progress is made in *language* when a child begins school and learns to read and write. Oral descriptions are arranged in new and sometimes stricter forms. Interest in reading varies considerably. This is not due simply to differing degrees of ability to understand the symbols necessary for reading, but also to the extent to which reading must compete with other interests. Persistent readers are frequently found among seven-year-old children.

School contributes much to the *adaptive behaviour* of most children, and provides active employment for the intellectual resources; although the child's response to the intellectual stimuli provided at school – as his response to other aspects of school life – may be conditioned by his home background. It sometimes happens that school is a disappointment to an intelligent child from an intellectu-ally stimulating environment. The demands made on the child's resources are not great enough.

In general it may be said that the seven-year-old takes a more realistic view of his surroundings. His imagination is more reflective. 'Let's pretend' games get less enthusiastic. Hesitant self-criticism and deliberation may slow down play. The gravity of reality is entering the child's life.

Socially this hesitation in relation to things and human beings represents a certain conflict with the external world. On account of the relative pliancy and sensibility of the seven-year-old, this conflict is usually not very noticeable. The child is more a recipient than a giver in his social life.

He is developing his sense of ethical conduct – the rules of games acquire importance; good and bad in the actions of playmates, and also in those of the child himself, are noticed. Crying openly is no longer the thing, and the crying itself has become less childish. It comes more from the inside, often (as Gesell says) from hurt feelings.

Social experiences are more intense and conscious. The child works hard to acquire the habits and the moral code of the family. Willingness to help and some sense of duty and responsibility appear, though the child's endurance in this respect may not be great.

EIGHT YEARS

The seven-year-old's cautious and expectant attitude towards his surroundings has disappeared in the eight-year-old. He has become accustomed to school, and playmates begin to occupy a more prominent position in his life. He is more assured in his associations with other children and with adults, and he embarks on adventure boldly. He eagerly extends his world in all directions. He is often extremely careless in his violent activity.

Differences in behaviour between individuals are observed earlier, naturally, but now they are usually more obvious and permanent. This is also true of differences between the sexes.

In his *motor behaviour* the eight-year-old can move faster and his movements are lighter and more graceful.

In *language* the child is extrospective, and is developing rapidly. An eight-year-old shows the same enthusiasm for language as he did at four, and sometimes now he uses language almost as an adult does. Pronunciation and construction of sentences are often good. Slang is an expression of new and independent contacts.

In *adaptive behaviour* the child shows expansion together with greater profundity. An eight-year-old begins to have an understanding of relationships that were formerly experienced only fragmentarily. He can more easily see similarities and differences in people and things. The hesitancy of the seven-year-old has, in many respects, been replaced by decided opinions, and the child now understands the difference between imagination and reality. Although the eight-year-old may be afflicted with unreasoning fear of darkness or fierce animals, he can mobilize forces to oppose his fears.

It is a suitable age at which to help children to overcome their fear of the dark, but it must be done carefully, and a child must not be left alone in the dark abruptly. The feeling of security a mother can give in this connection is of the utmost importance.

The eight-year-old begins to understand the impersonality of objects and the laws of nature, thinking gets less animistic, though traces of this mode of thinking still remain. Piaget gives an illustrative example. A child $8\frac{1}{2}$ years of age was asked if things were alive, and answered, 'They can't feel.' 'Well, but if this bench breaks, will it feel anything?' 'Yes!' 'Why?' 'Because it is broken.'

Socially the great activity of an eight-year-old plays a very important part and it may also be said to serve social ends. He likes to be in the company of grown-ups at home, but he demands more of them. He will both give and receive information. It is not only a question of physical nearness, he also strives towards interaction that will give him insight into the world of adults.

At eight years of age a child begins to see through the infallibility and omniscience of grown-ups. It amuses him to ask questions to which he knows the answers but his parents do not. He also seeks contacts outside his home, and he is very active in his group of friends. These groups keep together for only a short time, however. The child is not yet ready for complicated social rules and conventions. But he improvises, boldly and breezily, and is busy in many directions. Nothing seems difficult. He may sometimes lose heart, but it does not usually take long for him to regain confidence.

Although an eight-year-old may retain much true childishness, he is no longer a baby. At his best, Gesell says, an eight-year-old is so happy to be alive, so tolerant in his sympathies, so liberal in his eagerness to investigate the unknown that we may regard him as a promising first draft of an adult character.

NINE YEARS

Children nine years old have moved a good way along the path of development, and their behaviour has become highly differentiated. This makes it more difficult to generalize about them. A Norwegian, Åse Gruda Skard, has pointed out some circumstances which most probably contribute to this.

Collaboration between children and the community has increased, says Skard, and it must therefore be presumed that conflicts will be more serious. On the one hand, difficulties which have their origin in earlier years appear; on the other, the community does not always react favourably to this 'superlative' age. Madcaps may be accepted, but they may also be disapproved of and punished. In such cases, grown-ups not only regard children as 'impossible', they also place obstacles in their way in the form of prohibition, rules and punishment. The child reacts with rebellion and becomes really 'impossible'.

If, however, the age of nine years is compared with other ages, from the point of view of what may be called normal development, and ignoring the effects of idiosyncrasies in bringing-up and environment, can the nine-year-old be regarded as being particularly troublesome?

Gesell likes to provide a key-word to describe different ages. Perhaps he has found an adequate one for the age of nine in the term 'self-motivation'. By this he means a highly developed ability in a child to attack problems on his own initiative. This is a new and also an adult feature of behaviour, for a child to find out his own skill and compel himself to do his best for his own sake. It is expressed in various aspects of personality; the nine-year-old can resist temporary influences from his surroundings much better than a child eight years of age, and can become independent of the pressure of the group and the advice of adults.

Is there, in this striving towards an independent attitude, something that grown-ups find difficult to accept, and which therefore leads to conflicts? Or does our urban civilization with its crowded living conditions and many regulations offer too few possibilities for a nine-year-old to satisfy his natural aspirations? He wants and needs his maturity, his independence and his privacy respected. At the same time he needs his parents, who are expected to devote their time and interest to him.

In his *motor behaviour* the nine-year-old child has wider and more conscious interests than the eight-year-old, whose mobility, eagerness and contacts in practically all directions are now considerably restricted. The pace may still be fast but the nine-year-old has better control over it. Co-ordination of eye and hand is well developed; both hands can work independently of each other, and the fingers, too, can be used more freely and with greater diversity. One consequence of this is seen in the dog-eared pages of books, which are a result of finger activities that were generally impossible earlier.

Language is not so effusive as it was when the child was eight. Frequently there is a reversion to earlier grammatically incorrect expressions, due partly to the use of language for new tasks. It becomes more and more a tool for the dawning self-critical thoughts and a means of expressing feelings. Traces of secret language appeared when the child was eight, but now it is a common phenomenon. Interest in reading increases, but changes too; the fairy-tale age is over, and the 'Robinson Crusoe' age begins. This is a sign of intellectual curiosity and greater demands for realism.

The progress of *adaptive development* is signified not least by the evaluations and private norm system now emerging. A nine-year-old likes to think over and organize a task before he attempts to do it. These beginnings of methodology often give him a grown-up look and attitude, which should be met with respect and gravity. He is fond of collecting and classifying – unless the child's father is specially interested he will find himself inferior in ability to recognize different makes of motor-cars and types of aeroplane. The nine-year-old is eager to perfect his skill, and he is willing to keep trying.

For example, child psychologists are generally agreed in regarding nine as a suitable age for beginning the training of a child in handicrafts and elementary mathematics.

At this age, the child also attains *social maturity*, if by this is meant more stable and better integrated behaviour. This development reaches its optimum point at the age of about ten years. A nine-year-old's attitude to both himself and others may be extremely critical. He is sensitive to an attitude in parents that he may regard as too protective or – still worse – condescending. He is fond of his home, but has also a strong urge to make a position for himself.

Clearly a child's need of independence and of help and comfort must be met with understanding. At this age the need of independence in respect to the home becomes more profound, and it is experienced more consciously. At times friends mean more than parents, and Wolf Cub and Brownie outings may be considered much more attractive than a family trip. Socially, there is often segregation of the sexes: boys and girls form separate groups, and an attitude of contempt towards the opposite sex may develop.

This picture of a nine-year-old is on the whole pleasant and attractive. Why then is it regarded as a difficult age? It is clear that the demand for independence and unwillingness to accept authority is responsible for this. This attitude will sometimes lead to revolt. The revolt is not always open. Withdrawing into one's shell is one way of avoiding external strain; another common one is for the child to claim that he is 'not feeling well' when asked to do something he would rather not do.

TEN YEARS

Charlotte Bühler's fourth period begins at the age of nine years and ends at thirteen. For Gesell nine years of age is the final phase of the development sequence beginning after the age of five years. At ten the child's personality reaches a level of integration and rounding-off, which is reminiscent of the five-year-old stage. But while the five-year-old, contented and well adjusted to his own rather confined and self-sufficient world, sometimes seems like a finished product, the integrated personality of the ten-year-old child points forward to adaptation to the world of grown-ups (Fig. IV.5).

The control of various skills is expressed in different ways. A ten-year-old can, without interrupting its actions, carry on a conversation. Personal organization and attitudes to the surrounding world are usually more flexible. This means that the child of ten is very receptive to social and cultural influences. He often has considerable social intelligence which should be recognized and made the founda-

Fig. IV.5. The eleventh year is generally regarded as an uncommonly happy phase, which seems to anticipate adjustment to a grown-up environment.

tion of fundamental ideas of social broad-mindedness and tolerance.

Bühler claims that boys and girls are more like each other at ten than at any other age. Gesell, however, has quite the opposite opinion. He believes that a ten-year-old girl differs greatly from a ten-year-old boy with comparable education and experience. He emphasizes that girls are better balanced, have greater social maturity and more fundamental interest in problems concerning marriage and family life.

Differences of opinion among psychologists increase significantly when development from the age of ten onwards is under discussion, and it is not difficult to find more or less contradictory statements in the works of one author. This should not surprise us. Year by year an initially complicated organism becomes more complicated. Psychologists who devote themselves to the study of adolescents are faced with even more intricate problems than child psychologists. These problems will be further considered in Chapters XIII and XIV which deal with puberty.

Chapter V

PHYSICAL GROWTH

In this survey of development the stages distinguished are to be regarded as normative. Each provides an account of the forms of behaviour which are typical of its level. Study of a large number of observations shows that children in the western world may be expected to develop at about this speed and in this direction.

If the statements made in the survey are scrutinized closely, however, it will be found that they indicate many unsolved scientific problems. How far does behaviour depend on the influence of hereditary factors on the one hand, and environmental factors on the other? This problem underlies most psychological study, and it is also of great interest in any discussion of physical growth. For example, we know that an improvement in diet has a favourable effect on height and weight.

There is always the risk of confusing cause with effect. In contradiction to the assumption that a seven-year-old child is calmer than a six-year-old and therefore more fitted to begin school at that age (as he would in Sweden), it may be claimed that beginning school, or the knowledge that he is soon to begin school, may have a subduing effect on his behaviour. The environmental situation may thus contribute actively towards a certain change in behaviour which we may at first be inclined to regard exclusively as being due to maturation. We must avoid premature assertions that either heredity or environment is the cause of a particular pattern of behaviour. Nearly always there is a combination of both (cf. p. 154 ff.).

The psychologist, to arrive at valid conclusions based on strict scientific principles, collects data that can be treated statistically and by means of suitable methods. But in many branches of psychology, perhaps the most interesting ones, methods have not yet been evolved for collecting reliable and meaningful data in forms suitable for statistical treatment. This is illustrated by the observation technique used in the study of the social development of children (cf. p. 193). It is clear that methodological shortcomings here are due to the fact that we are concerned with an extremely complicated field of development.

Physical growth can usually be recorded with the help of reliable measuring methods. Child psychologists have begun to establish valid relationships between physical and mental development.

SKELETON AND MUSCLES

The development of an organism's behaviour is partly its striving to make effective use of the form of its body and of its organs. A quick-moving animal has a well-developed chest and powerful muscles; a slow one the heaviest parts of its body to the rear. Every organism must learn to make the most of the physical possibilities with which it is equipped. There is room for considerable adjustment in the event of accidental impediments to the organism's performance, such as injury.

Skeleton and the striped muscles attached to it are of primary importance for motor development. These and other tissue systems in the body do not grow simultaneously in all directions, as a previously shaped balloon does when it is blown up slowly.

Two important principles can be distinguished in physical growth: (*a*) growth is from the head towards the pelvis: the development of

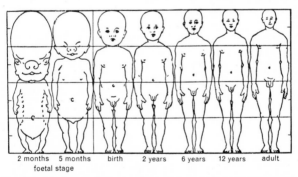

2 months 5 months birth 2 years 6 years 12 years adult
foetal stage

Fig. V.1. The human body, its shape and proportions change greatly during development. Notice particularly the relation of the head and trunk to arms and legs. (From M. C. Jackson.)

the head precedes that of the neck, and the neck develops before the chest and so on. This is the general *cephalocaudal* direction of development (Fig. V.1). (*b*) The growth of the different parts of the body proceeds in a *proximodistal* direction. This means that development is outwards from the central parts of the body. Thus the brachium is formed before the forearm, and the forearm before the hand. This principle applies also to the legs (Fig. V.2).

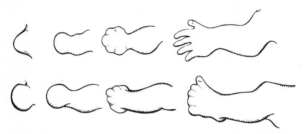

Fig. V.2. This figure illustrates the proximodistal development mentioned in the text (here from the fifth to the eighth week of the prenatal stage). The hand is in advance of the foot at the eighth week. (From Munn after Arey.)

Fig. V.1 shows how the human body changes in shape and proportion from the early embryo stage to the adult stage. The changes in the head are the most striking. In a two-month-old embryo the head is as large as the rest of the body, while in a fully grown human being it is approximately one-eighth of the total height of the person. The alterations in the proportions of the arms and legs are also remarkable.

The function of the skeleton is to stabilize movement and protect the internal organs. At first the skeleton consists of soft cartilage, and it is a long time before it hardens to bone. At birth a child has 270 bones. These are thin, flexible and loosely attached to each other. At puberty the number has risen to about 350, and is further increased by the age of twenty. After that some of the bones coalesce and the fully developed skeleton consists of 206 bones.

Alterations in the bone tissues can be studied best by means of X-ray photography. As the cartilage ossifies the tissues appear darker and more sharply defined on the plate. This development is illustrated in Fig. V.3 by X-ray photographs of the hand and wrist

of a boy and a girl at fourteen years. There is a clear distinction
between the sexes in this development, in that ossification is more
rapid in girls than in boys. As early as the age of four years girls are
almost a year ahead of boys, and during adolescence the average
difference is two years. At seventeen a girl's skeleton is practically
fully developed, while in boys this is not so until the age of twenty.

The development of the skeleton is measured primarily by the
hardness of the bones and is expressed by an index number giving
the relationship between the area of the ossified surface and the area

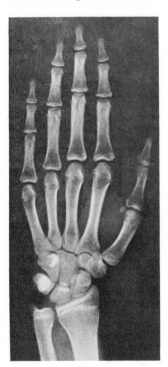 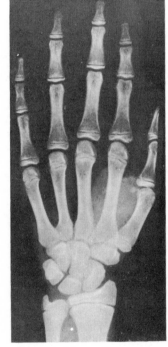

Boy 14 years   Girl 14 years

Fig. V.3. X-ray photographs reveal the great differences between boys and
girls during years of growth in respect of ossification. The girls are well
ahead. Cf. Fig. V.4. (Photographs from T. W. Todd.)

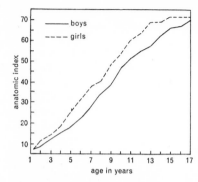

Fig. V.4 illustrates graphically that girls' hands are more ossified than boys' during the whole period of growth. (After Baldwin, Busby & Garside.)

of the part of the body as a whole. The curves in Fig. V.4 have been plotted from such an 'anatomical' index. They show that the index for girls is higher during the whole period of growth. Another, more simple criterion is the length of the individual bones. In this respect, too, girls have a slight advantage but when growth is finished male bones are, on an average, longer than female. There is some connection between the degree of ossification and the beginning of menstruation, as is shown in Fig. V.5.

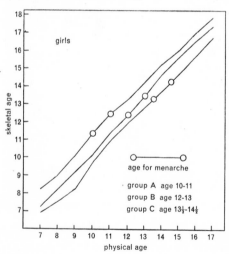

Fig. V.5. The curves show the relation between the 'skeletal' age, determined by the degree of ossification, and the menarche. The higher the 'skeletal' age, the earlier the menarche. (After Shuttleworth.)

Bodily movements and facial expressions are made possible by the co-ordination of nerves and muscles. The so-called striped muscles which, unlike the smooth muscles of the entrails, can be influenced voluntarily, originate from and are fastened to bones. There are a number of important exceptions to this rule, for example the mimetic muscles of the face and the final muscle in the bowels. The tongue starts from a bone but is not fastened at the other end. In a new-born baby the muscles represent about 23 per cent of the total weight. This proportion changes only slightly up to the age of fifteen years, when it is about 33 per cent. But only a year or so later it has risen to almost 45 per cent.

HEIGHT AND WEIGHT

The diagrams of increased weight and height are mainly illustrations of the growth of the skeleton and the muscles. If growth proceeded at an even rate, these diagrams would naturally consist of straight lines at a certain gradient. But this is not so. It is probably impossible to find one single case of such development. The diagrams are not even identical with each other, as will be seen from Figs. V.6 and V.7. If we connect the first and last points of the height curve by a straight line we will find a curve wholly above this line. The height curve rises rather steeply to the age of four years, after which it runs mainly linearly until adolescence. Then the gradient gets steeper again until full body height is attained during the late teens. If we draw a similar line through the weight curve we find that the first and last parts are above the line, while the central part shows that weight increases more slowly during the middle childhood years.

The curves for girls run practically parallel, just below those for boys up to the age of eleven years, when puberty begins in girls. At that age their weight curve in particular rises steeply. At the age of thirteen years the weight curves differ by rather more than five kilogrammes (ca. 10½ lb.) in favour of girls. After slightly more than a year boys again have the advantage, which they keep. Fig. V.8 shows how much the annual increase in weight varies. The first years of life naturally show the greatest proportional increase in weight, but regarded absolutely, the increase in weight is greatest during puberty.

These curves are based on examination of a large number of individuals who vary greatly from one to another in rate and rhythm

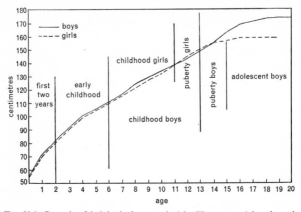

Fig. V.6. Growth of height in boys and girls. The curves (also those in Figs. V.7 and V.8) have been plotted by Cole from various American sources. These agree with the standard tables published for example in Sweden by Broman, Dahlberg and Lichtenstein. Considerable individual deviations from these normal curves occur throughout the whole period of growth. An eleven-year-old girl may vary in stature from 125 to 160 cm., and her weight from 20 to 50 kg. without there necessarily being any abnormality.

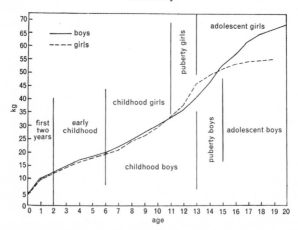

Fig. V.7. Increase of weight in boys and girls. Cf. text to Fig. V.6.

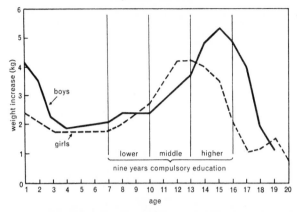

Fig. V.8. The annual increase in weight varies considerably during the period of growth, and accelerates rapidly during puberty. Great individual variations are found in both increase of weight and of height, due to how early or late puberty occurs. The school period shown refers to Swedish conditions.

of growth. It is therefore very difficult to speak of optimum weight or height during the years of growth – particularly during puberty and adolescence – since much depends upon the individual child's age at the onset of puberty. The inner secretions which guide this process have much influence on the development of both growth and behaviour. Menstruation usually occurs at about the age of thirteen years. It may occur as early as nine years of age or as late as eighteen, but all except about 3 per cent of fifteen-year-old girls will have had their first menstruation. It is more difficult to determine when puberty begins in boys, but it is normally between the ages of fourteen and fifteen. The variations are calculated to be between eleven and eighteen years (Fig. V.9).

OTHER ANATOMICAL CHANGES

The degree of ossification has been used to determine physical maturity, and the bones of the wrist in particular have been the objects of measurements to ascertain, for instance, the progress of motor development. But other anatomical growth processes have attracted the attention of psychologists. Important among these are the growth of the head, and the cutting and casting of the teeth.

Fig. V.9 shows the ages when boys and girls reach puberty. Each figure represents 10 per cent and the stage of development can be seen at five age levels. (After Keliher.)

Growth of the head and brain

The shaping of head and face begins early in the embryo stage. At birth a child's head is rather more than 60 per cent of its final size. Growth is rapid during the first year of life – at the age of two years the percentage is 87 – and slows down later until it ceases altogether around the age of 20 years. The brain goes through a similar course of growth. Its weight at birth is approximately 350 gm. and at the age of 20 years normally 1200–1400 gm. In a five-year-old the brain is about 80 per cent of its maximum weight, and at nine years of age 90 per cent.

No connection has been found between weight of brain and intelligence. It is not the weight but the number of convolutions which is most important. Nor is there any relationship between the measurements of the cranium and intelligence, even though a very small positive correlation coefficient of between 0·05 and 0·10 has been found. Very small craniums are often found among mentally deficients. An equivalent relationship is not so pronounced at the other extreme.

Greater agreement, though still weak and without diagnostic significance, is found between length of body and intelligence quotient (IQ). The fact that height has increased considerably during the past 50 years cannot be attributed to hereditary factors. The change is due mainly to better environmental conditions.

The theory is occasionally put forward that physically underdeveloped children are often compensated by better mental abilities. This is not correct; although there are striking exceptions, it is the rule that highly gifted people have, on an average, better physique than normally gifted people. L. M. Terman in particular has demonstrated this in his follow-up studies of exceptionally gifted persons. In adults, however, relationships of this kind have increasingly little significance.

Growth and casting of teeth

Teeth and their growth have been the subject of much uncertainty and ignorance. The first tooth usually appears when a child is six or seven months old, and the first complete set of teeth (milk teeth) around the age of four years. There are great differences in the cutting of teeth, both as regards time and sequence. Very occasionally – in one child in 2000 – the first tooth has been cut before birth. No meaningful connection between early teething and intelligence has been discovered.

Change of teeth begins normally at the age of about six years and until puberty the number of teeth increases fairly regularly from year to year. As in other respects, girls are ahead in this development. In the case of the milk teeth, however, boys take the lead particularly in the first years.

Two questions of psychological interest have been discussed in connection with teeth. The first is the effect of teething on behaviour, and the second the influence of thumb or finger sucking on the teeth. The first concerns the effect of a physical process on behaviour, and the second the effect of behaviour on physical development.

Both problems, which parents especially are apt to regard with anxious attention, are probably small ones. No evidence of a decline in standards of health during teething has been forthcoming. Children's doctors seem to be agreed that tenderness of the gums is common at the age of about eighteen months when the four central molars are cut, and when the last four molars in the milk teeth appear. A certain petulance in children at these periods is probably due to this tenderness, but the infections that frequently occur at the time have other origins. They may be due to the fact that the child is now capable of movement within a wider area and the number of contacts, with consequent risk of infection, is greater than before.

The other problem seems to be more complicated, and has not yet been solved satisfactorily. One investigation has shown, however, that finger sucking, particularly when the inside of the finger is against the teeth and when pressure is great, may cause certain defects in the gums and displacement of the teeth from their natural positions. In most cases these defects disappear when sucking is discontinued. Often too drastic and unwise steps are taken to compel children to break the habit of finger sucking, and these steps may have greater detrimental consequences than the sucking itself.

It is of the very greatest importance for the general state of physical and mental health to teach children mouth hygiene and care of the teeth as early as possible.

THE ENDOCRINE SYSTEM

Of the physiological maturation processes, those that are dependent upon the endocrine glands play an especially important role in physical and mental development. It is probable that these organs, more than any others, decide the course of physical development. They seem partly to function independently of each other, and as if they each gave rise to complex power fields, of which some are only active for limited periods of time and at different ages.

The interaction between the hormones is complicated. The hormones not only exercise direct influence on the course of maturation and on physical condition, but also affect each other in several ways. The mutual connection existing between the glands, metabolism and the nerve systems is difficult to determine experimentally. The science which covers such studies is called 'endocrinology'.

The endocrine glands

The endocrine or ductless glands include the pituitary body (*hypophysis cerebri*) and the pineal body (in the brain), the thyroid gland, the parathyroid glands and the thymus (in the upper chest region), the suprarenal bodies and the sex glands, i.e. the ovaries and the testes. The growth of all these glands seems to be similar during the foetal stage after they have been formed between the second and fourth months. After birth, however, they develop at very different rates, as shown by the curves in Fig. V.10.

The thymus grows rapidly during the first year, and in the years prior to puberty, when the gland attains its maximum weight. Then it is about 220 per cent heavier than at birth and 120 per cent heavier than at the age of 20 years. The thyroid and parathyroid glands and the pituitary body increase in size more steadily. The pineal body is up to 90 per cent of its final weight by the time a child is ten years old.

The suprarenal glands (see Fig. V.10) develop in a special way. By two weeks after birth they have lost half their weight, and it is not until about the age of twelve years that they have regained it. The sex glands grow rather slowly during childhood. The ovaries develop proportionally more than the testes up to puberty, but it is during the years following puberty that they increase most in weight. The ovaries attain their maximum weight at 20 years of age, but it is not until a few years later that the testes are fully grown. The weight of the testes is about forty times as great in an adult person as at birth.

If disturbances arise in the hormone production of the endocrine system, considerable disturbance may appear in growth, with serious effects on mental development. This is especially true of the pituitary body, which in many ways, both directly and indirectly – it produces more than ten different hormones – has great potential for influencing the course of growth. By means of growth hormones it controls directly the growth of bone tissues; overproduction results in giants and the opposite in dwarfs; and by the so-called gonadotrophic hormones (gonads = sex glands) it regulates the beginning of sexual maturity. If such hormones are taken from sexually mature animals and injected into sexually immature animals, sexual maturity soon appears. Some of the other hormones from the pineal body have a regulating effect by influencing various inner secretion centres, and other sex glands.

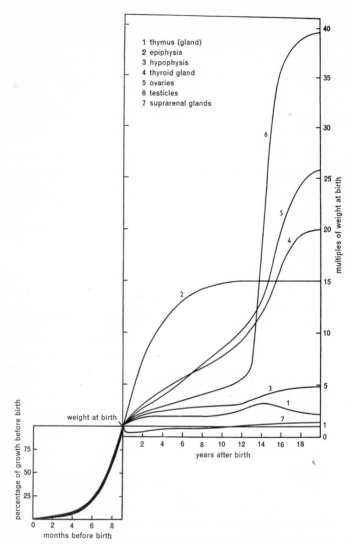

Fig. V.10. Development of the endocrine glands. Growth after birth expressed in multiples of weight at birth. (Cf. account in the text.)

The thyroid gland controls metabolism in essential respects. Disturbances in its functions not only cause physical changes, but the behaviour of the individual changes in character. Overproduction leads to general emotional instability and extreme sensitiveness to irritation.

The suprarenal hormone, adrenalin, on entering the blood, prepares the organism for attack or defence, both physical and mental. If the adrenalin secretion of an animal is stopped by operation, the animal becomes calmer and its activity is greatly reduced.

Mental changes generally do occur with changes in the physical condition, but physiological disturbances of a hormonal character have more fundamental and permanent effects.

General hormonal functions

This is no place for a catalogue of the functions of hormones. Only a few examples are given. The pituitary body, which is under the influence of the central nervous system, directs endocrinal interaction and its principal functions are the following:

(1) to stimulate growth
(2) to influence metabolism and
(3) to regulate physical development during the years of growth.

These functions are particularly active when sexual maturity has begun. The changes occurring then depend in many ways on the sex hormones. For thousands of years castration of domestic animals has been practised to make the meat more tasty or to make the animals easier to tame. The castration of men has been performed for various reasons, and is still carried out in the Orient. If this operation is performed before puberty, the result is often a very tall man, for the growing period of the bones is prolonged. The growth of hair round the sex organs is inconsiderable, the thymus gland does not atrophy, and sexual drive is completely lacking. Nor does the voice break.

Castration after puberty does not have the same physical or mental consequences. Sexual drives do not change in themselves, and the individual may still be potent, though sterile. Knowledge of the operation may, on the other hand, have profound psychological effects.

Such facts of experience, and extensive experimentation with

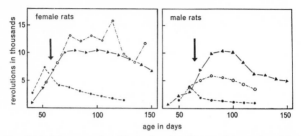

Fig. V.11. A large number of experiments with animals have shown that alterations in activity appear after interference with different glands. Here is shown the effect on rats if the sex glands (testes and ovaries) are removed, and injections of oestrogen (female hormones) made. The method is described in the text. Triangles = non-injected normal rats (control group). Open circles = injected rats with sex glands removed. Filled circles = non-injected rats with sex glands removed. (After Richter & Hartman.)

animals, make it clear that the sex hormones have independent and diverse tasks and effects. In addition, as already mentioned, it has been shown that gonadotrophic impulses, which start the sexual functions, originate from the pituitary body. The fact that, as far as can be observed, the gonadotrophic hormones have no effect before puberty is not because they are lacking. The presence of small amounts of such hormones has been observed in the pituitary body even at birth (cf. Fig. XIII.3, p. 218). But it is probable that these hormones are not secreted in large enough quantities to bring the sex glands to maturity before the beginning of puberty. It is not known why the increase in the activity of the pituitary body begins then.

The hormones and the activity of the organism

Finally a few words on the general significance of the hormones for the activity of the organism. This significance has been shown mainly by a large number of experiments on animals. If the pituitary body is removed, or if its communication with the central nervous system is severed, the activity of the animal is greatly reduced. This effect may be at least partly explained by the superior position of the pituitary body in the endocrine system. It has also been shown that interference with the pituitary body leads to atrophy in other glands, for example the thyroid gland, the pancreas and the sex glands.

As an example of how endocrine organs subordinate to the

pituitary body influence activity, we may study an experiment with rats. The experiment concerned the sex glands and the result is shown in Fig. V.11.

A common experimental method of measuring the activity of an animal is to shut it up in a treadmill arrangement to which a revolution counter is attached. The number of revolutions registered per unit of time sinks to about one-fifth for animals whose sex glands have been removed – if they have not afterwards been given injections of sex hormones.

Another method of measurement, however, has shown a much smaller decline. In the use of a so-called stabilimeter – the floor of the cage functions as a kind of scale which registers very exactly the changes in pressure caused by the animal's movements – the activity of castrated rats sinks by about only 10 per cent.

The aim of this chapter has been to illustrate some physical aspects of development. The various parts of the body do not grow at the same rate, nor do they reach maturity simultaneously. This should make us very careful when judging the importance of different factors. The closing section has, perhaps, more than the other parts of the chapter, been intended to illustrate how intimate is the interaction between physical and mental development. It provides an interesting background to the behavioural problems of puberty. No discussion of individual motivation can ignore hormonal processes.

Chapter VI

THE FOUNDATIONS OF
LEARNING AND PERCEPTION

The two terms used in the chapter heading stand for processes fundamental to the development of behaviour, whether we are considering
human beings or the simplest unicellular organisms. In order to
learn anything we must first be capable of perceiving: the written
and spoken word and the world of objects alike are experienced
through perception. They produce patterns of stimulation which, by
way of the sense organs, reach the central nervous system where they
are transformed into percepts. The consequences in the nervous
tissues of these percepts are what we know as learning.

There is something fundamental and right in the assertion that we
earn by experience. Experience is what we gain by perception, that
which we continually make use of when faced with new stimuli. If
we could not use past experience in this way the world around us
would seem completely disintegrated and disorganized.

As regards conscious mental life, we must imagine a newborn
child as very simple and unorganized. However diffuse the child's
reaction to stimuli may be the first time it is given the breast, it must
still be regarded as a kind of primitive perception, which releases
response reactions in the form of sucking and swallowing. When a
skilful cobbler repairs a pair of shoes, he reacts with adequate,
learned behaviour patterns in what are for him well-known stimulus
situations. It is the same in principle when a schoolboy repeats a
passage of poetry by heart. Frequently he hesitates and stumbles
through his homework. This implies that his behaviour has not been
sufficiently modified, which is the same as saying that learning is not
complete.

The examples given refer to learning of different kinds and on
different levels. What learning does is to make available, in certain

given situations, goal-directed responses. We are subjected to stimuli on the social and emotional plane, too. Intercourse with other people comprises a mixed skein of learned conduct, acquired from early childhood and onwards. Our emotional reactions in different situations depend on what the situation implies to us, and the meaning is practically always learned. We are continually concerned with stimuli. Our reactions depend on the relationship between the resultant percepts and the previously learned response patterns aroused within the nervous system.

UNLEARNED BEHAVIOUR

Active behaviour can be observed in an eight-week-old human embryo when, for instance, the cheek is touched with a hair (cf. p. 32). This reaction was described as the zero point of human behaviour. The use of the term 'behaviour' implies here that the organism responds to an external stimulus in a way that can be observed. Regardless of whether the embryo is actually able to experience anything like pleasure or displeasure – such a problem cannot possibly be solved – it reacts in a way that organisms during their whole life and development endeavour to do, that is to avoid unpleasant experiences and court pleasant ones.

Criteria of unlearned behaviour

Responses of this type seem to occur as direct functions of biologically given structures. By unlearned behaviour we mean non-modified expressions of these structure functions. Attempts have been made to lay down certain general criteria for the behaviour that is to be regarded as unlearned, and the following are usually given:

(1) the behaviour must be *universal* within the species,
(2) the behaviour in question must show *sequential* development,
(3) the behavioural acts must be distinguished by a peculiar *adaptiveness* which is evidence of a phylogenetic origin (see p. 15).

Phylogenetically conditioned behaviour must be regarded as being present in all normal members of a species. It also seems, however, that phylogenetically conditioned behaviour is the only form of behaviour that can be learned. No human being can learn to fly, for example, by practising arm-flapping; flying is out of reach phylogenetically. And, as a Swedish humorist has pointed out, 'Billions of bees can't write threes.' Man's greatest achievements, whether in the realms of art, science or acrobatics, are to be regarded as the results of phylogenetically derived structures the functions of which have been exploited to their fullest extent.

The significance of maturity

Some structures develop early, others late. Structures connected with sexual behaviour develop late. The processes behind the development of the functional structures are usually called *maturation*. The child's behavioural response to environmental influences is partly decided by the maturity level of the structures. Often the environment – represented by parents, for example – demands performances that are incompatible with the maturity level (incongruous demands for too early control of the evacuation functions, for politeness, for 'always being best' in various social connections, and so on). But the opposite extreme – exaggerated indifference to the development of the child – is also found. It is difficult to decide which of these two extremes is more to be deprecated.

Behaviour which occurs independently of environmental influences like training or observation of others may be described as unlearned. This definition should be regarded as a practical limitation rather than as scientifically conclusive. In essential respects it is only theoretically true, because we know that phylogenetic maturation is also stimulated by external influences. We are unable as yet, however, to measure and determine their significance.

ELEMENTARY LEARNING PROCESSES

Three important terms used in the study of unlearned behaviour are tropism, reflex and instinct. They are worth attention because modifications of such behaviour-types as a consequence of external influences or training must be regarded as elementary learning processes.

Tropisms

The term *tropism* can hardly be used about human behaviour. It is defined as an orienting response in an organism to an external source of stimulus. Some vegetable and animal organisms orient themselves towards a source of light, for example. Other sources of energy causing tropistic movements are heat, the gravitation of the earth and chemicals.

A well-known example of what is known as galvanotropism is the reaction of a larval salamander to a current of electricity through the body. If the direction of the current is from head to tail the ends of the body are pressed downwards, but if the direction of the current is changed the head and tail point upwards (Fig. VI.1). These different behaviour patterns are entirely compulsory.

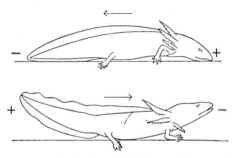

Fig. VI.1. An example of unlearned behaviour. Galvanotropism in the larval salamander. The arrows show the direction of current. See text. (After Loeb.)

Reflexes and their conditioning

Reflex differs from tropism in the following ways: it consists of a localized reaction, is not diffusely oriented but is specific and assumes an organism that has at its disposal synaptically connected nerve elements. The simplest of all reflex arrangements, the so-called reflex arc, consists of one nerve fibre leading inwards and one leading outwards between which is a contact point (synapse), which can transmit nerve impulses from one fibre to the other.

Efficient reflex mechanisms are present in an eight-week-old human embryo. This explains why the embryo then – but not before – can react to an external stimulus. This type of behaviour may be called a reflex.

Spelt (see above, p. 34 ff.) studied reflex activity, and was able to record a response to a previously neutral stimulus. This may, in principle, be compared with Ivan Pavlov's famous experiments on dogs, where the secretion of saliva was brought about as a consequence of the sound of a metronome, first associated with food. This is the conditioning principle, so fundamental to modern learning psychology.

The conditioned reflex has been regarded as the prototype of learning. Certain stimuli always provoke reflex responses. The lower part of the leg is involuntarily thrown forward if a blow is aimed at the sinew that connects the knee-cap and the shin (patellar reflex). Chemical substances on the tongue cause greater secretion of saliva.

A stimulus, which itself does not provoke a reflex action, presented immediately before or simultaneously with the effective (unconditioned or involuntary) stimulus, elicits, after a number of trials, a response without the help of any unconditioned stimulus. It is this reaction that is known as a conditioned reflex. In order to extend the use of the principle of conditioning to reactions that are not necessarily reflexive, reference is generally made to conditioned and unconditioned responses.

Classical and instrumental conditioning

The method of conditioning described above is the one that was used by Pavlov. It is called *classical conditioning*, to distinguish it from *instrumental conditioning*, developed later, mainly by B. F. Skinner. The methods differ in two essential respects:

(1) Classical conditioning produces the same type of response as in the unconditioned situation. It is concerned, for instance, with the secretion of saliva all the time. In instrumental conditioning we are concerned with different categories of responses. The conditioned depression of a lever (Fig. VI.2) acquires augmented strength, i.e. it is learned better because, with every depression, food falls into a dish. The conditioned action of lever-pressing and the unconditioned response of eating have little in common.

(2) The increased strength of response is controlled by the experimenter in classical conditioning. Regardless of whether the organism reacts to the conditioned stimulus (a bell, for example) or not, it is presented with the unconditioned stimulus (the food) after a definite interval of time. The rat in the Skinner box, however, controls the conditioning response itself, i.e. it receives the response-reinforcing stimulus (food) only if it makes the conditioned response of depressing the lever.

It will not be out of place in a discussion of conditioning to consider a few terms, beside those already mentioned. A conditioned response is brought about by *reinforcement*. If the conditioned stimulus is presented without the unconditioned stimulus, the conditioned response learned previously is said to be *non-reinforced*. In Pavlov this means that the bell rings but no food appears. In Skinner that the lever is depressed, but no food pellet drops into the dish.

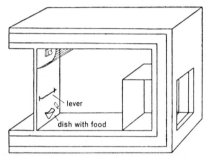

Fig. VI.2. The most famous apparatus for the investigation of so-called instrumental conditioning is the Skinner box. The animal used in the experiment (this type of box is for rats, but Skinner often uses pigeons) is placed in the box and when, during its endeavours to find food, it happens to depress a lever, a pellet of food falls into the dish. Gradually the animal learns to get food by pressing down the lever and instrumental conditioning has been established.

Repeated non-reinforcement tends to weaken the conditioned response or eliminate it completely. This is called *extinction*. It does not mean the complete abolition of the conditioned response, for after a period of rest following extinction, the conditioned response often appears again, but usually much weakened. This return of a response after extinction, without reinforcement, is called the *spontaneous recovery* of a conditioned response.

Conditioned behaviour is not merely something produced in experimentation with animals; it is generally considered to be an essential feature of all learning. One of the most important incentives to research in this field was provided by Watson's behaviourism. His far-reaching formulations like 'Man is a pure reflex machine' have been modified considerably, it is true, but his fundamental methodological and theoretical approaches remain. Thus Skinner, mentioned above, is to be regarded as a behaviourist.

Instincts

A third concept, side by side with tropism and reflex, is *instinct*. This term was covered by a cloud of obscurity for a long time, mainly because it was defined so diffusely. During recent years, however, the concept has been given content and definition by the brilliant research work for which Konrad Lorenz and Niko Tinbergen have

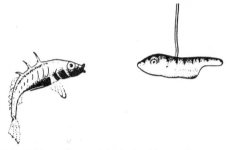

Fig. VI.3. A model of a female stickleback with a swollen abdomen elicits sexual behaviour in the male. On the other hand, a faithful model of a female without the swollen abdomen had no effect. (Model used by Tinbergen.) (Cf. text.)

been chiefly responsible. It seems very likely that their observations will also be of importance in the understanding of elementary human behaviour.

Tinbergen has suggested the following descriptive definition: 'Instinct is a hierarchically organized mechanism in the nervous system which responds with co-ordinated movements of significance to the perpetuation of the species, when influenced by specific releasing and guiding internal and external stimuli.' Tropisms seem to be completely stereotyped, while instincts, in addition to their greater complexity, have a certain – occasionally quite considerable – degree of adaptability. Typical examples are nest-building by birds, in which both site and available material may cause wide variations.

It has been shown that the stimuli causing instinctive actions are characteristic and simple. Of Tinbergen's many examples one is illustrated in Fig. VI.3. One of the 'sign stimuli' (or releasers) that produces mating behaviour in the male stickleback is the swollen abdomen of the female. A model of a female stickleback, not particularly lifelike, but with this swelling, is sufficient to elicit mating behaviour, while a faithful model without this swelling has very little effect.

It has also been shown that the natural impulse situation does not always provoke the maximum release. The oyster-catcher reacts with more intensive brooding when it has five eggs than when it has the normal three, and it appears to be happiest sitting on one egg four times as large as an egg typical of the species.

Artificial models of stimuli that excite the instinct mechanism, in which the characteristic features have been exaggerated, give augmented response effects. Such so-called super-optimal stimuli, maintains Holger Poulsen, a Danish zoologist and a pupil of Lorenz, seem to be of some importance in certain spheres of human behaviour. The sexual sphere in particular is rich in examples of instinctive behavioural tendencies, and 'dummies' representing feminine features in which the sexual characters are exaggerated are met with daily in advertisements and films. Ideals of beauty change, but women's clothes and cosmetics seem to have made use of super-optimal sign stimuli for thousands of years.

Instinctive actions are receptive to learned modifications. A primary learning element must be assumed to be present as early as the first 'following' response, sometimes called '*imprinting*', as Lorenz first demonstrated with newly hatched greylag geese. They have no inherited knowledge of the appearance of their parents, and when they are hatched they follow the first living creature they see, which is usually the mother. If the goslings are hatched in an incubator they may, in just the same way, follow a human being, and after an hour or so behave as though 'imprinted' with the image of the foster parent. After this, they pay no attention to other birds of their own species.

A more complicated type of learning that takes place at a later age but has obvious instinctual foundations is shown by Tinbergen in the following example. In Greenland sledge dogs live in packs of five to ten. Each dog defends the pack's 'territory' – it may be regarded as a kind of social life space – against strange dogs. The dogs within a region are well acquainted with the territories of the other dogs. This only applies to adult dogs, however. Puppies are outside these groups and do not defend any territory. They run all over the place, and when they enter the territory of strange dogs they are driven away. But even if they are bitten they are quite incapable of learning the boundaries of the territories. It is not until sexual maturity is reached that the young dogs learn to recognize the different territories, and within a week they have stopped trespassing on the territory of other dogs.

'Imprinting' and the development of human behaviour

It is not easy to make a balanced assessment of the significance of imprinting and similar phenomena in the development of human behaviour. It is tempting to credit them with being the deciding factors behind much that is puzzling and curious in this area of study.

Psychoanalysis has emphasized strongly the great penetrative power of certain emotional experiences of childhood. Although banished from the conscious personality, they exert great and permanent influence on behaviour. Sexual examples seem to illustrate this with particular clarity. Deviations from normal instinct-guided life can, at least partly, be interpreted in terms taken from the research work of Lorenz and Tinbergen. Their work provides a comprehensive empirical complement to the psychoanalytical approach.

Observations of this kind may help to illustrate how important is general theoretical discussion of fundamental learning processes to the central problems of child psychology. The solution of these problems must have far-reaching practical consequences. Comparative psychology, the object of which is to study behaviour at different phylogenetic levels, and which therefore embraces animal psychology, is frequently considered to lack interest, and is occasionally regarded – even by some child psychologists – with contempt. Certainly, care should be taken in the application of animal psychological findings to man, but such findings are undoubtedly worth careful study. We might notice that no one despises the common procedure of testing new medicines on animals; on the contrary, it is regarded as the only practicable method.

OTHER FORMS OF LEARNING

It is beyond the scope of a work of this kind to give a detailed account of the many problems of learning. However, we will make a brief survey of different forms of learning in connection with Fig. VI.4. Although it may be possible to discriminate between them in description it must be emphasized that they seldom or never appear in isolation but are interwoven into each other. That is why it is often

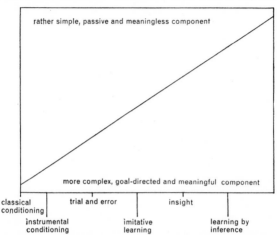

rather simple, passive and meaningless component

more complex, goal-directed and meaningful component

| classical conditioning | trial and error | insight |
| instrumental conditioning | imitative learning | learning by inference |

Fig. VI.4 shows schematically different levels of learning and how they increase in meaningfulness and degree of complication. (Cf. text.)

very difficult to illustrate principles of learning by everyday examples, for in such cases it is nearly always possible to show that forms of learning other than the one to be illustrated are also present.

The figure summarizes the developmental psychological aspect of learning, and shows how psychological and other components present in advanced learning become more and more complicated in structure. It also implies that the influence of environment becomes more important the higher up the learning ladder we get. Thus the maximum learning performances of human beings need linguistic symbols of various kinds, and these can only be acquired in a social environment.

It has been pointed out earlier that *conditioned reflexes* are a kind of prototype of learning, and may be regarded as fundamental elements. This is especially true of classical conditioning, described above. We have seen that it can be observed even in human foetus, and many experiments have shown that even unicellular animals such as amoeba and paramecia can be taught to modify their behaviour by conditioning.

Instrumental conditioning, which is more meaningful, makes greater demands on an organism. It is inconceivable in the embryo stage, and it contains in its higher forms many elements of the principle described below as trial and error. The rat which has to press down a lever in the Skinner box is an example.

Learning by trial and error

The term *trial and error* used in connection with a particular form of learning has been the cause of controversy among theorists about learning. Thorndike used it in the discussion of his experiments with cats in 'problem boxes'. His experimental set-up is illustrated in Fig. VI.5. In order to escape from the cage and reach food, the hungry animal – hunger is used as the motivating factor (see Chapter VII) – had to withdraw some bolts, and 'trial and error' describes the method by which the cat tackles the problem. The behaviour that does not lead to success gets less frequent, and there is a tendency to repeat actions that lead to satisfactory results.

Thorndike, on the basis of these observations, formulated his famous *law of effect*, which states that an action eliciting satisfaction becomes closely attached to the situation, while actions leading to contrary results are eliminated.

Much learning in both animals and humans – adults and children – contains elements of trial and error. We have all experienced the knowledge of failure and the need to begin again. Experience which

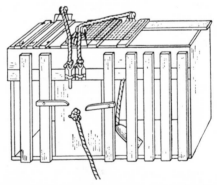

Fig. VI.5. Thorndike's problem box. (Cf. Fig. VI.2.) The Skinner box is much simpler and makes possible a more detailed analysis of behaviour.

is reflected in the sayings 'if at first you don't succeed, try, try, try again', and 'Better luck next time'. But on the human level it is hazardous to study the trial and error principle in any great detail.

Imitative learning

A small child learning to eat with a spoon does so by trial and error, but also by *imitative learning*. Parents try to show the child how to use a spoon effectively without spilling its food. The mother sits by the child with the child's hand in hers, and together they help to fill the spoon and carry it to the mouth as correctly as possible.

There are clearly simple imitative elements present, and the child's helper is to a certain extent prepared to utilize the growing ability of the child to imitate. Where social learning is concerned – for instance, problems of adjustment to group life during adolescence – examples of imitative learning are many and striking. The urge to be like others is very strong at this stage.

Insight

The next level in Fig. VI.4 is *insight*. This concept has been made famous by Wolfgang Köhler, in his experiments with chimpanzees. Insight is present in learning when one is faced with a situation that demands new adjustment, and when one is in a position to analyse the situation satisfactorily, understand the demands made by the problem and react in such a way as to arrive at a solution. Insight is discussed in the next chapter (p. 107 ff.), where Köhler's experiments will be critically scrutinized.

As an extension to insight, learning that makes still greater demands on mental activity may be described. *Abstract logical conclusions* belong to this learning level, and presume great ability in the use of symbols. Chapter VIII will deal with the development of this ability from the starting point of Piaget's researches. Intelligence tests for the measurement of the R factor (p. 143 ff.) have some connection with goal-directed learning at this level.

PERCEPTION

In the transition from an account of fundamental learning processes to perception, it would be convenient if valid assumptions could be made to connect these two subjects in a satisfactory manner. But in this respect general psychology seems to be in an embarrassing dilemma, which extends to developmental psychology.

We must assume that perception and the need to perceive are fundamental and it may be that Woodworth's formulation that perception is always incited by a directly inherited motive, which might be called the will to perceive, is correct. To see, to hear – to see clearly, to hear distinctly – to investigate what one sees or hears – little by little, such concrete, immediate motives come to control relationships with the surrounding world. It is impossible to stabilize and develop this urge towards organization without learning, and learning changes in one way or another the initial situation for new perceptions.

Primitive organisms begin life as practically finished products and are completely organized at an early stage. The higher up in the animal kingdom we get the longer is the growth and maturation period required. This implies that greater organizational demands are made on the organisms, which in return are provided with greater possibilities of behaviour. It is interaction between perception (becoming aware of a stimulus situation) and what has been learned (the retention of stimuli received earlier) that makes the organization of behaviour possible.

This is illustrated conclusively by experiments, in which chimpanzees from birth and for a long time afterwards (up to eighteen months old) were brought up in darkness. When, after that period, these animals were first introduced to simple visual stimuli, their ability to perceive was not much better than that of a newborn animal, and it took a long time for them to arrive at a normal perception level. Even six months later they were still much retarded compared with animals with a normal development.

Similar information has been obtained from people who were born blind, but who have been given their sight later by operation. One such patient was trained to distinguish between two simple figures, a square and a triangle, but after thirteen days' training he had only learned enough to be able to give the shapes of the figures by counting the corners one at a time.

The innateness of perception

Investigations and reports of this kind provide an essential part of the background to one of the most interesting contemporary works on the psychology of perception and learning, D. O. Hebb's *Organisation of Behaviour*. The connection between perception and learning is dealt with, and Hebb discusses the question of whether any components of perception may be regarded as innate.

Fig. VI.6. Rubin's famous reversible goblet-profile figure in which either a goblet or two profiles facing each other can be seen, but never both at the same time. The discrimination of a figure from its ground may be regarded as a fundamental ability.

In one important respect Hebb is in opposition to the Gestalt psychologists' theory of the innately structured general conceptions. Only in one form, he maintains, is the ability to perceive a figure present at birth, namely the ability to discriminate, diffusely, between a figure and its background. This is the ability investigated by Edgar Rubin in his well-known studies of the figure-ground problem (Fig. VI.6).

This primitive exercise of perception, the distinguishing of a figure from its background, is made possible by certain characteristics of the nervous system, related directly to the actual reception of stimuli. Hebb calls this simple perception product the *primitive unity*. It is exclusively sensory, i.e. determined by processes in the sense organs.

Hebb discriminates between this and *non-sensory figure-ground organization*. This latter is affected by and gets its content from experience and other non-sensory factors. He also isolates *identity*. This factor implies the possibility of recognizing and locating a meaningful connection in the perceived figure. This is due to the inherent associative features in perception, that is the ability to associate material learned earlier with that which is perceived. Identity is a matter of degree and is not innately given.

We must learn to understand even very simple figures. Behind our self-evidently experienced ability to recognize a circle at a glance, or distinguish between a triangle and a square, is a long and complicated learning and organization process. Every child must go through this process.

Another research worker who has also made valuable contributions to this discussion in our time, J. J. Gibson, has expressed this idea as follows: 'The visual world is an unlearned experience . . . meaningless when seen for the first time, and what one learns is to see the meanings of things.' Acoustic, tactual and olfactory impressions, and impressions from other 'worlds' of sensory experience – all communicated by the different sense organs – might take the place of visual impressions.

The primitive meanings of early visual impressions

Gibson, in the passage quoted above, seems to be closer to the Gestalt psychologists than Hebb and in a further analysis he approaches them still more closely, for he asks whether it is possible for a small infant, without the language habits acquired later, to have a wordless and crudely primitive meaning for certain of its earliest visual impressions.

It is naturally very difficult to answer this question. The results available are difficult to interpret and can hardly prove anything. But Gibson refers to an interesting experiment. Almost without exception children aged from two to six months fixate and smile at a face-like object. The face need not have a friendly expression, and need not even be attractive, but it must be in full face, not in profile. It must also move and be of a certain size; a child will not react to a doll's face. It is not until a child is six months old that its smile becomes discriminating; it no longer smiles at a strange face or a dummy, it recognizes its parents, reacts to disapproving facial expressions and begins to respond to a smile.

These latter responses are learned, but it is obvious that this is not the case with the former. Its effective sign-stimulus – the Lorenz-Tinbergen terminology seems adequate – is an indefinable pattern which shows only the most elementary features of the human face. 'The wordless meaning of this crude pattern', says Gibson, 'is equally primitive but it nevertheless is a discernible pattern and it has the meaning of something to be smiled at.'

 - It must be added that the smile is also primitive. Perhaps it is comparable with the behaviour of the inexperienced chickens in Tinbergen's experiment. He made a silhouette which was moved within the angle of vision of the birds. If the figure was moved so that it looked like a short-necked hawk the chickens ran away, terrified, to hide. If the silhouette was moved in the opposite direction it looked like a short-necked, harmless goose, and nothing happened. A small child cannot run away from danger or fetch the help it requires to satisfy its vital needs. But it can solicit pity with a smile.

Another example perhaps illustrates the same functional principle more adequately. When two wolves or dogs fight, the loser, to show that he admits defeat, lifts up his head and exposes his throat to his antagonist's fangs. But the bite is not given and the fight ends. The victor proudly lifts his leg, and the loser takes the opportunity of moving off. The exposure of a very vulnerable part of the body is here an effective means of averting danger. If we regard the primitive first smile as a kind of protective mechanism, we are very close to the conditions which Tinbergen asks that instinct should fulfil.

Many modern perception psychologists speak of perception as a series of assumptions made by the individual. We assume that the wall we see in front of us is vertical, that the floor we walk on is horizontal (although it should really appear to be sloping upwards slightly, when we stand looking down at it), that an object is a certain distance away, and so on. In most cases our assumptions are satisfactory and fully acceptable, but sometimes we may be very wrong.

When the apparatus with which a child organizes perception has begun to function, we may imagine that it develops the ability to make, on the basis of experience, better hypotheses about the surrounding world. At first they are tentative and erroneous, but they gradually become more stable.

THE MATURITY LEVEL OF THE SENSE ORGANS AT BIRTH

This discussion seems to lead towards an affirmative answer to the old question whether there are pure perceptions, that is sense impressions uninfluenced by experience. It seems difficult to find any valid argument why this should not be so when we realize how far the sense organs have progressed, at birth, in their ability to function.

Among what are known as the *cutaneous senses*, the *sense of touch* has already been discussed (p. 32). It was then pointed out that this sense organ functions very early – at the beginning of the foetal stage. There are no equivalent investigations into the *temperature senses*, but it has been shown that newborns react strongly to stimuli that are colder than the body surface. Heat stimuli are less effective. The sense of pain is not highly developed at birth, and it has been assumed that this retardation serves some kind of biological purpose.

The *sense of taste* seems to be capable of registering before birth, although normally activation does not occur. Of the taste qualities sweet, sour, salt and bitter, sensitivity to sweet is especially well developed in newborns, while response to the others is uncertain. The *sense of smell* is also developed before birth, but it is not considered to be capable of functioning normally until the nasal cavity is filled with air.

With regard to *hearing*, Spelt's experiments (p. 34 ff.) and several others show that acoustic stimuli increase the activity of a foetus during the last prenatal months. Although the mechanism of hearing seems to be well developed before birth, the foetus does not seem to be receptive to sounds of normal intensity until a few days after birth, possibly because the middle ear is filled with fluid and the outer ear is closed. Keenness of hearing increases during the first days of life. Hearing tests have shown that this improvement continues up to the age of ten years or so.

The mechanism of *sight*, which is unusually complicated and also includes important muscular factors for adequate movements of the eyes, begins to develop at an early embryonic stage. Light stimuli, even of high intensity, do not produce any definite retinal effect during the whole foetal period, although a certain ability to differentiate between light and dark has been demonstrated in children born two months too early. Ability to perceive the difference between coloured and white light has been observed in infants two weeks old. It is not until the age of six years that a child is able to discern the figures in a colour-blindness test.

The account in this chapter has been rather along the lines of 'in the beginning was perception'. Learning begins its modifying influence at a very early stage, however. It can be said about both man and animals that no activities are either wholly learned or wholly unmodified by learning. We are here clearly faced by difficult problems of definition, the solutions of which depend largely on continued experimental research.

The aspects of development to be discussed below will be seen to originate in various ways from the concepts outlined in this chapter. They may refer to social or emotional development or the general formation of personality. The vexed question of the relationship between hereditary and environmental factors during maturity is included in this discussion.

Chapter VII

MOTIVATION AND THE
DEVELOPMENT OF LEARNING

The mechanisms that enable us to perceive and to learn by perceiving are of fundamental importance in the development of all the forms of behaviour that a psychologist may want to study. Nevertheless, these mechanisms seem to be subordinate to the structures which determine *what* is to be perceived and learned. We are concerned with the highly developed processes of organization that guide individual human actions towards definite goals. We are also concerned with the aberrations in behaviour that often make it hard to discover why a person acts in a certain way.

WHAT IS MEANT BY MOTIVATION?

For centuries, philosophers in their studies of the will have pondered over problems relating to motivation. It has been asked whether free will exists, as claimed by so-called indeterminists, or does not – which determinists maintain. Early psychologists also paid great attention to the will, and regarded it as one of the three fundamental modes of consciousness along with feeling and thinking.

Contemporary psychology seldom uses the word 'will', but that does not imply that no interest is taken in the problems of the will, or that its importance is deprecated. On the contrary, the study of these problems is an essential task, not least in theoretical child psychology and in its application to upbringing and education. At present, however, such questions are discussed in the context of the study of motivation. If motivation were simply a more difficult word for will, nothing more would need to be said. But the development of the concept of motivation has changed discussion of will, like the change in outlook that occurred as the outlook of general psychology was changed when the word 'behaviour' took the place of 'soul'.

Behaviour is what can be observed and described of the activities of an organism, and the causes of behaviour are motives of various kinds and strengths. The process by which these motives influence actions in particular directions is called motivation. It is convenient to describe motives in terms of needs and drives.

Motivation directs activities towards definite ends in all spheres of behaviour, but perhaps most noticeably in learning. The question is: is it possible to learn anything at all without some kind of motivation? If one holds the view that no behaviour is possible without a motive, it must necessarily follow that no learning is possible without a motive.

Investigations of motivation

It is motivation that we are primarily concerned with when, to study how learning is affected by hunger in animal psychology, for example, we let animals suffering from different degrees of hunger loose in a maze to find their way to the end, where they will find food. A relationship between the degree of hunger and the rate of learning can be observed: the hungrier the animal is, the quicker it learns (fewer trips through the maze before the animal masters it without taking false turns). Thus the food is an attractive reward. If the animal is unrewarded, learning is poor or almost completely lacking. Fig. VII.1 illustrates this, and also shows how reward introduced later in the experiment accelerates learning. From this we can see that *something* has been learned even in the early unrewarded stages of the experiment. This 'something' has been called *latent learning* and seems to consist mainly of general adjustment to the experimental situation.

Again it is motivation that is being studied when an experimenter praises or finds fault with a certain performance to see how it affects the course of further learning. The experimenter is endeavouring to influence the subject's motives. If the result reveals changes, he has caused changes in the motivation which are of significance to the learning (cf. Fig. II.1, p. 26).

Behind any motivation there is some kind of need demanding satisfaction. In the first example given above, we are concerned with a physiologically conditioned hunger that drives the animal to perform certain tasks. If the animal is sated it will lie down and sleep in the maze, or manifest some kind of activity, perhaps because it feels uneasy in the confined space. The second example referred to learned

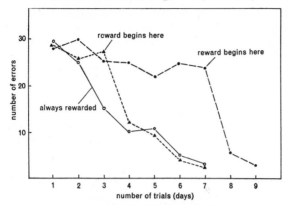

Fig. VII.1. These curves seem to show that some kind of learning, though of a latent nature, takes place even when the animals (rats) are not rewarded. The rats rewarded from the start improve steadily, while unrewarded animals show no improvement. But they learn very quickly when they are rewarded (given food). (From Blodgett.)

and socially conditioned formation of needs, which seem to follow the principle of avoiding unpleasantness and striving towards happiness. Freud introduced the concept of the 'pleasure principle' to account for our instinctive actions. He placed, in opposition to this, the 'reality principle' which adults have to follow to adjust themselves to the demands on behaviour made by the community. The concepts do not seem to be quite contrary to each other: even with the reality principle we choose the alternative that we consider least unpleasant.

If we are satisfied to describe motivation briefly as the *energy-creating and guiding processes behind the activities of organisms*, we find that motivation is a very general concept covering efforts on many different levels: we are able to consider under the same heading not merely physiological needs and drives, but also the highest human ambitions.

Motivation and upbringing

An essential end in all upbringing is to direct the motivation processes towards goals that are positive and meaningful for society and the individual. To create understanding of social values and norms in the individual is said to be the most important task of the school, together with the more direct acquisition of knowledge. When we say that there is joy in work in a class, we can usually also say that the children are well motivated in relation to the school.

Formerly children were often told that their will was in the birch, which meant that motivation was influenced chiefly by punishment. Whether a child's motivation can be prevented by corporal punishment from taking an undesirable direction is the subject of a debate that has been going on throughout the history of education. The alternative has been effort to achieve the desired results by positive measures to encourage interest.

A discerning psychologist (Coghill) has maintained that as long as the nervous system is growing, there is an internal behaviour motivation based on the maturation processes of the nerve cells. The child tries to perfect certain patterns of activity without any external influence. The living structure compels itself to function. The child attempts in innumerable ways to explore its surroundings on its own initiative, and since its surroundings are determined by parents, teachers and others, its activities are canalized in the direction of complicated cultural conditioning.

A decisive factor in this connection is the growing ability of the child to keep its attention focused for longer and longer periods. This is an important point in all discussions about school maturity, besides being a significant feature of general development. It is a question of maintaining interest in definite perception situations (the teachers' instructions, the textbook, table manners, and so on), so that learning will be possible.

Between the mostly unsettled, diffuse attentiveness of the baby years, by way of the struggles of early school days (with the difficulties of sitting still and persevering with one and the same task) and the adult's ability to work for distant goals there is obviously a period of decisive development. It embraces the growth of memory from relatively simple performances to the use of the material remembered for complicated abstract thought processes.

DEVELOPMENT OF MEMORY

'Memory, our memory, is a remarkable thing – erratic, unreliable, humorous, insidious, painful, enervating, comforting but above all – indispensable. We live by memory, we live in memory.' This description of the significance of memory, which opens a novel by Hjalmar Bergman, a famous Swedish author, is by no means exaggerated. The development of memory towards greater achievements and coherence is of vital importance. Without this development we should remain in the helpless, dependent condition of early childhood.

Every process in which memory is engaged may be described as symbolic. Language, which in itself is the most valuable and the richest system of symbols for describing what we experience and learn, and which man alone has at his disposal, is the most important instrument of symbolic behaviour at a high level. But the beginnings of simple symbolic performances can also be observed and studied in organisms where language is not present, and in children who have not yet learnt to speak.

The earliest recollection

An interesting question, partly connected with memory, is how far a person's first recollection dates back in time. Much attention has been paid to this problem, but no reliable method of investigation seems to have been developed. An American investigation of college students who were asked about their earliest recollections, and whose replies could be checked, gave an average of three years and seven months. They remembered incidents that were often associated with emotional experiences, fear and happiness in particular being connected with the first recollection.

Psychoanalysts claim to be able to trace very early childhood memories, and it is said that the use of hypnotism can reveal childhood recollections of any period selected. However, statements about exceptionally early recollections should be approached with critical caution. Quite frequently such memories are associated with incidents experienced by the whole family, and have often been the subject of conversation in the family circle. The child has then gradually reorganized the related incident into a personal and seemingly spontaneous recollection. Linguistic reminders and actual memories of perceptions cannot be kept apart by children. Dreams may, in the same way, be experienced as real events.

DELAYED REACTION

The investigations known as delayed reaction experiments that have been carried on ever since 1913, when W. S. Hunter, a Chicago psychologist, introduced the method, are based on principles which can be more reliably investigated by experiment. Delayed reaction means something really very simple: how long can an animal or a small child remember where an object has been hidden? The subject watches the hiding but is prevented from reacting (i.e. trying to find the object) immediately. Hunter's aim was to study in this way the length of a young child's or an animal's memory at various stages of its development.

Charlotte Bühler's tests

Data associated with such problems are given even in such an early work as Preyer's *The Mind of the Child*. It is stated that a child of

Fig. VII.2. Bühler and Hetzer, to study delayed reaction, used a ball from which a chicken popped out when the ball was squeezed. (See text.)

three to four months old looks round for an object that has been taken away, and shows emotional signs of missing it. Studies of infants made under standardized experimental conditions give more certain information. Charlotte Bühler and her co-workers, particularly Hildegard Hetzer, have shown great interest in this problem. Fig. VII.2 illustrates a contrivance used by these two workers to study delayed reaction. When the ball is squeezed a chicken pops out. This is shown to the child who is allowed to play with the ball for a minute. Then the ball is taken away and the child is given something else to do for a certain period of time. At the end of this time the experimenter gives the baby another ball, exactly the same as the first one, but without the chicken. The test is passed satisfactorily if the baby, after squeezing the ball, clearly shows, by expression or action, that it is astonished or disappointed when no chicken appears.

This test can be used first when a child is between ten and eleven months of age, when the average baby is able to pass the test after a maximum interval of one minute. At the age of fifteen to seventeen months an interval of eight minutes is considered normal, and a delay of seventeen minutes gives a satisfactory pass at 21 to 24 months of age.

It should be obvious that the strength of motivation that can be aroused in the child is a very important factor in this test, but the design of the contrivance must be regarded as especially apt from this point of view. We are interested here, as in most other tests, in inducing the subject to make the maximum use of his abilities.

Hunter's technique

The technique evolved by Hunter is more stringent and precise. A later adaptation of the method which he used with infants is illustrated in Fig. VII.3. Hunter's apparatus for experiments with animals was constructed in the same way. The animal was confined in a cage, from which it could watch the stimulus – food or some other stimulus that provided strong motivation – being hidden behind one of two or three doors. After a definite interval of time, the animal was allowed to react to the stimulus and it had to choose the right hiding-place.

Without going into a detailed discussion of how the results obtained by this method are to be interpreted – they have been analysed from a great many aspects – it is dangerous to give any figures. Rats have succeeded in passing a delayed reaction test after a few seconds, while the delay for monkeys under the same conditions varies from a few minutes to several hours.

An experiment has been made with 100 one-year-old children, 50 boys and 50 girls, using the apparatus shown in Fig. VII.3. Chance would have given 33 per cent correct responses, but a delay of 10 seconds gave 64 per cent correct responses. When the interval was increased to 20 seconds the percentage of correct responses dropped to 61 per cent; and 49 per cent of correct choices were made after a delay of 30 seconds. A further increase in the delay brought the percentage down to the level of chance. No differences were observed between the sexes.

Fig. VII.3. Allen's experimental set-up for delayed reaction. The mother sits with her child at a table on which there are three boxes. A toy is hidden in one of the boxes while the child is watching; after that, the table is pushed out of reach of the child. (See text for further details.)

Different results will be obtained if the child or animal is subjected to distraction during the waiting interval. As a rule an animal remains quite still with its gaze fixed intently on the spot where the stimulus object disappeared. Its behaviour is similar to that of a person who has been told to fix his eyes on an object a certain distance away which he must later localize in the dark with his hand.

This comparison is interesting; for the subject of the latter experiment is not only the object that disappears in the dark, but also the whole of the surrounding frame of reference. Nothing remains but to concentrate on retaining a conception of the *space* if he is to perform the localization demanded of him. The animal, owing to its poorly developed ability to organize its conceptions of the surrounding world, behaves like a man in the dark even in the simple situation prevailing in the trial described above. It does not seem to have a sufficiently developed memory to be able to retain a conception of which choice is the correct one in the stimulus field.

Elementary memory ability seems to be present in children towards the end of their first year. As might be expected, ability to succeed in reaction tests of this kind increases with age both in respect of length of delay and degree of difficulty of the task. Mastery of language facilitates the organization of these processes in a decisive way. With the help of the symbolic values of words, we can bind ourselves to perceived situations. Our memory functions in essential respects because we are able to describe our experience in words.

THE PROBLEM OF RETENTION

One of the most important problems in the psychology of learning is retention, that is our ability to retain material we have learned. This ability clearly develops and improves up to a certain age. But the ability to retain also depends on the quality of the learning. In the following discussion this means the motivation for learning rather than the extent of the learning, which is more a question of quantity.

The character of the learning material

General psychology teaches us that retention depends on the kind of material to be remembered. The more meaningful the material is, the better and more easily it is retained, and on the contrary, the more meaningless the material is, the more difficult it is to learn it and the quicker it is forgotten. The prototype of such material is a series of nonsense syllables such as *mev, jis, raf, xoj, zid, fep* as introduced by Ebbinghaus.

The fact that our early recollections are often so fragmentary is probably due to a great extent to shortcomings in organization ability, not least in language. We soon forget a series of nonsense syllables, although we may remember one or two of them. It is difficult to say which they may happen to be, and their positions in the list learned probably only gives an incomplete explanation. Similarly, it is difficult to understand why some childhood memories remain while others disappear completely. It seems likely that organizing circumstances favourable for retention were present in the perception situation. Ability to organize develops with increasing age.

We shall return to these aspects of the problem in the chapter on the development of language and thought. A simpler side of learning, which is more accessible for experiment, is the form of retention studied under the denomination 'immediate memory span'.

Immediate memory span

A simple delayed reaction test for two-year-olds is included in the well-known Terman–Merrill individual intelligence test. While the child is watching, a toy cat is put in one of three boxes, after which a screen is placed between the child and the boxes. The screen is withdrawn after 10 seconds, and the child must choose the box in which the toy is hidden. This is an excellent test, not least from the aspect of motivation.

Another type of test is introduced for children $2\frac{1}{2}$ years of age, and is also found later in the test scale at different ages. It is intended to test the span of what can be grasped and repeated at one time. This is usually called immediate memory span. For a $2\frac{1}{2}$-year-old to get a pass he must repeat two digits correctly, and the number of digits is increased with increasing age according to the following table:

Age (years)	3	$4\frac{1}{2}$	7	10
Number of digits	3	4	5	6

The test appears again for advanced adults, when eight or nine digits read in a monotonous unrhythmical series must be repeated correctly immediately afterwards.

The relation between this type of test and tests for measuring general intelligence is good during the years up to puberty. The correlation with other, more generally accepted, tests is usually about 0·50, but the relation is less significant during later school years and in adults. During the earliest years, particularly, this test, unlike the delayed reaction test, has very low motivation value, and $2\frac{1}{2}$- and 3-year-olds sometimes completely refuse to repeat the digits presented.

The figures given above are based on, and on the whole are in agreement with, a number of comprehensive investigations. Generally speaking, no differences have been observed between the sexes.

INSIGHT AND LEARNING

It may be that certain parts of this chapter seem thin and over-simple to some readers. The aspects of learning illustrated by the delayed reaction and memory span tests seem restricted and perhaps even uninteresting. Simple as they may be, however, they are still difficult to interpret psychologically. When we consider the concept of insight and the related area of study the difficulties increase until they become quite unwieldy.

In the 1920's, two famous Gestalt psychologists, Wolfgang Köhler and Kurt Koffka, produced a concept of insight based on experiments, and threw it like a firebrand into American psychology, which was then dominated by hard-boiled behaviourist theories. Man, like other organisms, was regarded as the plaything of reflexes elicited by external stimuli. But insight, said the Gestalt psychologists, was not mechanical. It was, instead, a response to meaningful relations in a given stimulus situation. With all the elements of a problem present, a solution would appear suddenly: insight supplied the missing link in a broken behavioural chain.

Educational psychology in particular received this theory with gratification. Something human and living came into the discussion, and educationalists felt that respect for thought and inspiration had increased. But although the discussion had been enriched and stimulated to a very great degree by the frontal attack of the Gestalt psychologists, it is extremely difficult to support their view with anything experimentally unambiguous.

Criticism of Köhler's experiments

Let us illustrate this by Köhler's well-known experiment with Sultan, the chimpanzee which succeeded in fitting two bamboo sticks together and using them to pull a banana into its cage. Köhler claimed that this was a completely new performance and that it was the result of some kind of original insight. However, Köhler's results with this and similar experiments have never been obtained by other experimenters.

In experiments with chimpanzees, in which the earlier history of the animals could be carefully checked, results quite different from those obtained by Köhler were reached. Animals which had not become acquainted with sticks and twigs in their early life could not solve the problem given above. Of six monkeys, only two could solve the simplest of Köhler's stick experiments, to draw a banana into a cage with only one stick. One of the animals solved the problem by chance, and the other had been seen manipulating branches of trees a few days before the experiment. When, after this test, the animals were allowed to play with sticks and then tested again, they all solved the problem very rapidly. Likewise, other seemingly convincing experiments by Harlow have shown that the acquisition of what we call concepts, principles and hypotheses can be made possible by giving the animal opportunity to practise. The learning curve is not characterized by sudden leaps, revealing flashes of insight; learning takes place successively. When the animal has acquired a concept, it becomes to a remarkable degree capable of altering the response pattern and adapting itself to the requirements of the situation.

This is obviously something different from Köhler's statement about a sudden and astonishing insight. A so-called perceptive attitude solution of a problem is here rather the result of extensive and versatile experience.

What has been said here does not detract from the value of Köhler's observation, which is still a fundamental and necessary link in the development of scientific theory in this field. It is certainly not in conflict with a basic thesis in Köhler and other Gestalt psychologists, that the learning organism, regardless of its level, always acts as intelligently as it can in the situation in which it is placed.

That human beings, both children and adults, behave as intelligently as circumstances and resources permit is an interesting claim. Naturally, we may protest that it does not always appear to be so, but that is clearly due to the multitude of factors, not least on the emotional plane, which make control over and use of the resources imperfect or even impossible. Investigations in the field of experimental neurology provide striking confirmation of this (p. 150 ff.).

Some of the things that make the discussion of insight so abstruse have been touched upon here. The learning process has many sides – particularly with reference to man – it is spread over a long period of time and, what is most troublesome for the psychologist, its mechanism is practically unknown. Nor does it seem possible to catalogue the various learning elements in the life of a growing person – we are even unable to determine what is to be regarded as important or unimportant in such a catalogue. Much that is most important is probably beyond our control, incidental things, which are apparently forgotten by the person experiencing them.

A modern behaviourist and prominent psychologist, B. F. Skinner, maintains that we can only predict an individual's behaviour from the base of a detailed knowledge of his life history. We must know which responses have been reinforced in the past and under what stimulus conditions this has occurred.

Chapter VIII

DEVELOPMENT OF
LANGUAGE AND THOUGHT

Language and its problems have occupied a prominent position in child psychology since the very early days. Preyer and many who have followed in his footsteps have paid great attention to the development of language. The gift of language has always been regarded as something unique to human beings. The Latin word *infans*, from which the English 'infant' is derived, means 'without language'. The acquisition of language is undoubtedly one of the most important aspects of the development of man.

Philologists have for a long time been interested in tracing the origin of language, but no universally accepted theory has yet been formulated. The same is largely true of its development-psychological aspects. How a child acquires language and thereby becomes possessed of an infinitely rich and versatile means of communication independent of time and space still contains much that is mysterious and wonderful (Fig. VIII.1).

HAVE ANIMALS LANGUAGE?

The discussion often starts from whether animals have language. Animals can communicate with each other by posturing, and by making sounds. Obvious cries of warning and calls are common. As everyone knows, parrots can be taught to 'speak', and after long training chimpanzees have learnt to articulate a few words. Chimpanzees can make certain reflex sounds, used only in strongly emotional situations and in an uncontrolled way. It is very difficult to cause a chimpanzee to make sounds deliberately, and it cannot be done without human intervention.

The fact that animals can, as a consequence of certain conditioning processes, make definite vocalizations does not mean, however,

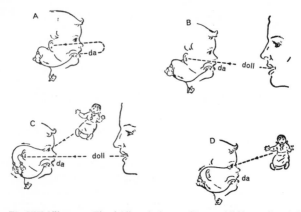

Fig. VIII.1 illustrates Floyd Allport's theory of how a child learns linguistic symbols. When a child makes the first meaningless sound, 'da', for instance, it reacts to it simultaneously as a sound stimulus. When the child has heard himself say 'da' repeatedly, the sound is gradually associated with the act of vocalizing. A 'circular reaction' is formed (A. Cf. text p. 120). The child can then be taught to associate 'da' with the word 'doll' (B). If a doll is presented simultaneously, it is associated with 'da' (for the child cannot yet say 'doll') (C and D).

that they can *use* language. A dog that has been taught to sit up and beg for a lump of sugar never behaves like that towards another dog, and no one has observed that parrots communicate with each other in the words taught them by human beings.

When animals react obediently to orders given by a human being, they respond only to certain superficial features of these stimuli, and there is no proof that words and phrases are understood as people understand them. The relation between a dog and its master can be regulated very sensitively by a complicated system of signals, but it never achieves or even approaches the conventional symbols of communication we call language.

Konrad Lorenz, the German student of instinct, has reported remarkable language performances by birds, and has pointed out that lovers of animals often attribute human characteristics to animals. They are convinced that the bird understands what is said to it. This is naturally out of the question. Not even the most skilful 'talking' birds, capable of connecting certain sounds and corresponding experiences, ever learn to make practical use of their knowledge. Lorenz continues: 'The complicated apparatus, with larynx and brain, does not seem to have a species-preserving function. One asks in vain why it exists at all.'

Chimpanzees and other superior apes have primitive organs of speech which could be capable of producing speech-like sounds if the ability to conceptualize were present. The vital reason for their failure to speak seems to be an insufficiently developed brain with no language centre. Nor have apes an innate need to begin to vocalize spontaneously or prattle like human infants.

THE EARLY DEVELOPMENT OF LANGUAGE

The first cry at birth may be regarded as a purely physiological phenomenon. It starts the process of breathing, so that oxygen can be supplied to the blood. The vocalizations that are made at a very early stage may be considered as the basic materials of language. They consist mainly of vowels, and they appear in children all over the world. The sounds are unlearned. As early as two months after birth a child has at its disposal all the linguistic sounds that the human voice can reproduce. As a consequence of reinforcement, the elements of which are determined by the language of the environment, certain sounds become dominant. Other sounds, not reinforced by practice, disappear. These pre-linguistic sounds have of course no symbolic value, but a certain organization of sounds can be discerned when a child is four to five months old, that is to say, when the prattle stage begins. Syllable-like sounds are made and often repeated.

It is a fact that deaf children do not prattle. This is evidence that a stimulus to speak emanating from the environment is of the greatest significance even in the prattle stage. Syllabic prattle may have the important function of providing practice in different partial processes which are later utilized in communicative language.

The pre-linguistic phase lasts for most of the first year, and the first words are usually crude – or more correctly – simplified imitations of something the child has heard. Sometimes these imitations have little or nothing in common with the words the child seems to be trying to say. This is due partly to lack of physiological maturity – the tongue being not yet sufficiently agile, for instance – and partly to the fact that adults often meet children at the linguistic level of the child, which contributes towards fixating a certain word formation. There are other reasons for this, too.

When a certain sound has acquired a representative connotation, that is when it stands for something definite and means the same to the speaker and the hearer, it becomes a word in the conventional meaning of the term. How far a child's first word satisfies these demands is difficult to say, but we may assume that much is parrot-like repetition. It is only gradually that words acquire distinct meanings in accordance with their use in the surrounding adult group.

But even a small child may influence the linguistic habits of the family group. If an elder sister named Miriam is called Mimmi by a younger member of the family, that name may be used for a long time to come. If an eighteen-month-old child points upwards and says 'apapa' when he sees an aeroplane, this curious word may easily become a synonym for aeroplane in the family circle. Sometimes onomatopoeic – imitative – words may be coined. After having called a ball by its right name, a fifteen-month-old child suddenly began calling it 'dap-dap', which described the bouncing of the ball. This was clearly for her a very interesting function of the ball, and required a special word.

The first word

Normally we may expect the first real word to come out when a child is about twelve months old. Parents usually give a rather lower average age than trained psychologists have found. Great individual variations occur, however. The claim that early speech and high intelligence go together is only partly justified, and contains a misleading generalization. Terman found among his superior subjects (IQ 140 and above) that the first word occurred at an average age of eleven months – according to information provided by parents – but among them were also children who did not begin to talk until they were between two and three years of age. At first a child usually uses single words, short ones as a rule. But they may be called one-word sentences, for the word often performs the function of a sentence. The word *ma-ma* may mean 'Mother, come here!', 'Mother, don't go', 'Mother look!', 'Mother, where are you?' and so on. Nor does a child's vocabulary reflect its ability to understand spoken language. On the contrary, a very young child often has a considerable understanding of language, which can be tested to some extent by giving commands which it is to obey. This aspect of language may be developed long before real talking begins.

THE DEVELOPMENT OF VOCABULARY

The first words are usually nouns. Interjections are also learnt early, but they are more difficult to determine linguistically. Not until later do verbs, adjectives, pronouns and adverbs appear – they usually occur in this order – and this increase in vocabulary makes possible a more complicated sentence pattern.

Extent of vocabulary

The growth of the vocabulary may be viewed from several angles, and the purely quantitative aspect is not the most interesting. We may speak of an active and passive vocabulary – the *active* vocabulary consists of the words a child uses in speaking, the *passive* comprises the words a child understands and to which it reacts correctly. The best-known study of the growth of the active vocabulary, containing data on the number of words at different ages, is that by Madorah Smith, 1926. Her average values up to and including the age of six years are given below.

These data refer to American children. The actual number of words is of rather limited interest, but the increment within each age

| Age | | Number of | Number of | |
years	months	children	words	Increment
0	8	13	0	0
0	10	17	1	1
1	0	52	3	2
1	3	19	19	16
1	6	14	22	3
1	9	14	118	96
2	0	25	272	154
2	6	14	446	174
3	0	20	896	450
3	6	26	1222	326
4	0	26	1540	318
4	6	32	1870	330
5	0	20	2072	202
5	6	27	2289	217
6	0	9	2562	273

sector is more illuminating. After the age of eighteen months a child increases its vocabulary rapidly, and by the age of two years seems to have discovered the general principle that things have names. (See the account of the development of language in Chapters III and IV above.)

Side by side with the quantitative increase in the language symbols comes a deeper understanding, which makes the meaning more precise and the range of meanings more varied. This process, of course, continues long after the age of six – even university studies are partly concerned with the enriching of the vocabulary. A child's vocabulary will cover a wider range of concepts as his contacts become more varied. Such factors must be taken into consideration when vocabularies are being measured.

Length of sentences

Another aspect of the development of language is the ability to combine words to make sentences. As a rule a child has a vocabulary of between 200–300 words before he leaves the one-word sentence stage. This usually occurs round the age of two years. Lengths of sentences at different ages have been calculated to give the following averages, but variations are great:

Age (years; months)	2;0	2;6	3;0	3;5	4;0	4;5	5;0
Number of words in sentence	1·7	2·4	3·3	4·0	4·3	4·7	4·6

Important stabilization processes occur in the development of language between the ages of three and four years. Speech becomes grammatically more correct, accidence more assured, and the proportion of unintelligible words decreases. Roughly about 25 per cent of the speech of a child eighteen months old is intelligible, and the proportion increases steadily until at the age of from $3\frac{1}{2}$ to 4 years it is practically 100 per cent. By the time a child begins school it has had a very comprehensive language training. It has been calculated that a four-year-old says normally about ten to twelve thousand words a day.

A difference between the sexes is found early, and it is present through the years. Girls are, on an average, verbally superior to boys, and can perform tests for measuring verbal intelligence factors better than boys can.

The individual age at which the use of language appears, is, as mentioned above, of small value in the prediction of general intelligence, but the positive correlation between general intelligence and the mastery of language increases with age. It is true that the level of intelligence is measured largely with the help of linguistic symbols, and in that way measurement has something of the character of a vicious circle, but it seems obvious that intelligent performances usually presume a skilful use of linguistic symbols.

Thought is impossible without language, and keenness and lucidity of thought are intimately connected with the logical construction of sentences. Observations of deaf and dumb children provide clear evidence of the significance of language. Such children live in an almost complete intellectual vacuum, until means of linguistic communication have been acquired with the help of arduous teaching methods.

LANGUAGE AND ENVIRONMENT

A large number of systematic and thorough investigations recently have shown how great the importance of environment is to the development of language. The influence of environment begins remarkably early, and its effects last a long time. The stimulating effect of a normal family environment cannot be exaggerated.

Children's homes

Children living at children's homes have, even when very young, distinctly fewer linguistic sounds than children living in families, which means that their use of language will be delayed considerably. This seems to be because children in institutions do not get enough language stimulation from adults. (It has been shown that twins are usually somewhat linguistically retarded because they are left to keep each other company more than other children. An only child, on the other hand, has a distinct advantage over other children in respect of adult stimulation, and tends to be forward in language.) Also, the monotonous and impersonal character of a children's home diminishes a child's desire to vocalize.

These results are worth consideration. They show how important the first practice of sounds is, and – still more important – they indicate how necessary it is to place children from institutions in families as early as possible. It is much more difficult to 'catch up' on language in later life than it is to improve the motor, social and adaptive insufficiencies which may have resulted from inadequate early experience. Gesell maintains that a defective linguistic environment has a cumulatively degrading and impoverishing effect upon intellectual development.

Different social and economic environments

Investigations tend to show that children at different social and economic levels differ relatively little from one another linguistically during the first year or so of life. The effects of linguistically poor environments do not appear until later. Distinct differences can be observed from the age of eighteen months. In well-to-do environments children of this age have, as a rule, richer vocabularies, and two- and three-word sentences appear earlier. Their command of syntax, accidence and the construction of sentences also develops earlier.

An informative investigation of these aspects was published in 1951 by E. Milner. Children in the first grade of the elementary school were tested with the *California Test of Mental Maturation*, a test which gives a good idea of the linguistic level in children. A group with very high test scores was selected, and another group with very low scores, and their family life was studied. Very distinct differences in the relations of parents to children were observed between the groups.

Children with good test results had on an average much better contacts with adults. The families usually had breakfast together, and the children were allowed to take part in the conversation, which was also the case at other meals. The children with low test scores usually had breakfast alone, after the mother had laid the table and gone to the other work she had to do. These children did not take part very much in the conversation at supper.

This and other investigations (cf. p. 242 ff.) show clearly that the attitudes of parents and family habits are extremely important for a child's linguistic development. The stress laid on environmental factors must not be interpreted to mean that hereditary factors are without significance: but the degree of their importance is still unknown.

It is clear, as Willard Olson and others have pointed out, that much that is important in the acquisition of language occurs before school attendance begins. The school often provides less oral language training now than formerly. At present a child's knowledge of language is enlarged at school mainly by listening and by learning other ways of using it, chiefly reading and writing. The child is also helped to master the larger symbolic units which he needs as his thinking becomes more advanced.

STAMMERING

Stammering is a disorder of speech often accompanied by emotional distress, which may partly retard linguistic development. The causes of stammering have long been the subject of speculation. Aristotle thought that a short thick tongue was particularly liable to produce it, and as late as the middle of the nineteenth century tongue operations were often performed, which not surprisingly led to even greater speech defects and frequently left the patient an invalid.

Wendell Johnson, an American, has published a comprehensive work on the subject, based on his own research, which has thrown new revealing light on the genesis of stammering. As mentioned above (p. 51), the trouble usually begins when children are three to four years of age. Johnson found that about twice as many boys as girls suffered from stammering.

The significance of parents' attitudes

One of the most interesting findings is concerned with the attitudes of the parents towards the child. A comparison of the reports submitted by parents of stammerers, and by parents of children who did not stammer, showed great differences in their attitudes to children's speech. Three- to four-year-old children are often eager, and it is quite normal for their speech to contain repetitions of syllables, prolongation of different sounds and hesitant pauses. Some parents consider these phenomena as the first signs of stammering, and tell the child to be careful in his speech, while other parents calmly wait and see.

It was found that most stammerers were the children of parents of the first kind. Children who were equally eager in their speech, but were not anxiously made aware of it and corrected, usually developed into non-stammerers. The anxiety of the parents was transferred to the children who began intensely and anxiously to take notice of their speech. The degree of a child's sensitiveness to the reactions of parents must naturally also be an important factor.

In more than 25 per cent of the children studied there were other members of the family who stammered, but, according to Johnson, care must be taken not to attribute this too much to hereditary tendencies. In families where stammering has been found for generations there is, says Johnson, a massive fund of experience of stammering, decided opinions upon it and a tendency to interfere in the child's speech maturation in a very upsetting way.

Besides being reasonable, Johnson's assumptions and explanations have also this practical implication, underlining the role played by the attitude of the parents. Its importance to the general development of language has been mentioned above. In this case it has been related to a special field.

Stammering has been regarded as being particularly common among left-handed children, but Johnson found no evidence in support of this theory. Trankell in Sweden has arrived at similar results in a comprehensive study of left-handedness among Swedish schoolchildren.

THOUGHT

'To think is to use symbols.' This may be a correct definition, but it is by no means sufficient. It was pointed out in the previous chapter that some symbolical processes are possible for children even before they can speak, and that even animals are capable of such processes. The classic examples consist of experiments based on Hunter's delayed reaction test (p. 101 ff.).

Even simple conditioning processes are symbolical in a way. Pavlov made a dog wait for its food half an hour after the bell had rung, and it was shown that the dog could delay its secretion of saliva for about 29 minutes. But we are not prepared to call that 'thought' in the real meaning of the word.

Nor is thought the recollection of something learned, although memory undoubtedly supplies the raw materials of thought and is a necessary condition of thought. Recollection is seeking certain definite concepts corresponding to earlier observations. Sometimes we do not experience any seeking at all – $2 \times 2 = 4$; Battle of Hastings, 1066; Declaration of Independence, 1776 – sometimes we must seek for a long time before we recollect a name that has just slipped our memory. 'I must think for a moment' may be the answer to such a question as 'What did you have for dinner yesterday?' or 'What did you do after we had gone?' However, this is still not thought in the real meaning of the word.

The meaning of thought

The use of symbols leading to the discovery of new relations is often given as a criterion for thought. To rise above the level of memory a person must produce something new – the concepts must be re-organized. Playing with ideas, as in daydreaming, for example, cannot be called thinking. Thinking is a more definite, goal-directed activity, aimed at solving some kind of problem.

It is probably quite impossible to give a comprehensive and satisfactory definition of thought that will stand the test of all critical scrutiny. The theories are also rather vague, and somewhat contradictory.

We are here considering the development of thought, and in this field the results of research work do not show much agreement. The difficulties of definition are to some extent to blame. There is general agreement that language and its development are of decisive importance – that is why thought and language are dealt with in the same section here – but it is probably impossible to isolate thought processes from other aspects of mental development.

Concepts are the tools of thought. They are the bases of such processes as generalization, differentiation and abstraction. The formation of concepts and their utilization and control in logical reasoning have been studied by means of a special technique that has not produced particularly comprehensive or unambiguous conclusions.

Jean Piaget has made one of the most successful attempts to produce a coherent account of the development of intelligence. He traces its origin back to what he calls sensori-motor intelligence.

Sensori-motor processes and intelligence

Towards the end of the first six months, new behaviour patterns can be observed arising from the combination of observation (the receptor or *sensory*) processes and motion (the effector or *motor*) processes. These, Piaget thinks, form the transition between simple, conditioned actions or habits, and intelligent behaviour. The co-ordination of sight and grasping, the importance of which Gesell has also stressed, provides a good illustration. Piaget exemplifies it as follows: A small child is lying in its perambulator. The hood is up and a row of rattles with a string hanging from it is fastened to the hood. When the child catches hold of the string and pulls, all the rattles sound at once. Astonished at the result, the child grabs the string again and repeats the procedure time after time. The first movement and the ensuing effect become a single action which, says Piaget, creates a need to repeat the action when the objects stop moving.

This is called a *circular reaction*. Such a reaction has certain features in common with the structure of simple habits, but it has still nothing in common with an action directed wholly by intelligence. These circular reactions are complete behaviour patterns. They are repeated as units without any previously determined goal and without any advantage being taken of coincidences that may appear while they are being performed.

It is not until later that such new elements are added to behaviour as make possible a certain degree of generalization, and the co-ordination of different patterns with each other. Circular reactions become more complex, and understanding of the relation of end to

Fig. VIII.2. The ability to take a roundabout way to reach a goal is a result of development. The child in the picture is still too young to understand that it must find the way round the sheet of glass to reach the toy. 'Detour' tasks of this kind are used in problem-solving experiments with animals and children.

means increases. New forms of behaviour, the intelligent nature of which is undeniable, begin to appear.

Concrete examples are the ability of the child to draw an object towards itself by means of the tablecloth, for example, or with the help of a piece of string fastened to it, and successful solutions of detour tasks (Fig. VIII.2). This presumes that the child understands certain relations and can co-ordinate them. It is not until the second year that sensori-motor intelligence is fully developed. Then rapid co-ordination processes can be observed which make possible what Gestalt psychologists have described as insight.

Thus, in these sensori-motor processes, Piaget recognizes the starting point of the development which leads to thought processes (reasoning). Thought originates from the sensori-motor intelligence, which continues to influence thought throughout life by observations and practical forms of behaviour. The schema formations of the sensori-motor intelligence are the practical equivalents to concepts and relations.

Development of thought proper

In the development of thought proper Piaget distinguishes four principal stages, from the emergence of the symbol functions to the thought operative groupings, that is theoretical intelligence.

(1) Symbolic and pre-logical thought develops from the age of $1\frac{1}{2}$ or two years to four years.

(2) Between the ages of four years and seven or eight years, what Piaget calls intuitive thinking begins and this progresses by phases, until the threshold of thought operations proper is reached.

(3) The organization of concrete operations, that is such thought operative groupings as refer to events that can really be manipulated or conceived intuitively, occurs from seven or eight to eleven or twelve years of age.

(4) From eleven or twelve years of age and onwards throughout adolescence, formal thought, the groupings of which are typical of fully developed theoretical intelligence, is finally established.

This brief survey of the stages in the development of thought requires a few comments.

Pre-logical or pre-operational thought

Both direct observation, and analysis of certain speech defects, show, Piaget maintains, that the systematic use of language depends on a general 'symbolic function' which makes it possible to express one's meanings by symbols which are quite different from the objects they represent.

All thought consists of relating meanings to each other, and meaning implies connection between the symbol and the reality represented by it. This connection is very incomplete during the first stage, up to a child's fifth year. The thought patterns are not yet general concepts although they are more than individual elements. Hence logical conclusions are impossible.

Piaget uses *transduction*, a term coined by William Stern, to describe the primitive conclusions that may be arrived at by direct analogy. The middle terms are incomplete and do not allow successful thought operative regrouping.

Intuitive thought

The second stage is characterized by a growing ability to form concepts with a gradually increasing co-ordination of logical relations. Thinking is still very imperfect, however, and is not superior to the pre-logical stage. It is concerned with intuitive conclusions based on observation. The following experiment illustrates the problem.

Two glasses, exactly the same size and shape, are each filled with the same number of beads. The child is allowed to put in the beads himself to see that there is no cheating. While the child is watching, the contents of one of the glasses are transferred to another glass of different shape. Children aged four to five years think that the number of beads has been altered. If the glass is narrow and tall they say that it contains more beads, and fewer if the glass is wider and lower.

At this age a child is aware of the constancy of objects, but cannot yet extend that idea to a collection of objects. The class concept has not been developed and erroneous reasoning is the result. This prelogical schematization imitates closely the perceptually given. It is reorganized, however, in a special way by the process Piaget calls intuitive thinking.

The difference between intuitive thinking and actual thought operations may be studied with a modification of the bead experiment. Let the child put beads in two glasses, different in shape and size, in such a way that the numbers of beads in the glasses increase uniformly, e.g. by the child's putting the same number into each glass simultaneously by using both hands. As long as the number is small – four or five beads – the child declares that the heaps of beads are identical. This seems to foreshadow a thought operation, but as soon as the columns differ greatly, the child no longer believes in the similarity. The budding thought operation is overcome by the misleading effects of perception.

Intuitive thinking dependent on perception is abandoned more and more and the remaining differences between it and thought operations proper emerge particularly clearly in questions of time and space. Time is intuitively related to objects and their individual movements, and is not experienced as something uniform and constant.

When two bodies are moved simultaneously from the same line to two points at different distances away, a four- to five-year-old child admits that movement begins simultaneously, but usually denies that the objects reach their destinations at exactly the same time, even though he has been watching the whole process. The concept of a common time for different speeds has not been developed; 'faster' also implies 'longer time'. Such difficulties are overcome by the co-ordination of the different elements of intuitive thinking. When this is achieved, the child acquires the concept of reversibility and the way is prepared for the thought operations which characterize the third stage.

Concrete thought operations

It is not until its ninth year that a child can co-ordinate chronological relations (*before* and *after*) with duration relations (*shorter* and *longer*), since until then they remain independent of each other on the intuitive perceptive level. As soon as they are combined into a unit, consciousness of a common time, valid for all movement regardless of speed, is created.

The qualitative operations, which determine the structure of spatial relationships, the combination of interval and distance, the appreciation of surfaces and length, the growth of a spatial co-ordination system, perspective and projections, and so on – also appear at this age.

Fig. VIII.3 is a representation of the world of a small child and

Fig. VIII.3. This photograph, by Herbert Gehr of *Life*, is an attempt to
reconstruct the world as it appears to a small child. Only the mother stands
out distinctly, everything else is diffuse.

may serve to illustrate the features of space mentioned above. Space
is naturally much more differentiated by the ninth year, but spatial
groupings cannot yet be manipulated abstractly. (Cf. Thurstone's
spatial factor, which is an important feature of general intelligence,
in Chapter IX, below.) We are still concerned with *concrete* not
formal thought operations, and they are related to external processes.
Though thought operations are often lucid and logical in structure,
and include appropriate linguistic expressions, this does not imply
ability to arrive at logical conclusions independent of actions.

What has been said here may be elucidated with the help of a common type of test devised by Sir Cyril Burt. Such a test may be formu-

lated as follows: 'John is taller than Harry. John is shorter than Tom. Who is the shortest?' It is not until the thirteenth year that it normally becomes possible for a child to answer such a question. (We ignore the fact that there are many normally gifted adults who find the problem difficult.)

If the problem is illustrated as in Fig. VIII.4 and the question asked, 'Who is the shortest?', the answer would be regarded as ridiculously simple by a twelve-year-old – and by adults. But if this problem is compared with that of the beads in the glasses it does not seem so simple by far, but shows that a considerable development of concrete thinking has occurred. The four-year-old child cannot understand that the number of beads is unchanged, but a seven- to eight-year-old can. The question that was beyond the understanding of the four-year-old seems silly to the seven- or eight-year-old child.

Formal thinking

The type of thought described as formal begins to develop during the eleventh and twelfth years, when a child becomes capable of thinking

Tom   John   Harry

Fig. VIII.4. With this picture before us we have no difficulty in answering the question which of the boys is the shortest, but if the question is asked without reference to the illustration (as in the test question in the text) the reply demands ability to think in concrete relationships.

hypothetically-deductively, in other words of drawing conclusions,

(1) on the basis of simple assumptions (hypotheses), which need not necessarily have any connection with reality or be related to what the person believes, and

(2) by relying on an internal power of judgement instead of having to make reference to experience.

Not until its thirteenth year can a child, with the help of linguistic means only, do what it could do as a seven-year-old with concrete equivalents to linguistic symbols. When the conditions for the solution of a problem are given only in language, the conclusion must be arrived at with one's own thinking, without direct concrete activity. That is why formal logic and mathematical deduction – to deduce implies inferring from the general to the particular – is nearly always incomprehensible to the child, and forms an independent field of study, that of the goal-directed 'pure' thought independent of all external operations.

This section is based wholly on Piaget, and his ideas on thinking have been given in some detail, for his work is outstanding in this field. In spite of its length, the account must still be regarded as an outline only, in which many of the views advanced by Piaget are omitted.

From the aspect of education, too, Piaget's theories are well worth serious consideration. Piaget himself is perhaps less interested in the purely educational measures that can be developed from his approach but their importance to the development of thought would seem obvious.

As is the case with other human characteristics, it is not difficult to find exceptions to the course of development described above. A girl aged four and a half years could add up $3 + 3$, then $6 + 6$, $12 + 12$, $24 + 24$, up to $384 + 384 = 768$, and a test question of the Burt type mentioned above was answered with practically no interval for thought. But here it is not the exceptions that primarily concern us.

Chapter IX

THE DEVELOPMENT OF
INTELLIGENCE

What we call intelligence is manifested in behaviour in many and widely different ways. It is not surprising, therefore, that the subject tends to crop up in chapter after chapter in a handbook of this kind. Some specimens of tests have already been given, and also of experiments intended to investigate phenomena connected with intelligent behaviour. In the account of Piaget's view of thought in the previous chapter, it was found that he stressed strongly the intimate connection between intelligence and thought.

Much of the research into and consequent discussion of intelligence has been concerned with aspects of development; and it was pointed out in the introduction (p. 23) that students of intelligence and test constructors are among the people most cited in the literature of child psychology.

SOME THEORETICAL VIEWS

There are many different kinds of intelligence, a fact that is often reflected in a confusing way in popular accounts and discussions. We may be acquainted with two ten-year-old boys, Harry and Tom, both of whom we are inclined to describe as intelligent, but we can see differences in the ways in which their 'intelligences' are expressed. Harry is perhaps very clever at arithmetic, while Tom has a remarkable gift for languages.

We sometimes regard ability to make social contacts as a sign of intelligence, perhaps quite rightly. From that aspect we consider Harry, for example, to be very gifted. It would not be difficult to find many features of intelligence that distinguish Harry and Tom from each other. In the same way we notice that people are 'stupid' in one way or another.

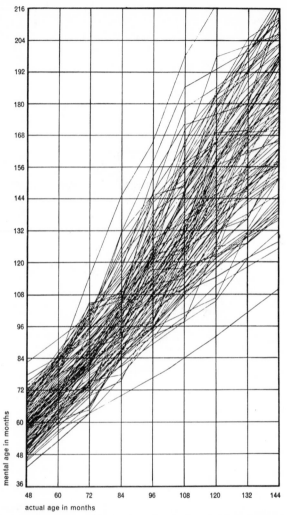

Fig. IX.1. Differences between individuals increase with age. The development of intelligence has been followed in 100 boys from the age of 4 up to 12. The curves form, as it were, a broom with the twigs spreading outwards (greater variation width). The figure exemplifies the *inter-individual* differences described in the text. The next figure illustrates the *intra-individual* differences.

Inter- and intra-individual differences

Two principal types of individual differences can be observed. The first refers to the differences between individuals, which are called *inter-individual*. This was the kind of difference that concerned us when we compared Harry and Tom. All selections made among candidates for posts, school marks, and so on, are made according to this type of difference.

The other type refers to differences in characteristics in one and the same individual. These are known as *intra-individual* differences. If we say that Tom is more linguistically than technically gifted, we are expressing an intra-individual difference. The school marks for a single pupil in different subjects also reflect such differences. The individual is compared with himself with regard to the prominence of different features.

The inter-individual differences increase with age (Fig. IX.1). The intra-individual differences and their development are more complex. But the popular view that a person poorly gifted in some respects will be better in others is not supported by the evidence that we have. On the contrary, highly intelligent persons are often endowed with good physical, emotional and other features. Certain types of intra-individual differences increase as the direction of education and interests is stabilized. Certain talents are neglected for lack of practice. Figure IX.2 illustrates a so-called intelligence profile referring to different intelligence factors.

Some technical questions of measurement

Common to practically all psychological traits – or variables – is the fact that the individuals measured are distributed according to the so-called normal curve. Imagine that we are testing a randomly chosen group of one thousand people, all of whom belong to the category for which the test is constructed. We will then find that the results of the majority of them will be rather close to the average value. The rest will be distributed in a fairly steadily declining number upwards and downwards. Very few will have extremely poor test results, and the extremely good results will be just as few.

We find this type of distribution when we measure the heights of a large number of people. Most of them will be near the mean value, and the numbers will be fewer the farther we get from this mean. Very short and very tall people attract attention because they are so rare.

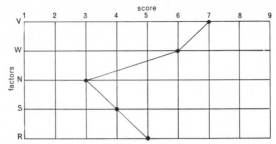

Fig. IX.2. Individual profile. One person is seldom equally gifted in all the 'factors' which make up intelligence. In the above case, the individual has more than average verbal gifts (V and W), less than average numerical ability (N) and spatial (S) factors. The logical factor (R) is about average. See also Fig. XII.2, p. 192.

One point must be stressed. When we measure stature we use the same instrument all the time, an instrument that is graded exactly into equal units of measurement. We can use this instrument to measure a newborn baby or a fully grown giant. But this cannot be done when intelligence is to be measured.

In the case of intelligence, different instruments must be used for different ages. A test suitable for three-year-olds is of no use for older children and adults. Instead of working with only one uniform 'rule', psychologists must measure with short fragments (the individual test items), which may differ greatly from each other. We must try, with the help of various methods, to decide what these fragments really measure, and to make them as uniform as possible.

Nor have intelligence tests of the usual kind any absolute zero point. The zero point of a rule is the beginning. It has no length at all. The same applies to weighing, and in timing, too, we have a zero point. But where is the zero point in an intelligence test, the point at which no intelligence is found at all?

Starting from the basic idea that features of intelligence increase in dispersion with increasing age, Thurstone assumed that the zero point would be found where no variation at all occurred. He found that the zero point of human intelligence should be at or immediately before birth. This view has little practical significance, but it is not without interest to compare this conclusion with those drawn from Spelt's experiments (p. 35).

The fact that no zero point exists on the scale we use implies, among other things, that we cannot say that a person with an IQ of 150 is twice as intelligent as one with an IQ of 75. But 150 lb. is twice as heavy as 75 lb., for weighing begins from a zero point.

Another system of measurement is, for example, the centigrade thermometer. It has an arbitrarily chosen zero point (the freezing temperature of water). We cannot say here that 10°C is twice as warm as 5°C. But at any rate the differences are uniform, and we can still calculate and compare them, because the distances between the scale marks are the same.

An intelligence test cannot even produce this last-named type of scale – it is called 'interval scale' in opposition to the first-named, which is called 'ratio scale' – because of the difficulty of obtaining the necessary equal scale steps. But during the work of constructing the test, when the tasks are tried out on a large number of persons, the frequency of correct answers to the separate items can be analysed, so that degrees of difficulty between the tasks may be increased as evenly as possible. That is what we try to achieve. It may be possible to describe meaningfully the units of measurement with reference to the interval scale. It may be reasonable to say, for example, that IQ 110 is as much more than IQ 100 as IQ 120 is more than IQ 110.

If we compare a well-standardized intelligence test with, for example, the items in an ordinary examination paper in arithmetic, we cannot, in the latter case, speak of any constant unit of measurement in the degrees of difficulty of the tasks. This provides an example of still one more scale, the 'ordinal scale', which means simply placing in order (from first to last). One often has to be satisfied with such a scale in psychology, as for example when a teacher is asked to place his pupils in order of intelligence, ambition or other features.

We have been able only to hint at some of the problems of the theory of testing. But information of this kind is important to give some understanding of the implications of psychological measurements.

The aim of factor analysis

The question of how intelligence is to be defined and measured in a meaningful way has given rise to a number of problems. Like chemists searching for chemical elements, psychologists have tried to break down intelligence into a limited number of fundamental abilities.

The research work in this sphere, which is dominated by the

so-called factor analysts, has sometimes been described as mental chemistry, and has led to the isolation of what are usually called intelligence 'factors' or primary abilities. The British tradition, going back to Charles Spearman and later represented by Sir Cyril Burt, Sir Godfrey Thomson and others, is very important. In America, L. L. Thurstone has made great contributions in this field.

Factor analysis, it is claimed, has revealed that the intelligent performance of any task involves factors (called s factors) specific to the particular type of task. Modern intelligence tests include some which aim to measure the various factors each as purely as possible. But there is also a general intelligence factor, the g factor, which must be taken into consideration, and which is involved in all types of task. Together the factors make what we usually call intelligence. Differences in intelligence are due to a considerable extent to the way in which these factors are distributed between or within individuals.

Some of this work is of particular interest to developmental psychology. Thurstone, together with his wife, made one of the most extensive studies and was able with his 'Chicago Tests of Primary Mental Abilities' to isolate twelve intelligence factors.

On the basis of an earlier study, Thurstone constructed a test battery intended to measure as purely as possible the seven most clearly defined factors (see p. 141 ff.). The battery was meant for college students, that is to say for young people in their late teens, but later parallel types of test for the fourteen-year and also for the five- to six-year levels were made.

It was shown that it was not possible in the lower age groups to distinguish as many factors, since the results in the different types of tests were not as distinct as in the higher age groups. Only five abilities could be identified.

This is an important finding, made and stressed by several research workers. The lower the age the more unstructured and clustered together the mental functions appear.

BINET APPEARS ON THE SCENE

One of the best-known events in the history of psychology is the request made by the French Ministry of Education to Alfred Binet to look into the problem of pupils remaining a second year in the same grade, and to find a way of picking out the intellectually weaker children so as to provide them with special tuition. Interest in handicapped children was rising round the turn of the century, and Binet, one of the leading experimental psychologists of his time, devoted himself to their problems.

Binet's first test scale appeared in 1905, and was a result of several earlier attempts to create an objective method of measuring intelligence. The test scale really succeeded in satisfying a practical need, and gave rise to research work that has been applied in many different fields and has encouraged the study of developmental psychology.

Binet's scale differed from earlier scales in several important respects. Formerly, with few exceptions, very simple tasks had been set, and experimenters had confined themselves to exact, but from the point of view of intelligence, somewhat inadequate psychological variables. Pure sensory physiological tests in particular were used widely.

More complex test items were introduced by Binet, of a type still in use, and it could now be claimed with justification that 'intelligence', in a wider sense of the term, was being measured. In addition, testing took only a relatively short time. The test items had finally been arranged in a rising scale according to degree of difficulty (although, owing to imperfect testing methods, this scale was a very unsatisfactory one), but without reference to the type of task.

Many of Binet's test items, and his views on the construction of tests, led the way to further development, mainly in America, where Henry Goddard introduced the method by a direct translation of Binet's revised (1908) scale, in which incidentally the concept of mental age was first used. However, it was chiefly through the efforts of another American worker, Lewis Terman, that the Binet test was finally developed and applied generally.

Terman's revision of the Binet scales

Terman's first revision of the Binet scales, the Stanford revision of 1916 (named after the university where Terman was working), became very well known, and there has probably not been any other test so closely associated in the public mind with the concept of measuring intelligence. The calculation of the intelligence quotient (IQ) was introduced for the first time. It had been suggested some years earlier by William Stern, but it was Terman who made it practicable.

Fundamental improvements were made in the Stanford revision

and it may be said to have marked the end of the first experimental phase in the measurement of intelligence.

In addition to the IQ, Terman introduced exact instructions for testing. He was also the first to see clearly the necessity of making a standard test scale by comprehensive and representative trials and the analysis of the individual test items.

Until that time testing had been used almost exclusively to select retarded children for transfer to special assistance classes. Terman thought, and stressed strongly, that testing could also help towards the understanding and guidance of average and superior children.

This Stanford revision held the field until 1937, when Terman and Maud Merrill published the second and still much used revision, which was standardized on almost 3000 children and adolescents between the ages of two and eighteen years. This revision has been used even more widely than the previous one outside the English-speaking countries.

From individual test to group test

The Binet–Terman tests represent a development of fundamental importance for practical testing. They are all individual tests, in that only one person is tested at a time by a trained psychologist. The group test, which enables several people to be tested at the same time, has another history. It was necessary during World War I to create an effective and rapid method of differentiating soldiers according to intelligence. Group tests proved highly successful, and there were obvious advantages in the saving of time and money. It did not take long for the group test to replace the individual test in many other spheres. Practically all tests now used on normal people are group tests. When preschool children are to be tested, and when testing is for clinical purposes – where observation of individual behaviour is important – individual tests are used, for practical reasons.

A modern group test usually consists of a series of sub-tests. Each part has a time limit and consists of a definite number of items arranged according to degree of difficulty. The items in a sub-test are uniform in type and are usually intended to measure, as purely as possible, one particular intelligence factor (see specimens on p. 141). Together the sub-tests are meant to cover and measure all the important areas of what we call intelligence.

The tests mentioned here comprise the main types of ordinary intelligence test. The subjects are given problems to solve, the solution of which demands a certain kind of intellectual activity; the solutions of the problems are exactly defined.

Projective testing techniques are quite different. In projective tests the subjects are shown pictures of various kinds which must be described, or a story made up round them, according to instructions. Such methods seem to stimulate the imagination in a more general way. The types of response differ considerably from subject to subject. Some of these methods will be described in the chapter on the development of personality (p. 188 ff.).

PROBLEMS OF RELIABILITY

Reliability and validity

One thing common to all tests is that they must have as high a degree of 'reliability' and 'validity' as possible. This means that they must give consistent results (reliability) when repeated and that they must measure what they are intended to measure (validity).

A test with a high degree of reliability, i.e. good resistance to random influences, need not necessarily have a high degree of validity – often the same as a high prediction value – but a test with low measurement reliability will certainly be not much use from the point of view of validity.

One check for reliability (the 'split-half' method) is to divide the test into two equivalent parts by, for example, separating from each other the answers given to all the odd-numbered from all the even-numbered questions, and then to compare the two sets of scores. A test whose separate parts give widely differing results is said to 'correlate badly with itself', and one cannot then, of course, expect it to show any correlation with, say, school marks, or any other external criterion of validity.

To produce a test which is both reliable and valid is a complex and difficult task, particularly when it is intended for the testing of small children. Yet it is desirable to obtain, at an early stage, an idea of a child's mental resources in order to make adjustments in its environment to suit its capacity.

An intelligence test intended for children aged two or three years, which gives a value normally showing little agreement with a test used for a later age, cannot be very helpful. As a rule it is the earlier test that has given the erroneous result and which has been lacking in validity. It has clearly measured something different from the later test, and has not really been suitable for measuring intelligence in any useful sense of the term (cf. Fig. IX.3).

Intelligence must be assumed to grow in one way or another according to some kind of sequential development. A person is not highly gifted one day and dull the next. Illness may, however, cause much mental deterioration, and radical changes in environment may affect the manifestations of intelligence and alter its functions (cf. p. 199 ff.).

Definition of intelligence

In defining intelligence it has become customary to make so-called 'operational' definitions, that is to refer to the operations, the measuring procedures, that have been used to evaluate it. It was an American psychologist, E. G. Boring, who produced the often-quoted definition: 'intelligence is what is measured by intelligence tests'.

If such a statement is to have any meaning, it must be possible to place the test in relation to some comprehensible idea of intelligence. This means that the need for validity must always be kept in sight – it must always be possible to show some relation between the result of a test and intelligent behaviour of the kind, for example, that leads to success in school. (Such success may of course be due to other circumstances as well, such as diligence, ambitious parents, and so on.)

Objections may be made to all attempts to find extraneous criteria for comparison with a test result.

If anyone claimed to be able to measure intelligence with a clinical thermometer we should be very sceptical. If we define body temperature as that which we measure with a clinical thermometer, on the other hand, the definition is sufficient as a basis for valuable decisions: for example, ought I to remain in bed, or can I go to work? We wish to get from an instrument for the measurement of intelligence information to help in arriving at practical decisions, so it is not unreasonable to relate this information to behaviour that is generally accepted as dependent upon the exercise of intelligence.

The diagnostic and prognostic value of the instrument

We think it insufficient to put a hand on a person's forehead and say, 'You have a high temperature.' All sensible people would say, 'Go and take your temperature.' We want the condition to be determined objectively. In the same way we feel that a general statement such as 'Henry is intelligent' is inadequate. A test is intended to be a measuring instrument.

Where the possibility of predicting a thing's development exists, a description of that thing's condition must have some prognostic value. This, from many points of view, is the most important function of intelligence tests. It means that the measure we have of intelligence, as expressed by the IQ, must remain constant through the years. A test for children and young people is standardized for a certain age. This should mean that a person with, for example, the average quotient of 100 in his fourth year should keep this average at later testings.

The fact that there is nearly always some degree of fluctuation in IQ value from one test occasion to another may be due to several factors. Development is by no means predictable in all aspects, and also – which is just as important – tests given at different ages do not always measure the same phenomena since more difficult tasks and sometimes new types of task must be introduced in order to study the growth of different functions (cf. p. 130 ff.).

The unsatisfactory prognostic value of very early tests is illustrated in Fig. IX.3, where two longitudinal investigations are compared. The results of a testing made with the Wechsler–Bellevue scale on persons eighteen years of age has been correlated with the results of earlier tests on the same subjects made mainly with the Stanford–Binet test and, in the earliest ages, the California Preschool Schedules. The test results have been transformed into uniform standard values, so-called z values.

The figure shows that the results obtained at eighteen years have little in common with the earliest results, but that the correlation increases considerably during the preschool years and improves successively later. Several investigations have shown that tests made before a child is a year old tend to show a slight negative correlation with results obtained in the fifth year and later. It is not until after the age of one year that the correlation coefficient moves over to the positive side.

Florence Goodenough has summarized the reasons why test results in the youngest age groups apparently have no prognostic value as follows: (1) The impossibility of guiding a child's response by means of verbal instructions, (2) uncertain and variable motivation, (3) difficulty of controlling and directing the child's attention, (4) observational errors in scoring, (5) lack of immediately useful criteria for selecting and weighing test items, (6) statistical problems arising from the low chronological age of the children, which makes small age difference count for much, and finally (7) the unsettled

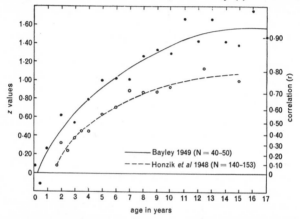

Fig. IX.3. Results of two separate studies, in which, on the basis of testings when a person has reached the age of 18, comparisons have been made with earlier testings. A test result at the age of 18 years shows little agreement with one obtained at 2 years, but correlation increases progressively.

problem as to whether or not true intelligence may be said to have emerged before the symbolical processes exemplified in speech become established.

EXAMPLES OF TEST:

Tests for infants

Existing tests for small infants may be said to have little prognostic value. However, the tests have been constructed side by side with detailed and protracted observations of behaviour, and have therefore provided much information on early intellectual development.

Pioneering work was done by Arnold Gesell, who published his 'Infant Schedule' in 1925. The test items in this, as in other tests for small children, are of the observation-technical type, and consist of observations of the kind mentioned in Chapter III, p. 37 ff. above. In the four-week stage the observations cover things like hand and arm positions, glance, and prattle. The weaknesses of this method are obvious, even at this early stage. Uniform judgements are extremely difficult, for however refined and standardized the observation technique may be, it seems impossible to eliminate differences in judgements made by different observers. Infant tests constructed later also have the same shortcomings.

In Europe Charlotte Bühler and Hildegard Hetzer constructed a *Kleinkindertest* in 1932, and in 1940 an American psychologist, Psyche Cattell, made a fairly successful test covering the ages of two to thirty months. It was intended to be an extension of the second Stanford–Binet revision towards younger ages. The items at the two-month stage are, for example, ability to react to a human voice, to follow a ring moving horizontally, and to prattle. The Gesell pattern is clear, and a common feature of all these tests is that they emphasize strongly sensory and motor development. The Cattell scale was standardized longitudinally (see p. 26) on 274 children aged 3, 6, 9, 12, 18, 24, 30 and 36 months. The IQ like the Stanford–Binet, is assessed on a basal age. Tasks for higher age groups are tried and mental age calculated according to the level of difficulty of the test items passed.

In respect of validity, the Cattell scale for the earlier years is no better than other tests, but its reliability is better. The reliability coefficient is, it is true, only 0·56 at the three-month stage, but it is as high as 0·90 at eighteen months.

Preschool tests

It is not until a child is eighteen months old that a tolerably valid test result can be expected. Then there are two well-known tests, the Merrill–Palmer scale and the Minnesota Preschool Test, both of which cover ages up to the seventh year. Among preschool tests there are also Gesell's Preschool Schedules for ages ranging from fifteen months to six years.

The last-named test has been of less importance in comparison with better formalized and standardized tests, particularly the Terman–Merrill scale, which has proved very useful even for the younger age groups. It begins at two years. A Swedish standardization of the Terman–Merrill scale covering the preschool years, published in 1950 by David and Rosa Katz, does not begin until the age of 30 months, as it was considered that earlier test results were too uncertain.

At the 2½-year-old stage this test scale makes use of well-known objects made as realistic toys, which the child is asked to name (What is this?), point to (Where is the cup?) or do something with (Put the spoon beside the cup). Simple memory tests are used at the three-year-level – to repeat two digits and to find, among four cards with pictures of animals, a picture that has been shown before.

The Terman–Merrill scale covers different mental functions. It consists of two parallel scales, which are known as the L and M forms, each of which ought to give the same IQ result. Comprehensive factor analyses have shown that the test measures a general intelligence factor (g factor), but it has been impossible to determine which types of specific factor (s-factors) it may involve.

No one has succeeded in constructing a group test for children younger than five to six years of age. The social experience of the kindergarten makes it possible to perform such tests at this stage. Among these are Thurstone's Chicago Tests of Primary Mental Abilities for children five and six years of age. Figure IX.4 shows a couple of items in this test. The upper one is an item from one part of the test, the object of which is to test a verbal factor. The child is instructed to mark the object that provides an answer to the question 'What do we look at when we want to know how cold it is?' The other example is part of a series of picture-rows designed to measure the factor that Thurstone calls perceptual speed. The children are told 'You must do two things in each row of pictures. First mark off

Fig. IX.4. Two items from the Thurstone group test for preschool children (5–6 years of age). The instructions are given in the text.

the picture that is alone at the beginning of the row. Then find the picture among the others in the same row that is exactly the same as the first one, and make a mark on that one, too. Do it as fast as you can. Do as many rows as you can before I say "Stop!" Are you ready? Begin!'

Tests for different ages at school

Group tests of this type are rather rare at preschool age, and it is not until children have been attending school for some time that they can be used generally. The Chicago Tests of Primary Mental Abilities constructed by the Thurstones, are meant for children aged eleven to seventeen years and may, as already mentioned, be regarded as patterns for many modern group tests. They were published in 1943. They were constructed in connection with the so-called group factor theory of intelligence, which states that intelligence implies the presence of several distinguishable and relatively independent mental functions. Most group tests are intended for children of school age, and many such tests have been constructed in practically all countries.

Tests for specific abilities and factors

Finally, we will give examples of some common types of test intended to measure different factors of intelligence. It should be borne in mind that the primary abilities that have been postulated have only relative equivalents in reality. Factor tests to measure these abilities always correlate more or less, which means that they, to a certain extent, measure the same thing, but they are particularly heavily 'loaded' with the factor they have been designed to test (see below). These examples illustrate a common principle of test construction: a series of items all cast in the same form but graded from very simple to very difficult makes it possible to cover schoolchildren at all stages of development with one and the same test. Figure IX.4 shows how two of them can be used for children as young as five to six years of age.

Verbal comprehension (the V factor). Antonyms and synonyms are commonly used here, and the correct response is often hidden among a number of so-called distractors, e.g.:

PUNISH: judge imprison enrich reward help
(Underline the word that means the opposite of the word printed in capitals.)

CONSIDER: calculate predict testify reflect investigate
(Underline the word that means the same as the word printed in capitals.)

Filling in missing words (Ebbinghaus's completion test) is often used to test verbal comprehension; e.g. A horse has .... legs.

Verbal fluency (W factor). The types of test for this factor are usually freer in form.

The task may be, for example, to write as many words as possible beginning with a given initial syllable. ('Write as many words as you can beginning with *in*!'), or constructing anagrams from a certain word ('Make as many words as you can with the letters in the word *Holidays*!').

W factor tests are not very often used.

Numerical ability (N factor). The term is perhaps misleading: this factor is by no means identical with aptitude for mathematics, which includes a number of still unsatisfactorily analysed components.

N factor tests are based on the four simple methods of calculation and are concerned with the ability to activate habits of thought that have become more or less automatic.

Two kinds of test used in the evaluation of this factor are:

Underline each number that is exactly three more than the number just before it.

6   5   9   12   15   11   8   4   7   9

Mark the correct additions

14	31	68	47
27	19	37	86
43	56	94	67
—	—	—	—
84	116	198	160

Spatial ability (S factor). This test demands ability to see, in different ways, certain spatial relationships.

One test is counting cubes and figures (Fig. IX.5, cf. also Fig. IX.8).

'S factors' (various kinds of S factor have been detected) play an important part in mechanical-technical aptitude.

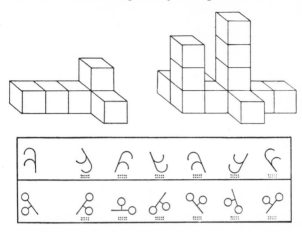

Fig. IX.5. Tests for measuring the spatial factor. Top, 'Cube counting';
some of the cubes are concealed, but they must be there, and the task is to
say how many cubes there are in each figure. Below, 'Figures'. A cross is to
be made under each figure that is the same (curves and circles in the same
direction) as the first figure in the row.

Perceptual speed (P factor). Specimens of tests to measure this factor
will be found in Fig. IX.4.

Another type of test for measuring 'P' consists of a word spelled
correctly, followed by the same word with the letters in different
order, one with the letters reversed.

> CAMP   macp   pmac   pamc   pacm
> (Underline the word spelt backwards.)

Logical reasoning (R factor). This factor is related in ability to draw
conclusions from given premises. It seems to be closely connected
with inductive reasoning (earlier it was also called the I factor),
but the letter R (for reasoning) indicates the more general logical
character of the factor.

Several types of test seem to measure this factor and it is therefore
difficult to isolate. At the same time, however, measurement 'R' has
come to occupy a prominent place in most group tests, and questions
like those given below occur frequently.

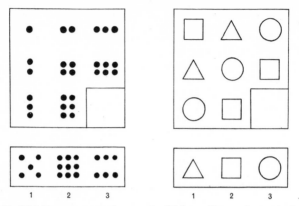

Fig. IX.6. Tests to measure the reasoning (R) factor. 'Progressive matrices';
the figures in the square are arranged according to a certain system, and one
of the numbered figures will fit into the lower right-hand corner.

Number series are very common. The questions consist of a series
of numbers arranged according to a certain sequence, which must
be detected. The next number in the sequence must be written on
the line after the series. e.g.:

$$7 \quad 9 \quad 11 \quad 13 \quad 15 \quad 17 \quad \underline{\quad}$$
$$21 \quad 20 \quad 18 \quad 15 \quad 11 \quad 6 \quad \underline{\quad}$$

Similarly, series of letters can be arranged according to a certain
system:

$$b \quad a \quad d \quad c \quad f \quad e \quad h \quad -$$

Verbal selection may also be included among these factor tests.
A word that differs in character from the others in a series must be
underlined. e.g.:

cow horse cart pig dog
never seldom often almost always

This is the factor tested by the so-called progressive matrices
illustrated in Fig. IX.6.

The above is intended only as a brief survey of the types of test
items that may be included in modern group tests covering various
ages.

SEX DIFFERENCES

Are there any innate differences between the sexes in respect of intellectual potential? The question has stimulated much controversy, and a good deal of very thorough experimentation. Some clear, unambiguous results have been reached with regard to certain abilities, but it looks as if intelligence in the general meaning of the term is about the same in both sexes.

It is very difficult to arrive at a meaningful conclusion, for we can define intelligence only operationally from the test instruments used. This is true of intelligence in both the general and specific meanings of the term, of course. It is necessary in the construction of a test to begin from certain rather arbitrary starting points. How far these favour one or the other sex it is almost impossible to discover. Also, different attitudes towards the education of boys and of girls may influence the development of intelligence.

If a series of tests comprising the Thurstone primary factors is given to both boys and girls there will be differences between their average results for some of the individual factors, but no significant overall difference when all sub-test results are combined. Nor are any sex differences revealed as a rule by the Terman test, but in this test possible tendencies have been neutralized at the construction stage, partly on the assumption that no general intellectual sex differences exist.

It is not difficult to construct a test that will favour one or the other sex. Thus girls are superior in verbal tasks – particularly those measuring the W factor, but also those measuring the R factor – and boys achieve better results in tests measuring the S factor. Some very detailed and well-planned Scottish investigations, the earliest in the 1930's and the most recent published in 1949, have shown, among other things, how sensitive a test may be to sex differences. In the investigations made during the 1930's, in which the Stanford revision of 1916 was used, no differences were detected between the sexes, but in the 1949 report, which was based on the Terman–Merrill scale of 1937 and a group test, the first-named test showed a statistically significant advantage for boys, while the result of the group test was in the opposite direction.

The test subjects were children aged ten to eleven years, and the sampling was made with an unusual degree of care. It is generally very difficult to make a selection from a large population so that the sample is a correct representation of the population. An error in the sampling procedure may produce, among other things, an apparent difference between the sexes that does not reflect the truth about the population as a whole.

A report published by the Swedish National Board of Education, based on a large-scale investigation of the experimental nine-year comprehensive school, throws some light on the problem of sex differences. Figure IX.7 gives the average profiles for the pupils in grades 8 and 9 (aged fourteen to sixteen years).

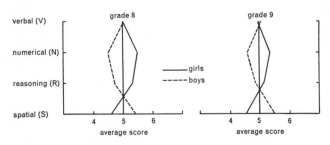

Fig. IX.7. Average profiles for grades 8 and 9 (of the Swedish comprehensive school) according to Härnqvist's F-test, which shows sex differences in three of the four factors studied.

Sex differences give rise to difficult but very interesting problems. Witkin, an American worker, has shown clearly that sex differences exist in certain spheres of perception, and he has been able to relate them to intellectual factors, mainly to the S factor.

In Witkin's best-known experiment a room, capable of being inclined, is built up in the laboratory, and a chair, which can also be inclined to the left or right, is placed on a level with the missing fourth wall (cf. a theatre stage). The subject can see only the room from the chair.

The table gives the results for different age groups of two types of experiment.

In Series 1*a* the chair and the subject were placed at an angle of 22° to the right or left and the room was sloped at a gradient of 56° in the same direction. The same gradients were used in Series 1*b*, but the room and the chair were then inclined in the opposite directions.

The task of the subject in both experiments was to adjust the room to an objectively correct horizontal position, while remaining in a tilted position.

Age group (years)	Series 1a Mean value (degrees wrong)		Series 1b Mean value (degrees wrong)	
	Boys	Girls	Boys	Girls
8	17	17·5	21·5	24
10	16·5	22·5	19	28
13	13·5	21	18·5	22·5
15	9·5	12	25·5	25·5
17	8·5	12·5	16·5	23
Adults	11·5	17·5	23	30

This task is a rather difficult one, and not very pleasant for the subject, for the horizontal and vertical planes that are so important to us seem to disintegrate. But the interesting point is that clear sex differences appear. The female subjects were less successful in adjustment to the true upright, a result which is valid for all age groups from eight years upwards. It is only at the fifteen-year level that the values in Series 1b are the same. This is interesting, for in other experiments (cf. below) this age level reveals a striking neutralization of the differences between the sexes. The differences are greatest among adults.

Witkin has also used, in other experiments, so-called Gottschaldt figures, in which the task is to find a figure that is embedded in a confusing pattern of lines. Two such figures are illustrated in Fig. IX.8. They may be regarded as typical spatial tests (cf. p. 142), and the sex differences they reveal, which increase with age and are most marked among adults and least noticeable at the age of fifteen years, are in the direction that is to be expected from the findings of other similar experiments, that girls usually take longer over the task and their behaviour is generally more uncertain. (It is very difficult to apply this test to ten-year-olds and it takes them on an average twice as long as children of thirteen.)

Of special interest in this connection is the fact that there is a clear relationship (about 0·50–0·60) between this test and the experiment referred to above. The reliability, checked by retesting after an interval of more than a year, is very high, which shows that individual stability in these performances is considerable.

Similar experiments have been carried out in Sweden by Sandström, independently of Witkin. They have revealed significant sex differences, particularly among adults, but none at all at the age of about fifteen years. One of these experiments is carried out as follows. The subject sits at a table, the top of which consists of a sheet of wallboard, painted white with a small black spot. The subject must fix his gaze on this spot, and the task to be performed is to stick a pin into the underside of the sheet of wallboard immediately below the spot.

Fig. IX.8. Two pairs of Gottschaldt figures. The left-hand figures are to be found in the respective patterns.

Deviations from the exact point are, on an average, much greater for women than for men – the mean value for men was 17 and 18 mm. (right hand and left hand) and for women 28 and 25 mm. Among younger age groups the differences were very small, and in this experiment, too, there were no differences between boys and girls about fifteen years of age; in fact there was a slight tendency for girls to be better. Differences between individuals may also vary greatly – from the immediate vicinity of the spot to 8 to 10 cm. away.

It is interesting to note, too, that the differences between right and left hand are usually insignificant. The mean values show that there is not even a tendency to be better with the right hand (only right-handed subjects took part), which might have been expected in view of the lower motor precision of the left hand. This and the very high degree of stability in the performances of the same subject suggest that a kind of personally focused localization mechanism exists.

No tenable theory has been advanced to explain what may be behind these sex differences found in the experiments reported above. We are concerned here with a border region between perception and specific intelligence factors that is very difficult to define.

Chapter X

EMOTIONAL DEVELOPMENT

The behaviour associated with what is commonly called 'the emotional life' presents innumerable difficulties to the psychologist. The problems themselves are very elusive owing to the difficulty of studying them in laboratory conditions. Even elementary definitions are difficult to make. If one goes outside strictly operational definitions (by which phenomena are defined solely in terms of the results of experiment, no wider generality being claimed for the definition), there is great risk of getting caught in the quicksands of hypothesis.

The word 'emotion' is derived from the Latin *emotus*, the participle of *emovere*, to move or to be put in motion. The word 'emotion' is used in psychology to describe a state of excitement in the organism, but if we equate emotion with feeling, which in everyday language we tend to do, it becomes clear that under this heading we are concerned with more than the physiological response to emergency situations.

Anger and fear, sorrow and joy are typical emotions. But emotional life does not consist only of powerful and violent feelings but also – and more usually in normal people – of a calm and temperate emotional condition.

The close relation between feeling and perception is often emphasized. The etymology of the word 'feel' tells us a lot about feeling. It is derived from the Anglo-Saxon *felan*, and is related to *folm*, the palm. It meant originally to obtain knowledge tactually, that is, by touch. The French word is *sentiment*, which is related to the Latin *sensus*, from *sentire*, to feel, to perceive, to be sensible of. Thus etymology relates feeling to a means of gaining knowledge. What this knowledge is and exactly how it is acquired has long been a subject of contention among philosophers.

EMOTION AND MOTIVATION

A hungry baby can hardly experience its hunger except as an emotional condition caused by the hunger. Like every other organism, it increases its activity as a consequence of unsatisfied needs. It may kick and wave its arms, but most usually it screams. An adult observer cannot know anything about the baby's emotional life, but it may be assumed that it is lacking in nuances, and that it gradually becomes – like other features of personality – differentiated and enriched with growing experience gained through learning and perception.

Thought and feeling affect each other during this development, and some psychologists maintain that it is the emotional life that prepares the way for thought. Susan Isaacs, an English child psychologist, maintained that it is the child's first experience of disappointment, of unsatisfied longing for food during the intervals between meals, that first stimulates it to make evaluations of the surrounding world. It seems likely that there is some truth in this view. Unsatisfied demands compel an organism to become active, leading it to make use of its resources in various ways.

This brings us to the connection between motivation and feeling. Several research workers have emphasized the need for a theory of motivation capable of bringing order into the discussion of emotion. One theory – that of Susan Isaacs – has already been cited.

Motivation is usually described in terms of needs (see Chapter VII, p. 98 ff. above), and every need is connected to an emotional state. Behind every manifestation of behaviour is a need, and emotion (or feeling) is present in all the activities an individual is engaged in. This is true of the infant, as well as of sub-human organisms. Pleasure and displeasure are the terms generally used to give broad, unspecific descriptions of affective states: pleasure accompanies behaviour which improves the individual's welfare, displeasure that which frustrates motives and plans.

Frustration

The term frustration is often used to describe a state characterized by baffled impulses giving rise to irritating dissatisfaction. The blocking of an impulse leads to frustration, and individuals are subjected to such blockings at all stages of development: the grown-up at work, the schoolchild at his homework, and the baby when its needs remain unsatisfied.

If an individual is continually exposed to serious frustration, it is clear that harmful disturbances may appear in his personality. There has been, ever since Freud, much lively discussion about how this condition affects the development of personality. What at least seems clear is that a child's physical or mental development can hardly be fostered if the child is neglected in such important respects as security and protection, with all the affection, consideration and material care that they involve.

Illustrative experimental work in this important field of developmental psychology has been performed by, among others, Norman Maier, an American psychologist. He considers that his results are applicable to both human beings and animals. Maier used Lashley's experimental set-up (Fig. X.1). The rat has to jump from a platform towards one of two cards each carrying a different design. The 'correct' card gives way and the rat is rewarded (with food), while the other card is fixed and the rat is punished (falls into a net).

Fig. X.1. Lashley's jumping apparatus. The rat has to jump at one of the cards. (See text.)

In Maier's experiment the rat was set an insoluble problem. Reward and punishment were meted out arbitrarily. There was no definite arrangement or pattern of the cards which would allow a predictable result. In such a situation the animal refuses to make any choice, even though it may be very hungry. A new form of persuasion must be introduced before the animal will jump: Maier directed a puff of air at the rat. Compelling a choice in this way often leads to behavioural fixation of a highly stereotyped kind; the animal jumps again and again at the same card or at the space between the cards. Fixation may become so permanent that no changes occur in the behaviour pattern if a card is removed and food is placed, clearly visible, in the opening.

Main types of frustration behaviour

Maier distinguishes between three main types of frustration behaviour: fixation, aggression and regression.

In *fixation* the behaviour pattern cannot be modified, and may
seem unintelligent; it does not allow adjustment to a specific situation. Such behaviour can sometimes be observed in children with
strictly formed habits, and at school futile efforts to keep up in a
certain subject may lead to a pupil's being unable to grasp something
really quite simple. Difficulties with mathematics at school sometimes provide examples of such fixation. At times fixation takes the
form of resigned disinclination.

Aggression implies that the individual makes blind attacks as a
reaction to frustration. Aggression is not always directed against the
immediate cause of the frustration. A schoolchild who has been
subjected to criticism or ironic comments by his teacher, or an adult
who has been reprimanded by his superior at work, often works off
his irritation on those he can command, but who are quite innocent
in this connection, or he bangs doors and kicks the furniture. The
need for a scapegoat is a general phenomenon, besides being a
fascinating theme in the history of religion.

Aggressive behaviour may also be directed against the individual
himself as a consequence of an exaggerated sense of guilt.

Regression means a return to earlier and more primitive forms of
behaviour. A grown-up who cannot have his own way may scream
and act like a child, while a child may revert to the baby stage to gain
its ends. Bed-wetting and thumb-sucking, or marked dependency
on the mother at a stage when this dependency has usually been
overcome, are examples of what may be signs of regression due to
frustration.

Other defence mechanisms

Among the defence measures adopted against frustrating internal
tensions are certain other mechanisms intended to bring the organism
into mental equilibrium. The whole of this discussion is based on
parts of Freud's theory of personality dynamics.

Rationalization is the justification of an act after it has been performed, to avoid feelings of guilt from blameworthy behaviour. It
also appears in eager assurances of, for example, enjoyment of a

situation which is actually experienced as disturbing and unpleasant. A pupil who has failed in his work at school may make excuses to himself by claiming that the teacher was unfair, or that he had a cold – which he makes seem more serious than it was.

Compensation means that failure in one field of endeavour leads to greater efforts to succeed in another and there gain longed-for approval. A boy who finds it difficult to shine in intellectual subjects at school may instead devote himself eagerly to gymnastics in order to be all the better there.

Projection is a method of avoiding guilty feelings by attributing one's own mistakes and bad features to others. A lazy person accuses others of laziness.

Repression – regarded in Freud's psychoanalysis as a central defence mechanism – is a process by which a person endeavours to defend himself against painful impulses, not accepted by society, by banishing them to the unconscious.

Still another way of avoiding frustrating conflict situations is to retire within oneself, a method that seems to require less energy than the other measures mentioned here. Different forms of *withdrawal* are daydreaming or wool-gathering, general lack of interest and the abuse of drugs, such as alcohol.

Excessive employment of the mechanisms mentioned here as a consequence of continual frustration is very similar to neurotic behaviour, but a distinction is usually drawn between the two. The behaviour pattern evoked by frustration is attached to a certain situation, while the neurotic pattern is more generalized.

People resort to defence mechanisms in order to achieve a tolerable existence, and individuals differ greatly both in respect of the situations which evoke such defences, and in the particular mechanisms they employ. Some understanding of how they function is necessary as a background to an account of emotional development.

Defence mechanisms begin functioning early. Their development and employment depend on a large number of factors, about which we know very little. Disappointments and frustration are not due only to external stimulus situations, but also to the mental condition of the person faced with these situations. Hunger and fatigue are liable to increase irritability – in all age groups – and the intensity of the frustration also depends upon how much is at stake.

THE DIFFERENTIATION OF THE EMOTIONS

There has been much discussion about how to describe the emotional life of a newborn baby. What content is to be attributed to it? Psychoanalysts and others closely associated with them have claimed that from the moment of birth – indeed, even before birth – human beings are capable of emotional experiences. Isaacs has maintained that knowledge and insight are lacking at birth, but that desire, fear and anger, love and hate are present from the very beginning.

How far such a claim may be considered meaningful is clearly dependent on what is meant by emotion. If by fear and anger, for instance, is meant the attitude the organism adopts to protect itself against danger, and the defensive or offensive actions that follow, the same words could be used to describe the behaviour of an individual cell.

To describe the defence of a normal cell against, for instance, a cancer cell as an active struggle is acceptable. It is more difficult, however, to accept the statement that these antagonistic cells are in a state of fury, in spite of the fact that their behaviour – the word behaviour is also fully acceptable in this connection – is the same as that of more complicated organisms in similar situations.

Emotional, as well as intellectual, terms become less meaningful the lower down in the animal scale we get. This seems to be due to the fact that the simpler the organism, the more reason we have for regarding its behaviour pattern as autonomic, i.e. not dependent on conscious initiative, and not guided by highly differentiated mechanisms in the central nervous system. We are hardly prepared to speak of a frightened or angry amoeba. Only in imaginative fiction would such a thing be possible.

Heredity or environment?

The view that emotional development depends chiefly on maturation processes predetermined by heredity is held in particular by Gesell. However, the opinion that this development is due mainly to environmental factors has many advocates. It is pointed out, for example, that a snake let loose in the vicinity of a child does not arouse fear if the child is younger than two years. Children three years of age, on the other hand, show some caution, and from four years upwards they show an even greater inclination to keep at a distance.

A prominent supporter of the environment theory, Harold Jones, has said:

> As a child develops, his intelligence innately matures, and his perceptions become enriched through experience. New things startle him because of his keener perception of the fact that they are new and unusual. . . . Fear arises when we know enough to recognize the potential danger in a stimulus, but have not advanced to the point of complete comprehension and control of the changing situation.

This view is similar to Hebb's (p. 164 ff.).

In Sweden Wilhelm Sjöstrand has stressed that the puberty phenomenon, the attitude of young people to the authority of the community and its social behaviour, is considered by an almost unanimous scientific opinion to depend on social and cultural influences, while the defiant periods appearing around the ages of $2\frac{1}{2}$ and 6 years are attributed by Gesell, for example, to genetically conditioned changes in the nervous system and are therefore part of his general sequential theory. 'It has clearly not occurred to Gesell', says Sjöstrand, 'that when children reach a certain motor development, they may be placed in such a situation by the social environment that behaviour will be similar for all of them.' This interpretation is worthy of attention. It may also help us to understand why comparisons based on anthropological results are so risky.

The sequence of emotions

Figure X.2 is from a study by Bridges, and is intended to give a survey of the approximate ages at which the different emotions first appear. The emotional content of the first month of life is designated 'excitement'. By this is meant that specific reactions, even as responses to strong stimuli, cannot be detected during the first weeks. Only very general and uncontrolled muscle reactions can be observed.

During the first months distress and delight are differentiated, distress somewhat earlier than delight. Anger, disgust and fear appear at between three and six months, and during the months around the first birthday delight splits up into satisfaction, and affection for grown-ups and children.

Data of this kind are naturally unreliable, owing to the lack of relevant measurement techniques and the fact that available observation methods leave the field open for subjective judgements. Others have considered that they could observe other emotions: Bühler adds anxiety and surprise in the seventh month, and Goodenough, in her list of emotions shown by a ten-month-old child, includes obstinacy, dissatisfaction and anticipation. Lists of this kind easily lead to confusion because scientifically we do not know what we are talking about: a valid, reliable system of definition does not exist.

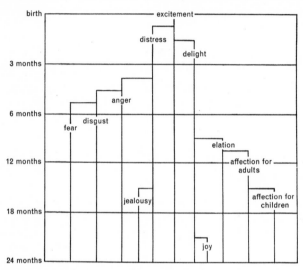

Fig. X.2. Approximate ages for the appearance of emotions in children according to Bridges.

Learned and unlearned expressions of emotion

Studies of the above-mentioned kind suggest strongly that many different expressions of emotion are largely learned. They can no longer be regarded as a number of primitive, natural patterns. Watson, the behaviourist, was one of the first to study this problem. He came to the conclusion that there are only three unlearned types of emotional expression, and they are related to fear, anger and love.

Sudden loss of bodily equilibrium by the violent removal of a support or by a loud noise was regarded by Watson as always arousing fear, while anger was evoked if a child's freedom of movement was restricted. Love, in which term Watson, like Freud, included sexuality, appears when a child's erogenous zones are touched, when a child is patted or fondled, or allowed to lie on its back in someone's lap.

It has been impossible to confirm Watson's statements. His theory has been shown to be too simple, and the uniformity of the response patterns is open to question. The only emotional pattern that is now regarded as unambiguous and which appears very early is the response of starting with sudden fear. This startle pattern is thought to be a preparatory defence measure by the organism.

Nevertheless, although emotional development is highly dependent on learning, it seems impossible not to attribute a nucleus of primitiveness and universal applicability to emotional expressions, for they are intimately related, among other things, to various physiological conditions that cause the tissues to expand or contract. This restricts the possibilities of expression, and leads them into definite channels.

It is true that we can weep for joy and even laugh in our sorrow, but such reactions seem to be exceptional expressions of emotion or due to extraordinary conditioning. They are not normally the primary expressions of these emotions.

Emotionally differentiated behaviour patterns

Many aspects of child training in the western world aim directly at differentiation of the emotions – above all at control of displeasure reactions. Training to increase a child's resistance to fear usually begins early, in the games that grown-ups play with even very small children. 'Pat-a-cake, pat-a-cake, baker's man', for example, begins slowly and gently, but leads up to a violent climax, 'Put it in the oven for baby and me'; while riding games such as 'The ladies they go nim-nim-nim-nim-nim', on to 'Old Farmer Brown goes gallopy-gallopy . . .' are realistic reproductions of wild rides. The more wildly Farmer Brown's horse is allowed to gallop, the more delighted the child seems to be.

Children expose themselves to stimulating situations containing reasons for fear – swinging, climbing high trees or, in Sweden, for example, jumping from one ice-floe to another. The attraction of dangerous situations is present in all ages. As spectators, adults enjoy similar dangers in detective stories and books of adventure, at cinemas and theatres, at amusement parks and sports arenas.

People in our modern society remain ambivalent in many respects. They are repelled by a dead body (students of medicine have to overcome feelings of nausea in anatomy classes), blood and grave bodily injuries. At the same time they read reports of murders in the newspapers with delight. 'A good axe murder is definitely more attractive than a poisoning, and a poisoning is better than natural death' (Hebb).

Observations of this kind suggest that there are energies linked with certain defence mechanisms in the organisms, which are not normally or sufficiently often released in our community. Animals in captivity may, for example, show signs of violent motor fear reactions for which adequate stimuli do not seem to be present.

EMOTIONAL MATURITY

However we may choose to classify emotional development, its differentiation and the forces that govern it, we can observe that on the whole emotional behaviour seems better integrated as the child grows older. Ability to govern and control emotional impulses increases so that emotional resources can be used spontaneously and for life-enhancing purposes.

Any theory of emotional maturation, says Jersild, an American educational psychologist, must take into consideration all a human being's resources, and his ability to enjoy making use of these resources. Emotional maturity, at any stage of growth, reflects the results of development of all parts of a child's personality that can affect each other.

The concept of emotional development must therefore be considered in relation to the age level. Jersild has indicated a number of aspects of development that seem to be characteristic, some of which are given here:

(1) A change from helplessness to a greatly increased capacity for self-help, with a consequent progressive freedom from the frustrations and fears that beset a helpless creature.

(2) A shift from abject dependence on others to increasingly balanced independence, with consequent openings of channels for enjoyment of self-help and an increasing degree of psychological as well as physical self-support.

(3) A shift from capacity to appreciate and react to only the immediate present to increasing capacity to encompass the past and

to anticipate the future, with resulting changes in anticipation of both good and ill.

(4) Increasing intellectual capacity, including increased capacity for dealing with aspects of life on a symbolic level; increased ability to plan; increased 'attention span', bringing increased ability to see beyond, and thus to be immune to, momentary or temporary frustrations.

(5) Development of capacity to identify oneself with a larger social group, and the ability to participate emotionally in the fortunes of the larger group.

These and similar claims can hardly be said to have any scientific foundation, but are general descriptions of the progress towards the greater stability and better equilibrium, in agreement with the educational aims of most Western societies.

The psychoanalytical viewpoint

In spite of the pressure of environment and in spite of his own efforts, man is, throughout his whole life, the 'victim of his feelings'. The factors that promote or handicap progress towards a richer and more controlled emotional life have been discussed widely by child psychologists, and particularly by psychoanalysts. Psychoanalysis has focused its attention on certain aspects of early training; for example the effects of sudden or too early weaning, or exaggerated demands on the early control of bowels and bladder.

A central part of the psychoanalytic theory is that of infantile sexuality: that a child experiences sexual pleasure in various ways in the earliest periods of its life; and that the foundations of sexual disturbances and deviations, and therefore of the whole personality, may be laid down during the early stages of development, if the child's environment reacts mistakenly to its needs.

There is no doubt that genital reactions are present very early. Baby boys a few days old can have erections. Young children of both sexes find pleasure when, in the process of investigating their bodies, they touch their sex organs. The need to suck, either inherent in the child or acquired very early, is satisfied adequately by the breast, or by finger or thumb sucking. Emptying the bladder and bowels also gives pleasure, and frequently there follows a period when the child delights in playing with its faeces.

The two main periods of pregenital development are called the oral and anal stages. During the first (oral) period, the mouth is the principal erogenous zone, and later interest is transferred to the anal zone and its functions.

The significance of the mother

If the child is to pass through these stages without profound disturbances, it is presumed (and this seems reasonable whatever theoretical approach is adopted) that the needs intimately connected with them must not be subjected to grave frustrations.

The mother, or the person who takes her place, plays·a fundamental role in this connection. A 'primary affection hunger' is often spoken of to stress the child's need of mother-love and other emotions contained in the mother–child relationship. A child shows early its need for human company, and the old view of the mother's significance in this respect is being confirmed all the time. The emotional situation existing between the two provides, therefore, the best starting point for discussion.

The problem of breast-feeding versus bottle-feeding, for example, must be viewed from this angle. No investigation has shown decisively that one is better than the other. The bottle-fed child, if cared for lovingly and with understanding, is undoubtedly better off than the breast-child whose mother regards feeding as a nuisance, and restricts her care of the child to a minimum.

Weaning is also part of this problem, for it must in any circumstances give rise to certain feelings of frustration in the child. The breaking-down of the pleasurable habit pattern – breast-feeding – should naturally take place gradually, and not be subject to the mother's casual whims and fancies.

Training in cleanliness

The importance of the development of control of bladder and bowels is often discussed. Early and brusque demands made by parents may lead to grave disturbance of a child's progress towards emotional maturity and balance.

It takes a long time for a child to gain the muscle control necessary for regulating these functions, and cleanliness in a child should not be expected before the age of two to three years at the earliest. Growing tendencies towards fear, anger and anxiety are results of too early and too strict demands on cleanliness, and many behaviour problems in later years – even among adults – have been traced back to frustrating experiences of this nature.

Torsten Husén tells of a nine-year-old country girl in the south of Sweden who had a curious and apparently inexplicable fixation.

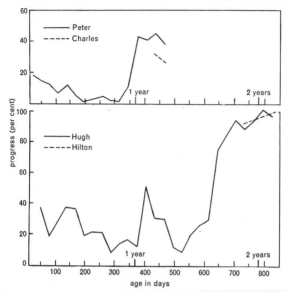

Fig. X.3. Early and energetic toilet training is harmful, and the curves show that training has little effect before the necessary degree of maturation has been reached. Myrtle McGraw experimented with two pairs of identical twins. One child in each pair was given toilet training very early but made for a long time no progress at all. The definite rise in the curve may be assumed to be due to the development of the nervous system, for when toilet training of the other twin began later, he learned very quickly. Success is measured as a ratio between the total number of urinations per day and the number of toilet urinations.

She refused to go to school when it was raining and the roads were wet, and when the sugar-beet crop was being lifted and the roads were muddy and sticky she would not go out at all. The only reason given by the girl was that she was 'afraid'.

A child psychiatrist studied the case and, during the case history (see p. 188) the mother, who was a dominating and exacting woman, related that the girl had had trouble with bowel control. Just before she was two years old the child, alone in the nursery, had a bowel movement and spread the faeces over a patch of floor. The mother, in a violent rage, had pressed the child's face to the dirty floor, after which the girl had never done 'anything forbidden', but had sat obediently on the pot.

The analysis showed clearly that the girl's terrified refusal was mainly rooted in this incident. Such examples are abundant. We can assert without fear of contradiction that parents who continually regard their children as troublesome encumbrances, who make exaggerated demands and are over-ambitious with reference to training in cleanliness do their children a disservice by undermining their chances of achieving emotional equilibrium.

A study of the investigation illustrated in Fig. X.3 is of interest in this connection.

FEAR AND ANXIETY

Much of this chapter deals with various aspects of fear and anxiety. There is no doubt that these emotional states are very important elements in the life of an organism. Many features of behaviour that seem to be directly opposite to them – marked aggressiveness and tendencies to show superiority over others, for example – often originate from fear and uneasiness.

A person has different ways of facing his uncertainty, and the method he chooses seems to depend on both previous experience and inherent reaction tendencies. Hidden behind many manifestations of human conduct, including self-assertiveness, are feelings of insecurity and uncertainty.

Definition

Fear may be regarded as sentry and first line of defence for the organism. It obviously contains a large element of usefulness. But on the human level at least, and already during the early years, it is manifested in such an exaggerated way that it may appear as a threat to integrity and emotional well-being.

It is not enough to define fear as an emotional condition appearing when danger threatens an organism – fear may be aroused by stimuli that only hint at the possibility of danger. We may, perhaps, differentiate between fear and anxiety by saying that when fear is present there usually exists a clear idea of what the threat is, while an anxious person is often quite unable to explain to himself and others just what it is that makes him uneasy.

Children, too, are often subject to such emotional conditions, which are inaccessible to rational understanding, and this seems to be part of the price we must pay for the distinction of being human.

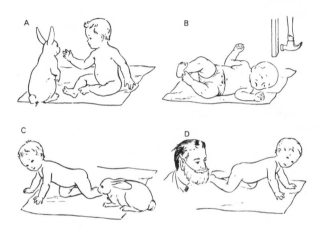

Fig. X.4. Watson's famous experiment to produce conditioned fear. The child plays cheerfully with a rabbit (A). A sudden loud noise is made and, according to Watson, causes an unconditioned stimulus for fear (B). The noise is assumed to be associated with the rabbit and fear of the rabbit arises (C). The fear spreads to other objects similar in appearance to the rabbit, a bundle of white waste or, as here, a Santa Claus beard.

Hebb has said that development of the ability to think rationally runs parallel to development of the ability to act and think irrationally.

Reasons for fear

Numerous investigations have shown how causes of fear change with age. We have already mentioned (p. 154) how fear of snakes is hardly present before a child is in its second year, after which fear increases in frequency to become practically general after four to five years of age.

This also occurs in chimpanzees, and the strength of the recoil reaction increases with maturation. Adult chimpanzees brought up in captivity without ever seeing a snake are just as afraid of snakes as are other chimpanzees. These animals also become terrified at the sight of a sculptured chimpanzee head or a death mask.

Chimpanzees (and other animals), like human beings, differ individually in respect of objects and situations that arouse fear. Common to all is that the higher up in the animal kingdom we get, the greater are the variations found in the causes of fear. This is also true of the reasons for aggressive behaviour.

It seems necessary to assume innate tendencies to fear certain objects – the examples above are of such types of fear – while fear of others is acquired as a consequence of conditioning. The classic example of this has been given by Watson (see Fig. X.4).

Sudden noise in association with something living, soft and furry, seems to be an effective conditioning combination in contrast to many other situations; a child is not afraid of a tricycle, for example, even if it has fallen off one and hurt itself. If the animal in Watson's experiment is replaced by a wooden block or a piece of glass, the conditioning process is usually quite unsuccessful.

Learned and unlearned elements

Hebb maintains that the fear of animals shown by children is only partly the result of conditioning. It should be regarded primarily as a means of reinforcing a response tendency in which psychological maturation is concerned. 'Such fears are not learned, but they require that certain other learning has taken place.'

This learning comprises the perceptual development that has occurred through contact with the usual environment of the organism.

> Though we have no detailed information about how it works, there is some form of conflict between the effects of the present sensory input and the reaction patterns set up by past experience. The normal environment of the species establishes certain ways of reacting to common sensory events; after this has happened, and only then, the sight of a snake can have its disrupting effect.

A still better example is fear of strangers, which holds for both chimpanzees and human beings. It appears first at about four months in chimpanzees and at about six months in children (cf. p. 94 above). Fear does not usually appear if the baby chimpanzee or child has always been surrounded by many individuals, but in a normal environment the reaction appears at full strength at the first sight of a stranger.

So far, therefore, the reaction is not learned. But if the chimpanzee has been reared in the dark, or if the child was born blind and given its sight by an operation at the age of six or eight months (cf. p. 92), fear does not appear immediately. The child must first become visually acquainted with a small group of people. This is also true of the chimpanzee, which requires about one month to get accustomed to its environment. Not until then does the baby chimpanzee show fear at the sight of a stranger. This, therefore, is the learning element. 'The reaction is not produced by a generalized susceptibility to any new stimulus,' says Hebb, 'it seems instead that "fear of the strange" is a fear produced by events that combine the familiar and the unfamiliar – not by the totally unfamiliar event.'

Hebb illustrates his claim as follows: Dr R. and Mr T. were regular attendants at a nursery for chimpanzees, which were very fond of them both. They were allowed to embrace them when they arrived. In sight of the young chimpanzees Dr R. put on Mr T.'s coat, and suddenly the young animals showed fear of the same type and degree as when a stranger appeared. An unusual combination of familiar and unfamiliar objects may therefore incite a powerful emotional reaction.

We have discussed the problem of fear of the unknown in some detail because it presents some particularly interesting problems. Similar reactions undoubtedly survive in adults, too, and it would certainly be fruitful to study, for example, hate of foreigners and aggressive reactions to people of another colour or religion from this standpoint.

IMPROVEMENT OF CONTROL OF EMOTIONALITY

We have described motivation as the inciting and driving processes in an organism, and in doing so 'need' terms have been used.

Need or drive implies something that provides the organism with behavioural energy, but like the motor in a car, it cannot determine what the behaviour is to be. The stimuli received by the organism have two behavioural consequences.

The first, which Hebb calls the arousal function, activates the organism generally without affecting the actual form of activity.

The second, the cue function, directs the response reaction and determines whether the aroused activity shall culminate in flight or aggression, for example, whether the child will remain out-of-doors or indoors in obedience to what mother says, or not.

The direction of the cue function

A practical question, and a very important one, too, is how far we can alter the cue function by the influence of environment. That is clearly what we must do when we want to achieve better control of a child's emotions or our own.

It seems possible to define periods, usually referred to by such terms as the defiant age, puberty crises and the like, when the organization of stimuli comes to a standstill as a result of certain conflicts. This causes, in its turn, disrupting disturbances in the cue function.

Certain circumstances connected mainly with fundamental needs are clearly of importance for a favourable development of the cue function. A child who gets sufficient food, who gets his need for sleep satisfied and whose health is cared for in a wise way, tends to develop emotional stability.

Care that leads to a feeling of physical well-being reduces emotional stress. This is also valid for the child who is made to feel the affection and appreciation of his environment – without being 'spoiled' of course – and who feels affinity with his group.

The importance of the attitude of parents

Wise attitude on the part of the parents must have a profound effect upon a child's control of its emotions. Such attitudes include allowing the child ample opportunities for its own activities, accepting its playmates, and giving it a say in decisions affecting it and its group. This is far from allowing it to run wild or terrorize the neighbourhood, which no one can call training in co-operation. It is the very antithesis of a desirable social life.

Behaviour that causes frustration in a child is harmful. A child who is always made to feel an outsider, who, for one reason or another, is not accepted by his parents, who feels that he does not satisfy their expectations or is continually compared unfavourably with other children and subjected to sarcastic comments, does not live in an emotionally beneficial atmosphere. If to this is added a continual threat of corporal punishment, there will arise emotional strain, which may cause grave injury.

Human beings neither do nor can dole out their expressions of affection in standard doses in their association with others, but it is obvious that some kind of moderation in emotional interchange favours the emotional development of a child.

Emotional coldness expressed in different kinds of repudiation, or a negativism which continually finds faults and shortcomings in a child, with perpetual reprimands, is strongly to be deprecated. But over-demonstrative affection and 'fussing' can be harmful too.

A child, like an adult, should have the right to look after itself, and to devote itself to its own affairs. What is usually known as 'spoiling' or 'coddling' may easily lead to wrongly directed development.

The problems we are concerned with here usually originate from defects in the emotional maturity of the parents themselves and of other adults in the child's environment – defects that cannot easily be described, but which are present in all people, though not to the same degree. Married couples cannot always regard each other with the same degree of enthusiasm. Warmth in relations between parents and children is also subject to such variations. It is one of the conditions of life that even the best person must sometimes become a source of disappointment to the people among whom he lives.

It is important to avoid premature judgements of what is good and what bad in the bringing up of children. As in other fields, behaviour varies greatly, the conceptions of strictness and spoiling are liable to be regarded subjectively. The aim should be to create conditions for self-realization. This self-realization must be led in such a direction that the individual finds joy in being considerate to others.

Chapter XI

SOCIAL DEVELOPMENT

In his gospel of man's return to Nature, Rousseau dreamt of the 'noble savage'. He imagined him as a highly developed and enviable type of man who had, in his upbringing, been influenced as little as possible by grown-ups. The inherent goodness of man would ensure that development would lead to ideal human goals.

These ideas are found in modern views of upbringing when it is claimed that the child, for its 'self-realization', must enjoy a measure of freedom to prevent its becoming impeded or misdirected in its development. The child must also be allowed a positive and creative role in the interaction between the generations.

The idea that a civilized community can, in itself, be a serious obstacle in the way of the development of personality is absurd. On the contrary, it is with the help of society that higher forms of personality can be created, and human resources be provided with the conditions necessary for full development.

GROWTH OUTSIDE HUMAN SOCIETY

Stories of children being brought up by animals are as old as the hills. The best-known in the western world is the legend of Romulus and Remus, who were suckled by a she-wolf. Romulus became the first king of Rome and after his death was worshipped as a god. In more modern times there are stories that tell of infants put out to die being rescued and nurtured by animals. When they have been found later, their adjustment to human life has been practically impossible.

It seems possible here to speak of behavioural imprintings (cf. p. 88) that cannot be effaced. Some of these reports seem fairly reliable, among them one of two girls in India, Amala and Kamala, who were found in a wolf's lair. A number of very unusual behavioural patterns have been observed in such children. They never learn to walk upright

– when they move slowly they do so on hands and knees, and they run on hands and feet. They have no language in the human meaning of the word, but can only make sounds similar to those made by the animals among whom they have lived. Their senses, sight, hearing and smell, are highly developed – ability to see in the dark is remarkable. Their emotional life is undeveloped; they can register great rage and impatience, but do not react with laughing or weeping when such reactions seem natural. Sex activity is either non-existent or oriented towards very diffuse or general ends.

Against such a background, the injury our cultural society may cause an individual must be regarded as very small. On the other hand, a human being brought up in society is mentally far more vulnerable, for he is in possession of a much richer and more versatile system of apprehension. We cannot form even the vaguest idea of the mental world of creatures brought up outside the society of human beings. Before we can begin to understand them we must make use of linguistic concepts, which do not exist for them. It is no exaggeration to say that such an individual is nearer to the she-wolf by whom he was brought up than to other members of his own species, human beings.

These facts show that we grow up into human beings by reason of our contacts with an older generation of adults. In almost every section of this book there have been references to the growth of social behaviour. The modifications of behaviour we call learning are mainly caused by the influence of other people and the objects man has created for himself.

A newborn baby is *asocial*, and it is the interaction between himself and his surroundings that makes him a social being.

SOCIALIZATION

The general term 'socialization' is used to describe the process by which a young person adopts forms of behaviour that are in accordance with the norms and values of the adult environment. The concept is closely connected with the intricate problems of bringing up children to become good citizens of the community to which they belong.

One may say, with Gordon Allport, that the most important task of developmental psychology is to throw light on the process of changing an asocial child into an adult with organized likes and dislikes, duties, interests and the capacity to take its place in a complicated society.

This transformation is brought about by what we call upbringing, the aim of which is to create conditions for the development of a well-integrated individual who is able to undertake in the community the responsibility for which his gifts suit him.

The contribution of social anthropology

Several sciences have concerned themselves with these problems, and among them social anthropology – the science dealing with the history of human development – takes pride of place. Social anthropologists have been able to show more clearly than others how socialization affects and canalizes human behaviour and what variations it may produce between one society and another.

What is regarded as natural behaviour – the 'right thing' – in one society is unknown or taboo in another. The persistence of these variations among people of different races and cultures must be due mainly to social learning passed on from generation to generation.

The developmental aspect was stressed early, as the titles of Margaret Mead's books, *Coming of Age in Samoa* (1928) and *Growing up in New Guinea* (1930), show. This aspect, which has of late become of fundamental interest in anthropology and other sciences, has opened up new vistas in child psychology.

Examples from zoology

In 1958, at a zoological congress held in London, a report of a Japanese investigation showed how even in monkey communities stable behaviour patterns may be passed on from one generation to another by learning. Among these learned habits were preference for or avoidance of certain foods and the washing of sweet potatoes before they were eaten. Monkeys belonging to groups which had the fixed habit of washing sweet potatoes could travel great distances to wash their food and then return to the group to eat it.

It is usually rare to find the leader monkey looking after two-year-olds after new baby monkeys have been born, but in one group this occurred for generation after generation. As a rule the habits of the group were accepted by each new generation, and new habits were always introduced by young individuals. It was found that the dis-

persion of habits from one group to another was practically unknown, when the groups were closed to outsiders.

Excellent examples may also be found in the works of Lorenz and
Tinbergen (p. 86 ff.).

Psychoanalytical points of view

In addition to the findings of social anthropology, mention must be
made of the emphasis laid by psychoanalysts on the significance of
childhood experiences on the personality of adults. In this branch,
too, interest is centred round the progress of socialization and the
problem of how learning affects development. Attempts have been
made to solve this problem by studying the effects of weaning
customs among primitive tribes.

It is very difficult in studies of this kind to isolate the influence of
a particular factor, but there are interesting clues. For instance,
members of the Trobriand tribe, where children are never weaned
but are given the breast until they give up of their own accord, seem
far more peaceful than the belligerent Kwomas, who stop breast-
feeding suddenly and strictly.

SOCIAL LEARNING

As implied above, social development must be described largely in
terms of learning. Such concepts as reinforcement (see p. 85) are used
to explain the effects on social behaviour of the influence of environment. Some actions meet with the approval of people in the environment, others with disapproval. There is a tendency to repeat
actions that gain approval until they become firmly fixed, according
to Thorndike's law of effect (cf. p. 90).

But whatever examples we may choose to illustrate social behaviour – even apparently very simple ones – we are concerned with
complex learning processes, partly because there are always influences coming from a number of different quarters, often with widely
divergent ideals of social behaviour.

Conflicts between parents and children

The views of parents on how children should behave are seldom in
agreement with the children's own views, which are largely determined by their schoolfellows or the 'gang' to which they belong.

There is seldom agreement on how children should dress, how relationships between the sexes should be regulated, how one should behave towards older people and so on.

Conflicts are frequently very sharp, and, like Winston Churchill, one sometimes feels uneasy at the thought of what children of the next generation will do to shock their parents. Papyrus documents more than 4000 years old have been found expressing uneasiness and anxiety over the behaviour of young people.

There has clearly always been opposition among young people to the social behaviour accepted and defended by an older generation. Social anthropology seems to have shown without any doubt that this opposition is greater and more active the more complex, varied and demanding the society is.

Puberty crises are more serious in western society than among most primitive peoples. 'Cultural puberty' is a term sometimes used to designate the difficulty encountered by young people in the western world in adopting and accepting the organized forms of habits, ideas, attitudes and values that are typical of our culture.

Bühler's social types

Social learning does not function independently of the nature of the individuals. Certain innate behaviour tendencies must be assumed, varying from one person to another. This is a line of thought found in many workers, and Charlotte Bühler has made the following classification:

(1) *The socially blind type*, which takes no notice of other children, but keeps mainly to itself.

(2) *The socially dependent type*, clearly influenced by the presence and activities of others, and showing great interest in other children.

(3) *The socially independent type*, which, though conscious of the presence of others, does not allow itself to be affected by them.

Social behaviour patterns that conform more or less with these descriptions seem as a rule to occur independently of the home environment, though it is very difficult to demonstrate this experimentally. It is circumstantial evidence that has given rise to the assumption that these patterns are due to innate dispositions.

Views similar to those held by Bühler are also found among psychoanalysts. Karen Horney, for instance, starting from the child's feelings of loneliness and helplessness, propounds a theory of three possible ways of meeting and overcoming these feelings: to approach other people and develop dependence (*go to*), to avoid (*go from*) them and isolate oneself, and to *go against* others and maintain one's independence, often aggressively.

Child psychologists seem to be thinking in terms of such classifications when they attempt to plot the social development of children and observe and calculate, for instance, the frequency of contact-seeking during group games.

The social learning we have spoken of must be assumed to emanate from varying and partly innate states of preparedness for different expressions of social behaviour. It may perhaps occur in the same way as mentioned in the previous chapter, where, on the basis of Hebb's theory, it was shown how certain types of fear are generated (p. 164 ff.).

THE BEGINNINGS OF SOCIAL INTERACTION

If there is to be social interaction the child's perceptual faculties must be developed. This is a necessary condition if the social stimuli to which the child is exposed, e.g. mother, father, brothers and sisters, are to be experientially available. During the second month of life the first social reactions usually appear, among them the child's first response by smiling (cf. p. 94 ff.), cessation of screaming when he is picked up, and ability to discriminate between human and other sounds.

Charlotte Bühler, who is very often cited as an authority on social adjustment, notes the following norms in later development.

Between the second and third month, smiling in response to the smile of an adult. The child begins to show dissatisfaction between the third and fourth month when an adult disappears from his field of vision. By the middle of the first year the child begins to distinguish between well-known and strange faces. A month or two later the child endeavours actively to attract attention by prattling animatedly, stretching out his arms towards the adult person, and by screaming when the grown-up stops talking to him.

These tendencies become more marked around the ninth month by the child's attempting to hold on to an adult by his clothes, for instance. The following month the child may be expected to stretch out his hand to give something to an adult. At this stage, too, the beginnings of organized play appear.

Contacts with children of the same age

Grown-ups dominate the life of the child during the first year, and the child shows little interest in children of his own age. An investigation of 92 children aged six to twenty-four months has shown how social contacts develop between children of the same age. Two children were put in a play-pen and observed through a one-way screen (p. 28) in situations which were experimentally quite well standardized. These were the main results:

From six to eight months of age the interaction between the children was quite impersonal. A friendly smile could occur, but the other child was mostly treated as a kind of plaything. Attempts to take anything from the other child were also made in an impersonal way.

The tendency to fight increased between the ages of nine and thirteen months, and quarrels were of a more personal nature, particularly when one child had a toy and the other had none. No actual enmity between the children could be observed, however. The beginnings of co-operation and the social use of playthings, e.g. rolling a ball to each other, occurred at this age, too.

The period fourteen to eighteen months brought a change of

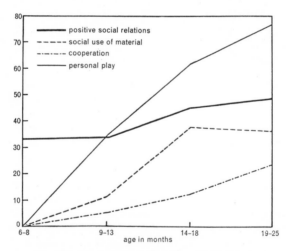

Fig. XI.1. Some aspects of play and social development.
(Cf. text.) (Based on Maudry and Nekula, by Munn.)

interest from objects to the other child. Co-operation and the social use of playthings became more marked and, apart from the fact that playthings were taken rather roughly from each other, relations were much more amicable.

Willingness to make social contact increased during the last half year before the second birthday, whenever playthings happened to be in the play-pen. The children showed greater indulgence towards each other. Games increased in both number and length during the investigation period, and became more personal in that behaviour was better adapted to the other's activities.

Even up to the age of three or four years a child is not normally able to maintain active contact with more than one other child at a time. It is not until the end of the preschool age that groups of three or more become usual – due partly, naturally, to the development of the forms of play, which in their turn depend on the social maturity level. It is clear that language is essential here, as in other spheres, for wider contacts. Some of the aspects of development mentioned here are presented graphically in Fig. XI.1.

PLAY

Children's play has long been a fascinating field of study for child psychologists, and the developmental processes behind play have been the subject of much, often speculative, discussion.

Play theories

The first real theory of play was advanced by Herbert Spencer. He regarded play as an outlet for surplus energy, with a consequent reduction of tension. He stressed particularly that healthy children play more than delicate ones and adults. Critics have pointed out that this theory does not explain why different forms of play occur, why surplus energy cannot just as well be discharged by work as play, and why children go on playing when they are tired out.

At the beginning of the present century, a German psychologist, Karl Groos, advanced the theory that play is preparation for adult life. He claimed to have found support for this theory in his studies of play among animals, and in the children of societies at various cultural levels.

Stanley Hall's famous recapitulation theory of play aroused much attention, too. It was based on the so-called biogenetic law propounded by Ernst Haeckel, the biologist. This theory maintained that during his lifetime an individual has to pass through the same course of development as the species has passed through earlier, and according to Hall, play is a particularly clear manifestation of this.

There is no doubt that play contains more and more social elements, and when endeavours are made to characterize different forms of play these are the elements most emphasized. Development towards greater social co-operation is not a sequence of clearly marked stages. A child may often revert to earlier forms of solitary play when he encounters problems of adjustment. He may also be a participant in one kind of associative activity, and a spectator in another, or have his own special interests which may induce him to abandon his group for a time.

Forms of play

Bühler attaches much importance to play, and maintains that all important maturation occurs during play. Among other things, playing teaches a child the rudiments of social co-operation, and Bühler claims, as do psychoanalysts, that a child who has never learned to play properly will continually meet with difficulties in his later development.

In her classification of kinds of play activity, Bühler discriminates between functional play, imaginative play and constructional play.

Functional play dominates the first year of life and originates from a general functional drive expressed in animated activity. The child finds pleasure in the observation of its own movements. It is not until towards the end of the first year, when the child begins to discover form, that its attention is attracted by toys.

A one-year-old usually knocks over a tower built of blocks. About two months later he may be expected to let the tower remain standing and examine it.

Imaginative play gives meaning to the actions: they must 'stand for' something. At two years of age, for example, a child may throw the pillows out of bed on the floor, lie down on them and say: 'I'm asleep.' Imaginative play predominates at the age of three to four years, after which it gives way to constructional play.

The child's great longing for contacts is expressed in imaginative play. He pretends to be mother or father, and copies their actions. Imagination makes it possible for children to invent playmates or other living creatures in order to satisfy social needs.

Solitary children frequently surround themselves with these products of imagination. A well-known Swedish author, Hjalmar Bergman, felt ugly and rejected as a child, and took refuge with the 'babiloons' and 'flapoxen' he had created in his imagination.

Constructional play becomes most common after the age of $4\frac{1}{2}$ years. Bühler gives a good example of how this type of play differs from imaginative play. While mother takes down the washing, her two boys, one three and the other six years of age, help her to collect the pegs. The three-year-old boy puts his pegs in his pocket and sells them as biscuits, while the older boy joins his together in various ways and asks the younger boy to guess what they are – a rocking-horse, an aeroplane and so on.

The older boy wanted to see a result, and was not content with the occupation as such. *Joy of achievement* is related to *joy of functioning*.

From solitary to social play

Types of play may also be classified by social content according to the following categories: (1) solitary play, (2) looking-on play, (3) parallel play, (4) associative play and (5) co-operative play.

Solitary play is the only possible form of play for the very youngest children. Later solitary play implies the will to be independent and alone with the material available to others, too. No attempts to associate with others appear during play. *Looking-on play* may mean verbal contact, or only watching what others do. *Parallel play* means that all the children use the same playthings but play side by side rather than with each other.

One feature of *associative play* is that children take ideas from each other, borrow and lend toys or tools. They may also 'supervise' each other's actions, but follow their own inclinations. The object of the play or work is outside the actual group interest.

In *co-operative play*, on the other hand, the object is to achieve a certain result together, and the task is organized with this end in view. The term implies conscious co-operation between the members of the group.

In 'activity method' teaching, strong emphasis is laid on co-operation, and endeavours are made to construct tasks suitable for joint activities, for they are of the utmost importance in fostering better social co-operation.

It is perhaps of interest here to observe how, as a rule, co-operation has become more necessary in scientific work. This is shown by the fact that scientific papers and works written by more than one author are becoming more common. Figure XI.2 illustrates this trend.

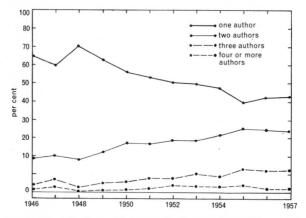

Fig. XI.2. Training for social co-operation is stressed strongly in modern schools. A rather interesting parallel is found in the increasing tendency towards scientific collaboration. The curves refer to articles on psychology mentioned in Psychological Abstracts during the period 1946-1957. (From *American Psychologist.*)

This is due mainly of course to the increasing complexity of the sciences, and the consequent difficulty for one person alone to master more than a very limited specialist field, but it also places new emphasis on the value of the co-operation we strive to establish during the early years of life.

The development of play rules

There are innumerable conventions and compacts in human corporate life. Many of them are deemed so important that laws have had to be made to enforce their observance. As society develops, new social forms appear which must be regulated by legislation, while old laws are modified to make them suit the demands of modern society.

Even without official legislation there exist codes of behaviour which are obeyed to the letter, and it may be dangerous to violate such codes. This is also true of many aspects of play. This acceptance and recognition of the 'rules of the game' by a child is an important stage in its social development.

Up to the age of three years a child rarely applies any hard and fast rules in its play. After that age rule-making begins. The rules apply only for the time being, and are altered as soon as it suits one of the participants. If children play at smugglers and customs officers, the open floor may represent water and the carpet land. If anyone steers on to the carpet he is told that it is 'against the rules'. The next time someone does it and is told he is breaking a rule, he may say that the rule does not apply any longer. Thus rules may change rapidly, and usually it is the dominating members of the group who make and alter the rules of the game.

A later stage has been described by Piaget as the coercive stage. Then rules are fixed once and for all, and may not be changed. One of the short sides of a football field may be much too short, but the goal must still be the right size and corners must be played properly. Rules sometimes seem to be verbally inspired by a higher power.

Then finally there comes a stage that may be described as realistic, when rules are subjected to discussion. This stage begins in the teens, when other actions and elements of behaviour are also debated and questioned.

It does not seem possible to keep these stages separate from each other. The application of rules may also vary in an adult community with the predominating type of society. Most frequently laws must be applied coercively if they are to be obeyed.

GROUPS, GANGS AND CLIQUES

One of the chief tasks of social psychology is to study group behaviour and observe how the private individual adjusts himself to and is influenced by membership of different groups. When we speak of the social development of children, we mean mainly their ability to form groups or participate actively in them.

Developmental psychology has been able to draw upon a number of very carefully designed and controlled studies of the social activities of the preschool child. It has been difficult to follow these up in such detail with older children. Interest has then centred mainly around leisure activities, the origin and structure of gangs and clubs, the changes in the circle of friends and the like. Such problems during and around puberty are dealt with in Chapter XIV (p. 219 ff.).

Social learning, which has been mentioned earlier, occurs to a great extent through the medium of the group. Attitudes to all kinds of things are determined by membership in a group. Demands for conformity in clothes and linguistic habits are often binding, and schoolchildren will seldom dress differently from their schoolfellows. ('But nobody in the class has such a silly cap!')

A case has been recorded concerning the eight-year-old daughter of a Swedish family that had settled in Denmark. She said hardly a word to the children in the neighbourhood during the first month, but after that she began speaking Danish almost at once. Good and rapid linguistic adjustment is also needed by children who move from one part of a country to another and meet with different dialects. For various reasons the parents may not change their modes of speech, but the child usually experiences the 'gang language' as more important than the 'mother language', and takes pains to learn it quickly.

The need for identification with friends and peers increases with the years, or at least is expressed more positively. In the same way and side by side with this, the need to be alone or with only one friend also develops. ('I have got hold of a good book and must go home to read it', or 'John and I are going home to sort out my stamps'.)

The social climate of the group

Under the title 'Patterns of Aggressive Behaviour in Experimentally Created Social Climates', Kurt Lewin published, together with R. Lippitt and R. K. White, a now famous report of an investigation made to elucidate the influence of different types of leadership on group behaviour.

Four equivalent groups of ten-year-old boys were collected in small clubs under the supervision of an adult. The leader was instructed to act in an *authoritarian*, a *democratic* or a *laissez-faire* manner during different periods. The groups met twice a week to make masks.

In the *laissez-faire* situation the leader remained mainly passive.

The members of the group were allowed to do as they liked and make decisions without any interference. If the leader's advice was asked for, he gave it, but he never made comments about the results of the work. He maintained an attitude of friendly passivity.

The leader was instructed to help the *democratic* group as much as possible and discuss all projects with the members. He allowed them to criticize all suggestions, but made no decisions himself. The responsibility had to be taken by the group as a whole.

In the *authoritarian* climate the leader decided everything, and divided the work according to his own ideas. He praised or blamed the boys without giving reasons, and remained aloof from the group.

Different behaviour patterns were observed in the social climates created in this way.

Under the *authoritarian* leadership three groups became very dependent on the leader and behaved very submissively. If the leader left the room, the speed of work sank. The fourth group showed hostility towards the leader, and the members had difficulty in getting along together.

The climate was much more amicable and confident in the *democratic* situation. Whether the leader was there or not, the members worked just as well.

In the *laissez-faire* system the speed of work improved when the leader left the room, for then a member of the group often took the initiative and the leadership of the group.

The results of this investigation have been interpreted in several ways, and have, perhaps, sometimes been generalized to apply to situations that cannot be compared with the experimental conditions. But it seems clear that the arrangement described as democratic encourages social feelings, while the *laissez-faire* climate leads to slackness and lack of initiative, and prepares the way for autocratic interference at opportune moments. The authoritarian spirit tends to release aggressive feelings or lead to submissive dependency. However, the forms of behaviour mentioned here cannot be completely isolated from each other.

The investigation seems to show, however, that a democratic attitude in relations between people encourages consideration for others, and creates joy in work on the basis of mutual agreement. A democratic attitude does not exclude stringency and discipline.

The sociometric method

The investigation described above made use of a well-designed observation technique to arrive at results. A method quite different from such techniques is the 'sociometric' method. It is used principally on groups of children and young people, and is intended to

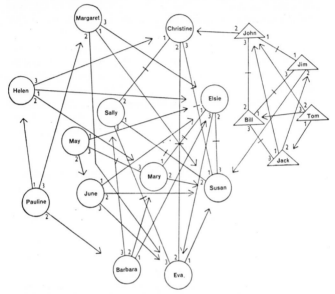

Fig. XI.3. A class of children aged about 13 years (12 girls and 5 boys) had to choose companions for group work in geography. The result (3 choices were made by each child, in rank order; the figures by the circles refer to the rank) is shown here in a sociogram. ——→ = single choice, —|— = mutual choice. Tom is an 'isolate' (not chosen by anyone) and Susan is a 'star' (chosen by many). Triangles are present, too; John, Bill, Jim, and Christine, Sally, Susan. (After Sterner.)

give a graphic picture of the social contacts within a group. The method was introduced in the 1930's by Moreno, and has since been used in a number of studies.

In principle the method is to allow each child in a school class, for example, to say which of his classmates he would like to have as a partner in some project. On the basis of the replies, a sociogram is made to illustrate the interpersonal relations within the class. One or two pupils, '*stars*', are usually found to be chosen very frequently, and at the other extreme there are one or two who are not chosen at all, called '*isolates*'. Further mutual attraction occurs in '*pairs*', as well as in '*triangles*', where three members of the class are attracted to each other. A series of social constellations can be discerned in this way (Fig. XI.3). In principle, certain social experimental variables can be introduced into the group situation, to see how they affect interpersonal relationships.

Moreno himself made practical use of the method by allowing the girls of a reformatory school, of which he was the head, to decide by choice their placing in different houses. The girls were allowed to make new selections every sixth week, and he found that girls in houses with a good social climate chose among themselves, while in houses where conditions were not so good the choices were mainly of girls in other houses. By transferring girls from one house to another the proportion of isolated girls was kept at a minimum and the spirit of community was improved.

Such results, including the report that the frequency of attempted escapes decreased, may be due to other factors, however. They may, for instance, have been produced by the experimenter showing interest in the well-being and adaptation of the girls.

The Vineland social maturity scale

The 'Vineland social maturity scale' is intended as an instrument to assess social development. This scale, constructed by an American, Edgar A. Doll, contains a large number of descriptions of situations standardized for different age levels.

The social maturity level is determined on the basis of observations and interview data referring to the way a child behaves in different situations. The measuring unit is called the social maturity quotient, SQ, which, like the IQ, has a mean value of 100. The observation method is used for young children; an increasingly advanced interview technique is used with older subjects.

Not all the items – 117 in all – are exclusively social, but most of them refer to social behaviour and the attitude of the growing children to supervision by adults. The items are divided into the following eight categories: (1) self-help general, (2) self-help eating, (3) self-help dressing, (4) self-direction, (5) occupation, (6) communication, (7) locomotion and (8) socialization.

There is a Swedish standardization of the method made in Gothen-burg by Olof Magne and Gösta Wahlberg. The reliability coefficient they obtained was higher than 0·90, which implies satisfactory reli-ability (see p. 135). The correlation of the scale with the Terman–Merrill test is very high (the correlation coefficient is about 0·80). This means that it measures, on the whole, the same factors as an ordinary intelligence test. The correlation coefficient varies with chronological age, and tends to sink with older subjects. The social maturity level is reflected in several of the above categories, but here we will take two items from category 8 and follow the Swedish standardization.

One task in the scale is usually performed successfully by children a couple of months after their second birthday. It is: 'Participates in games with other children.' The child must really play *with* other children, not, as earlier, play alongside other children. For example, playing with bucket and spade in sand, or motor-cars, building with blocks of wood, such children's games as 'Ring a Ring o' Roses' and the like. It is the co-operation that is rated, not the choice of occupa-tion or the degree of skill.

At 5½ years of age a child normally 'Takes part in simple party games' – another category and activity. The level is above that of the kindergarten child. Activity is less on the physical plane alone. The task demands co-operation with others in simple party games, watching for one's turn, understanding and obeying rules, showing judgement and friendly competition. Tiddlywinks, simple card games, dominoes, snakes and ladders are typical examples.

This chapter and the previous one on emotional development bring us to what is known as the 'development of personality'. The term has arisen without any clear description of its implications. It is obviously an overlapping and summarizing concept, which seems to cover almost all psychological variables.

For practical reasons we can isolate certain seemingly separable sectors of personality, often ignoring the connection of each to the personality as a whole. It must be stressed that this isolation, though often necessary for the purposes of research, may tend towards over-simplification. If, for instance, an IQ is used to assess general personal-ity – which such a quotient cannot do – a serious error has been made.

Chapter XII

DEVELOPMENT OF PERSONALITY

There is no doubt that one of the most presumptuous terms used in modern psychology is 'personality', and its use in developmental psychology is no exception. In reality the concept is scientifically unwieldy, and it has meaning only as a summarizing construct.

Personality implies all the physical and mental qualities of an individual put together. The nature of a personality, which, as the product of environment and heredity, is always unique, is decisive for behaviour in any given situation.

To say that personality is difficult to use as an object of research is not to deny the value of the concept. On the contrary, it seems important to keep it well in the foreground. It is absolutely necessary in applied child psychology. The more versatile and integrated picture we can obtain of a child, the better we can understand the child and adapt our actions accordingly.

It is perhaps characteristic of modern child psychology that it tries to observe a child within the context of the total behavioural situation. We must try to retain this fundamental view when we are studying, experimentally or otherwise, any very restricted sphere of behaviour.

It was stated in the previous chapter that behaviour is essentially a product of the influences that reach the individual through interpersonal relationships with other people. The most powerful influences are undoubtedly those active during childhood.

At present, great stress is laid on the school as a place where the development of personality must be fostered, a task that is often thought to be in opposition to the school's task of imparting knowledge. It is not easy to see where the opposition lies. It seems unreasonable to claim that living contact between teachers and pupils can in itself adversely/affect teaching and learning, or give rise to worse conditions for tuition. We must look elsewhere for reasons for the difficulty which schools find in problems of upbringing. It is not easy to penetrate the surface of the problem and get down to essentials.

Psychology has been able to give some help with a few simple elucidations – simple in relation to the complexity of the problems – but the fact is that educational aims must be fixed and decisions made in the light of the never-ceasing demands and criticism of the community. Developmental psychology cannot provide scientifically verified solutions to these complex problems. The question is touched upon here because these problems, and the hopes of their solution, are usually linked with the psychological discussion of personality. The most influential educationalist of the present century, John Dewey, conjured up a picture of an 'ideal personality', in his enthusiasm for what education might achieve. His exposition of his ideas of society and personality, however, owed its inspiring effect more to the strength of his convictions than to any experimental evidence.

THE COMPONENTS OF PERSONALITY

If, when watching a small child, we feel inclined to say that he is already a 'little personality', we usually mean that certain relatively stable and uniform features are discernible in his behaviour. It may be characteristic of one child to clasp his hands behind his back, incline his head and look studious, or smile openly and make social contacts in a special way. Such a child is often described as precocious, by which is meant that the elements of behaviour observed seem mature in one way or another, or at least well developed for the age level of the child.

The concept of 'trait'

The idea of 'trait' occupies a prominent position in modern personality psychology, and it may be said that it is a more up-to-date method of description than the attempts that have been made to classify human beings according to type. The so-called typologies, associated with such names as Jung, Kretschmer, Sheldon, Sjöbring and others, have not been applied very successfully in the context of developmental psychology.

Traits may be defined as functional units within the wider patterns that constitute personality. All languages have many words to describe them: honest, brusque, ingratiating, kind, childish and so on.

In the 1930's, two Americans took the trouble to count the words used in the English language to describe personality traits; they arrived at the imposing number of 17,953. Many of these are more or less synonymous, but even so it is impossible to construct any easily applied system with such a number.

One of the most energetic students of personality, Raymond Cattell, has compressed this enormous list of words and, with tne help of factor analysis, obtained twenty 'sectors in the field of personality'.

These sectors are intended to be components, with the help of which important aspects of personality can be described. In comparison to dimensions referring to height and weight, for example, which can be measured uniformly with adequate units of measurement, many psychological variables – particularly personality variables – are difficult to measure.

A general temperament factor?

The traits related to temperament have been the subject of special attention. Such adjectives as calm, impatient, energetic and impetuous describe temperament. Temperament may be defined as the characteristic pattern of the development of energy. It seems possible to maintain that this occurs in a relatively permanent and, for the individual, uniform way. It is clear that the temperamental variables are closely related to the emotional life – words like emotional, when used about people, are intended to describe temperament.

In many of the type theories, types of temperament are related to physical features, and attempts have been made to demonstrate correlations between these components. Sir Cyril Burt considers that there is a general emotionality or temperament factor, which finds expression in a person's conduct in a large number of situations. People with high 'loading' in this factor often show great fear, fly into a temper easily, are irritable and so on. The opposite is found in people who are characterized by few and weak emotions.

Burt calls this general temperament factor the *e* factor, and thus draws a parallel with the *g* factor of intelligence research which, together with certain specific factors, is assumed to contribute in one way or another to all intellectual achievements (cf. p. 132).

In addition to the *e* factor, Burt works with two other important factors. One refers to the dimension introversion-extraversion, i.e. the tendency to direct one's attention and actions inwards towards the self or outwards towards external phenomena, and the other refers to whether a person tends to experience received stimuli as mainly pleasant or unpleasant.

Concrete examples of the components used in judging personality will be given later in this chapter.

INVESTIGATION METHODS

Owing to the vagueness of the concept of personality, there are no definite criteria that allow us to decide unambiguously to what extent an investigation refers to personality as a whole, or only to parts of it.

It may be justly maintained that no test can claim to describe personality with any pretentions to completeness. Often there is nothing to go on but the researcher's own statement of what his instrument is supposed to measure. Such statements differ greatly in the claims they make. They imply, too, that it is very difficult to determine the validity of such tests.

The following methods are those most frequently used in investigations of personality. There is some overlap between them:

1. Case-study.
2. Questionnaires and rating scales.
3. Observation of behaviour in standardized situations.
4. Projective methods.
5. Psychoanalysis.

In addition to these methods there are complementary tests of various kinds, which we cannot concern ourselves with here. One widely used method, which is covered to some extent in the above list, is the interview method. It is dealt with below under case-study.

Case-study

This method may be described as a mainly clinical method. It is often used to find the cause of some peculiarity in behaviour. The main task of the examiner is to plot as exactly as possible the person's past, chiefly by interviews with the patient himself and those who know him well (parents and teachers, for example). This mapping of the main events in the patient's life is spoken of as the *case history*.

A less comprehensive type of case-study is often made as a final, complementary item in connection with the assessment of a person. It consists mainly of an interview made on the basis of a careful study of available test data collected at earlier examinations. An interview of this type is often called an *exploration* and may be regarded as a final control and complementing of the test results. Such an exploration can only be made by a trained psychologist.

This mode of procedure has been applied since World War II in the armed forces of many countries and similar testing methods are used for schoolchildren who are to be placed in different kinds of special class. Data are collected by most of the methods mentioned above, but psychoanalysis in the full meaning of the term can only be used in special cases, however.

In the investigations mentioned, the psychologist has usually to compose a short descriptive account. It may contain the following items:

1. *Environment:* parents, position in family circle, school and so on.
2. *Interests and general horizon*, including leisure activities, and orientation in the surrounding world. A number of questionnaires and 'interest schemata' are available.
3. *Aptitudes* judged by general and special aptitude tests.
4. *Character and personality traits* such as maturation level, temperament type and general personal organization.
5. *Attitude* to the circumstances the exploration is intended to investigate (for example, army or school).

Comprehensive and well-systematized descriptions concerning the application of the case-study method are available. There is also a good deal of important research on record concerning interview techniques. Interviews with children of different ages are attended with special difficulties – one of which is to avoid leading questions. The ability of the psychologist to make contacts naturally always plays an important part in obtaining good results from interviews.

Questionnaires and rating scales

The methods included under this heading are undoubtedly the most commonly used, and are those that perhaps come to mind first when personality tests are mentioned. The number of instruments is very great and many of them are rather uninteresting and of little value. Others are very well planned and some are important standard instruments for the testing of personality.

Both questionnaires and rating scales have been constructed in many ways, but subjective judgements have always to come into the picture at some point or another. The questionnaires, often also called personality inventories or personality schemata, are usually designed so that an individual rates himself, while rating scales are intended for a judgement of a person by others. As mentioned above (p. 22 ff), these methods were introduced into child psychology at an early stage by Stanley Hall.

Rating scales list a number of personality traits. The extent of their presence in an individual must be assessed. This is usually done by indicating a digit on a scale between 1 and 5 or 1 and 7, where 1 means that the rater considers that the individual has little of the trait in question, and the highest number means that he has very much. The digit in the middle of the scale marks an average occurrence of the trait. Each personality trait is assumed to be normally distributed, i.e. most individuals fall on or around the middle digit on the scale.

It does not really matter how many traits are included, and choice is practically unlimited. The types of trait usually chosen are co-operativeness, ability to make contacts, energy level, emotional control, ability to lead, alertness, ability to arouse sympathy, and so on.

Naturally, the raters must be well acquainted with the person to be rated. Ratings are often used as validity criteria for tests or questionnaires. Sometimes specially trained raters are employed who observe the persons to be rated during a certain period of time. Endeavours are always made to obtain as many raters as possible.

A particular difficulty in the subjective rating of personality traits is what is usually called the *halo effect*. This is the tendency to be influenced during rating by knowledge of the quality of other traits in the individual, or by a general impression of the individual's superiority or inferiority.

This tendency is one the psychologist must be on his guard against. He must try to rate each personality trait as an isolated phenomenon. When rating a group of persons, a class of schoolchildren, for instance, at least part of the halo effect will be eliminated if one trait is rated at a time throughout the whole group, instead of making all the ratings for one person at the same time.

The traits to be estimated must be defined as clearly as possible so that they can be rated uniformly by different raters, and the significance of the scale steps must also be clearly given.

The questionnaire also implies a rating, but a rating of oneself. One has simply to answer a number of questions as truthfully as possible. This may be done by putting a cross in a square meaning 'yes' or 'no', or by putting a cross somewhere on a scale line, one end of which means a definite 'yes', and the other end a clear 'no', while the middle means 'doubtful'. There are several other designs – Fig. XII.1 shows a simple form meant for schoolchildren – some of which compel the subject to take a definite stand.

	always x	often x	sometimes x	seldom x	never x
1 I enjoy lessons at school					
2 I want school to finish earlier					
11 I sit thinking about other things during lessons					
16 I feel nervous when we have exams					
30 They feel nervous at home when I have exams					

Fig. XII.1. Some questions from a form belonging to a Swedish study of well-being at school. The pupils were told to put a cross under the heading that suited them best. A five-point rating scale is used here.

One such method is the method of *paired comparisons*, frequently used to discover directions of interests. If, for example, nine different spare-time activities are taken and paired in all possible ways, 36 pairs are obtained, and in each pair the activity preferred must be underlined. In this way graded numerical values are obtained for each activity, and in the example given an 8 means that an activity is preferred to each of the others given.

Most questionnaires include a number of differently-framed questions for each trait to be assessed. The replies to the questions referring to a certain trait are counted together, and the number of points obtained for each trait indicates the strength of the trait in question.

The *Vineland Social Maturity Scale* (p. 183 ff. above) shows the sort of category that may be used, and other examples are provided by the *California Test of Personality* (Fig. XII.2). It consists of 144 questions, to be answered 'yes' or 'no', and it can be used from the age of ten years upwards. In the test the questions are read aloud, and the subjects have to draw a circle round 'yes' or 'no' on a reply form. Two main traits are measured with this test, personal adjustment and social adjustment. Each of these is divided into six sub-groups.

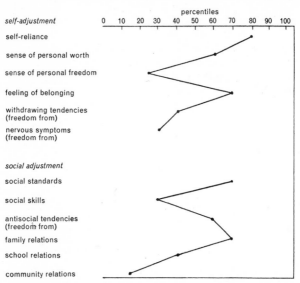

Fig. XII.2. The answers in the California Test of Personality calculated for different groups in percentile values, brought together to form an individual personality profile. High values indicate a high degree of the trait in question. The percentile 80 means that only 20 per cent have higher values, 50 is a median value, etc.

Thus, under personal adjustment are measured self-confidence, feeling of personal worth, feeling of personal freedom, feeling of solidarity with others, freedom from isolationist tendencies, and freedom from nervous symptoms.

Social adjustment is divided into social norms, social adaptability, anti-social tendencies, attitude to family, attitude to school, attitude to the community.

Personality tests of this type also include temperament inventories, as well as interest and occupational schemata. One temperament inventory by Thurstone (who has constructed several instruments of a similar kind, and also made important methodic improvements in this sphere) is intended for adolescents, and contains seven variables, namely activity (degree of need for action), energy (physical activity requiring a great expenditure of strength), impulsiveness, dominance in relations with others, stability, sociability, and inclination towards reflective theoretical activities.

Similarly, an occupational and interests scale, constructed upon the same principle, may relate preferred occupations and interests to contact-seeking or isolation needs, dominance or submission, and so on.

Observation of behaviour in standardized situations

The methods falling under this heading have been touched upon in different connections in the present work. Gesell in particular has applied and developed various techniques for this type of investigation. Most tests for small children consist of standardized observation techniques.

Once again mention must be made of the Vineland Social Maturity Scale, which is in many ways typical of this method. Much work is being done at present to construct more social tests, mainly for preschool children and children in their early school years. But it seems extremely difficult to arrive at standardized measures of social behaviour.

One method is so-called *time sampling*. Observations are confined to brief periods of time, e.g. of three or five minutes' duration, during which attempts are made to observe and record, with the help of coding procedures, as much of the behaviour as possible, or certain features of behaviour determined beforehand. The observation periods are distributed over a number of days or weeks at definite times in the mornings and afternoons.

One difficulty of this method is to select such features of a child's behaviour as can really be considered to have prognostic value. The frequency of social approaches, for example, in a group play situation, or to what extent the child makes use of the available playthings, is not easily related to later social and general developmental tendencies.

Observation of behaviour seems for several reasons to be a natural

Fig. XII.3. Observation of behaviour through a one-way
screen. (Cf. p. 28.)

starting method in psychology, not least in developmental psychological research. It makes possible the collection of fundamental
facts from which significant problems and testable theories can be
derived (Fig. XII.3).

Projective methods

The projective methods are being adopted more and more by practical child psychologists. This is true not only of the projective play
tests constructed especially for children, but also of tests intended
originally for adults, e.g. the Rorschach ink-blot test and the Thema-
tic Apperception Test (TAT). There is a special variation of the
latter intended for children, called the Children's Apperception Test
(CAT).

The general assumption behind all tests of this type is that, during
testing, the subject reveals underlying strata of personality in the
handling of, for example, play material, or the interpretation of
pictures. The replies given by the subject are 'projections' of his
personality. Repressed aggressive tendencies appear in some replies,
in others stress and causes of uneasiness. This is assumed to occur

unconsciously and in a way relatively uninfluenced by the examination situation.

Application in therapy

Besides being useful instruments for research in the study of personality, the projective methods are extensively used for diagnostic and therapeutic purposes, particularly with children.

Some projective tests may be described as continuations of the methods of observation mentioned above, but instead of merely registering the superficial behaviour, they direct attention to the underlying causes of the behaviour.

Why does a child choose to play with worn, broken toy animals instead of whole ones? Why does a child put a doll in the oven of her toy cooker, to injure it? Why does a child anxiously build a fence without a gate round a house?

There is no question of fixed or 'correct' responses of the type required in most other tests, which attempt to measure specific personality traits (general intelligence tests, for example). In the case of projective tests interest is centred round the subject's unique organization of the material at his disposal.

Projective play therapy is arranged so that the child requiring treatment is allowed to play in a room which is usually equipped with standardized toys. There is often a box of sand in the middle of the room where the articles are placed and where the child is to play. A bowl of water placed beside the sand is usually part of the equipment.

As a rule, the therapist is present, and her task is, besides making observations of behaviour, to establish good relations with the child so that he is encouraged to play without anxiety. Ability to gain the confidence of children, many of whom are extremely inhibited and shy, is consequently of the greatest importance for child therapists (Fig. XII.4).

Finger-painting is one method used in play therapy. The children dip their fingers in the colours and smear them on paper on walls. The *mosaics test* consists of a large number of different coloured triangles and rhomboids, with which the child is required to make designs. Choice of both colour and *motif* is revealing to the psychologist (Fig. XII.5).

This is not the place to attempt detailed evaluations of these testing

Fig. XII.4. Play therapy.

methods, but it is obvious that they must throw much light on disturbed personalities and can be a guide in treatment.

Rorschach and CAT

Two testing procedures more directly 'projective' in method are the Rorschach ink-blot test and the Children's Apperception Test. A leading feature of the Rorschach symmetrical ink-blots or the situation pictures of the CAT is that the material is unstructured or only partly structured and capable of being interpreted in many ways. The ink-blots do not really represent anything in particular, but their outlines and unevenly coloured surfaces give free play to the imagination in the interpretation of the blots.

What the subject 'sees' in the blots and the variety of his responses provide the basis for the evaluation of the results. Distinction is made

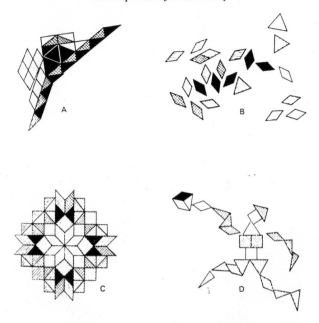

Fig. XII.5. Different results of Margaret Lowenfeld's mosaic test. No attempt is made to interpret them here but the totally disintegrated figure (B) is evidence of at least temporary grave disorganization or perhaps mental defect.

between the tendency to respond to the whole blot or to some detail, good or bad perception form, whether the object seen in the blot is at rest or in motion, and so on. Some of the ten Rorschach blots are coloured, and the number and type of colour responses have important influence on the evaluation of the responses (Fig. XII.6).

Development reflected in Rorschach and CAT responses

As already mentioned, projective testing methods have begun to attract the attention of child psychologists. An American, N. Ford, has demonstrated, with the help of Rorschach tests, some interesting trends of development.

According to Rorschach theory – which we cannot discuss in detail here – the relation between the number of movement responses (re-

sponses indicating that the figure observed in the blot is in motion –
'dancing bears', 'flying birds', 'a person walking') and the sum of the
colour responses shows the degree of introversion or extraversion of
the subject. A majority of motion responses suggests introversion,
but mainly colour responses imply extraversion.

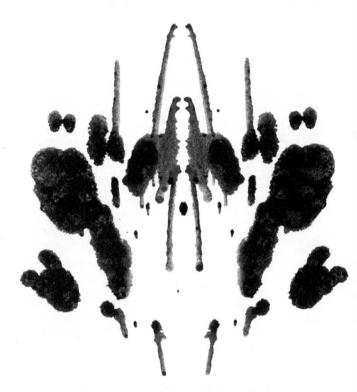

Fig. XII.6. Figure of the type used in the Rorschach method. Ink is
splashed on to a sheet of paper which is then folded down the middle, so
that a symmetrical figure is formed.

Figure XII.7, from an investigation by Ford, shows how, for children from three to seven years of age, the number of motion responses
increases in relation to the number of colour responses; according

to the theory this should imply development in the direction of greater introversion. This need not necessarily mean anything more than that a child discovers itself more and more during this period of development, and takes greater interest in itself. But it is most interesting that a test of the Rorschach type can reflect such a development.

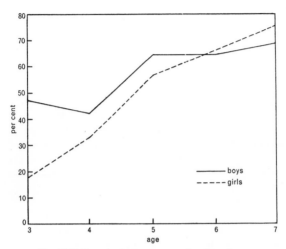

Fig. XII.7. Rorschach response as a function of age.
(See text.)

Of perhaps even greater interest is a study carried out at Fels Research Institute. The development of the IQ of 140 children has been followed continuously from the age of $2\frac{1}{2}$ years and between the ages of six and ten the children were given projective tests (Rorschach and CAT) in order to investigate the relation between changes in personality and alterations in the IQ.

Many striking exceptions, which cannot be explained by, for example, changes in environment, or illness, are found to the general tendency of the IQ to remain relatively constant through the years. Changes in IQ upwards or downwards have therefore sometimes been explained by reference to personality factors.

The researchers at Fels selected four personality variables, on the hypothesis that all might be expected to have some relevance to the development of the IQ, namely *the need to achieve something*, *the drive to compete*, *the desire for knowledge* and, at the opposite pole to these variables, *passivity*. It was assumed that changes in these variables would be reflected in the CAT and Rorschach responses.

It was expected that increases in the need for achievement would produce more fantasy achievements in the stories told by the children in response to CAT pictures. The hero in the picture might be said, for example, to be dreaming of becoming world-famous.

An increased desire to compete might be shown in the Rorschach test by aggressive interpretations: animals or people fighting, explosions, such as volcanoes and bombs, fires, articles or parts of animals usually regarded as weapons of aggression, e.g. spears, clubs, knives, horns and claws.

Intellectual curiosity might be reflected in CAT stories by the hero's interest in natural phenomena, and in the Rorschach test by an increased frequency of anatomic responses (including parts of skeletons and X-ray photographs of lungs which are quite commonly 'found' in these blots). The experimenters' hypothesis was that increases in the frequency of the above-mentioned types of responses would correlate positively with rises in IQ.

The number of CAT responses in which the hero of the story was said to look tired or sleepy was taken as the measure of the fourth variable, passivity. It was expected that greater passivity would be accompanied by a decline in IQ.

The method used resulted in evidence supporting a number of these hypotheses. The two extreme groups of subjects, one consisting of children with rapidly rising IQ values and the other of children with declining IQs, differed significantly from each other in respect of responses given in the projective tests.

Much of the discussion of this investigation is interesting. Competition with schoolfellows is, according to the hypothesis propounded for the investigation, a socially accepted way of working off aggression, as is shown by the fact that a person inclined towards competitive behaviour unconsciously gives Rorschach blots more aggressive content.

This investigation shows how projective and other methods can be combined, and how even very complex problems may be attacked and elucidated. It must be borne in mind, however, that the use of projective test methods in experiments has its dangers, scientifically speaking. For example, it is difficult to determine the validity of the tests themselves. The earnest endeavours that have been made to determine validity can hardly be said to have given unambiguous results, and a modicum of critical hesitation seems justified. This does not mean, however, that we cannot anticipate valuable results from the continued application of projective methods in child psychology.

Psychoanalysis

The above section on projective methods does not attempt to do full justice to their importance in child psychology, and this is even more true of any brief account of psychoanalysis. Psychoanalysis has expanded into an enormous field of research, and its sphere of influence extends over innumerable problems. We have several times found reason to mention psychoanalytical points of view.

From its very earliest period, Freudian psychoanalysis showed great interest in the years of childhood, because disturbances in adult personality were found during treatment to be traceable in one way or another to childhood events or experiences. It was on the basis of this that the theory of psychoanalysis was built up. This theory attributes decisive influence to childhood experiences and gives them a far-reaching sexual content.

Modifications made in the theory have not decreased interest in the applications of psychoanalysis or reduced its possibilities of stimulating the solution of new problems, as shown by the references made to psychoanalysis in this book.

Freud's interest in children and their development was a consequence of his clinical experience of adult neurotics. Their continual recollections of childhood, nearly always heavily loaded emotionally, made him regard childhood and infancy as decisive periods of development.

Psychoanalytical treatment in the usual meaning of the term has proved inapplicable to children, for whom modern play therapeutic methods have been evolved. It is interesting to see how these have grown out of psychoanalytical theories. Sigmund Freud's teaching was the starting-point for the two perhaps most prominent advocates of play therapy, Anna Freud and Melanie Klein.

According to psychoanalysis, the behaviour of the young infant is wholly determined by its innate drives, which have their origin in the most fundamental layer of personality which is called the *id*. But the child soon has to come to terms with reality and a part of the id becomes differentiated into the *ego*, or self, which has the function of trying to reconcile the often contradictory demands of the id and of the environment, above all of the parents. At a later stage these parental demands, prohibitions and culturally determined moral attitudes are taken over by the child itself and incorporated into its own personality in the form of an irrational conscience-like mechanism, the *superego*, which makes its own demands upon the ego. An upbringing that warps or unreasonably hastens these processes may result in neurotic disturbances, often of a sexual nature, in the adult personality.

Later writers have formulated revisions in psychoanalytic theory, in particular in the direction of reducing the emphasis laid by Freud upon the primacy of the sex motive. In general, neo-Freudian theorists have tended to play down the biological and give more weight to the social factors responsible for the patterning of personality.

Chapter XIII

PUBERTY AND THE YEARS AROUND

An account was given in Chapters III and IV of child development up to and including the eleventh year. An attempt was made to follow the changing pattern year by year in terms of certain particular aspects of personality – through the early stages it was possible to trace development during still shorter periods of time, but it was shown that towards the end a strict chronological follow-up becomes more difficult.

The intricate period of development dealt with in this and the next chapter can hardly be described in the way used earlier. To seek for a 'statistically' average eleven-year-old, twelve-year-old, etc., is impossible, for the behaviour variables have such a wide range (a strictly scientific view would claim that this is true far earlier) that general statements have but small validity. The more varied is the environmental situation, the greater will be the variations in personality.

PUBERTY AND SOCIETY

We know that changes in society during the present century have caused puberty to occur earlier. But while physical maturity has been arriving at an increasingly early age, the age at which social maturity is attainable has become steadily higher.

It is certainly correct, as Gesell and many others maintain, to consider development in terms of inexorable maturation determined by inner sequences, but these maturation sequences are in danger of being overwhelmed by external strain caused by society. The sequences are difficult to grasp and analyse. In a simple society, the demands made upon an individual – at whatever age he may be – seem generally more uniform and clearly defined.

In a modern society, however, there are hardly any clearly defined roles even for the different sexes; the tasks of men and women are no longer distinctly differentiated. An interesting example from Sweden is the question of women clergy, which caused unusually lively and protracted discussion. Sex roles have always been extremely important in religion. It was only to be expected that their annulment would meet with violent opposition.

Our industrialized society makes it in most cases impossible for parents to lead their children naturally into the working life of adults, which they were able to do in the old farming society.

Neither the study of old western forms of civilization nor anthropological findings from primitive cultures seem to provide any information that can be applied to present-day social problems.

Adolescence has been described as a conflict situation. Psychoanalysis (which has paid remarkably little attention to the period round puberty) has drawn attention to its neurotic features. The discussion of frustration in Chapter X is also relevant here. Typical of a conflict situation is inability to choose among different motives for an action. Frustration arises as a consequence of baffled need impulses. Causes of conflict and frustration undoubtedly reach a peak during the years of puberty, and experimental work has shown the importance of both these factors in the development of neuroses.

The problems of puberty do not appear like lightning from a clear sky. Difficulties accumulate rapidly during puberty, but if security and self-reliance have been developed during earlier years, it may be assumed with a fair degree of certainty that resistance to the destructive effects of these difficulties has been built up. Further, the hereditary mechanism of resistance to external strain should not be ignored.

AN ATTEMPT AT AGE GROUPING

The years from eleven to sixteen may be divided in various ways. Most commonly, perhaps, the years eleven and twelve are regarded as the last years of childhood, and puberty marks their upper limit. The disintegration of the usually well-balanced personality pattern of the ten-year-old, which seems to occur almost without exception and often rather violently during the twelfth year, and which also contains the germs of something quite new, assigns these years to early adolescence. The term pre-puberty seems to be an adequate designation for the years eleven to twelve.

Puberty may be assumed to begin at the age of thirteen years, although physiologically its appearance varies from one individual to another and between the sexes.

The duration of puberty is usually said to be about two years. It is reasonable to define the commencement of adolescence in terms of physiology, and identify its beginning with puberty. The process of sexual maturation is not merely physiologically fundamental – the whole chemistry of the body changes and new features appear – but also psychologically revolutionizing, for it is a process of liberation from earlier dependencies and a deepening of social and emotional relations.

Psychological terms, the implications of which are determined by the culture in which we live, must be used to describe the duration of adolescence. If the social environment allows the individual to take responsibility and play the part of an adult at an early age, maturation is speeded up. Here, as in other connections, maturation must be understood as a relative concept, related to the type and degree of difficulty of the demands made by society.

TO BE GROWN-UP – TODAY AND YESTERDAY

There is, in our western societies, no direct initiation into the world of adults in line with the initiatory rites found among many primitive peoples. Religious Confirmation has lost much of its significance. In old farming societies it often meant that a son or daughter could begin helping more independently in the work of the farm.

The social changes induced by industrialization have weakened the concept of adulthood. In Britain, for instance, a young person may leave school at fifteen, marry at sixteen, drink in the public bar and fight for his country at eighteen, and vote at 21. No single symbol of maturity remains.

Outer signs of adultness are permitted to young people earlier now than formerly. Dress, the use of cosmetics, and so on, give the impression that the young are growing up early, but this does not by any means imply that young people are fully accepted in adult society. The gap between inner and outer maturity, between physical and mental development is getting wider. Many difficulties and numerous extremely controversial problems may be attributed to this circumstance, caused and exaggerated by profound social change and technical progress.

Many results – favourable in themselves – of socio-economic

advance, such as the higher standard of living, for example, have given rise to an enormous range of needs, which society is struggling to direct into desirable channels. This struggle may be compared to the conflict of puberty. In many situations definite rules of social behaviour are lacking. Formerly laws and regulations were of long duration, but nowadays, owing to the continual changes in social life, many regulations become quickly out of date, and the authorities hardly have time to formulate adequate new legislation.

It would be remarkable if these often intrusive changes did not influence the periods of life during which young people are growing into the world of adults. It is one thing to be accepted as an adult in a primitive society – perhaps the difference is simply that between the moments of time before and after an initiatory rite. But it is another thing to find oneself in an environment where the process requires several years of wearing and trying adjustment. On the Samoan Isles, Margaret Mead could not observe any nervous disturbances, in the form of conflict-filled anxiety and uneasiness, at the transition into the adult stage. It takes place almost directly. The differences found between girls before and after sexual maturation are mainly physical changes.

PHYSICAL DEVELOPMENT

Study of the physiological processes that begin to assert themselves strongly during the years prior to puberty, and of which the culmination marks its beginning, is of fundamental importance. These processes also affect directly the development of personality. Puberty involves becoming functionally capable of procreating offspring. The maturation of the sexual functions is clearly the principal feature of the changes that take place.

Hormonal changes

During the years immediately prior to the age of ten, increased secretion of sex hormones can be observed in both boys and girls and the amount of secretion increases successively. This secretion appears in cycles rather more than a year before a girl has her first menstruation (menarche). The increased activity of the sex glands or gonads (ovaries in females and testes in males) is regulated by the pituitary gland. This activation leads to the physical and mental changes that characterize puberty (Fig. XIII.3, p. 215). Points of importance to this account have been given in Chapter V under the heading 'The endocrine system' (p. 74).

In addition to increased secretion of these groups of hormones (which are called gonadotrophic hormones because they stimulate the gonads) there is also great activation of the growth-controlling hormone. This too is produced by the pituitary gland.

Disturbances in growth and sexual maturation are caused by too late or early, too strong or weak, too slow or rapid activation of these hormonal processes, and variations even within the normal range are considerable. The differences are caused not only by heredity. Environmental conditions have much influence on these processes, too. The fact that puberty occurs earlier now than it did only 50 years ago cannot be attributed to changes in heredity factors, but must be due essentially to generally improved living conditions. Diet in particular has changed and has played an important part in this development.

We are really concerned here with a principle that is valid for the growth of all organisms: the more favourable the conditions, the earlier maturity is reached. Conditions that are biologically, and also of course psychologically, 'favourable' for the organism cannot easily be defined, however. Maturation processes which occur slowly and in poor circumstances will not necessarily lead to worse results.

Figure V.8 (p. 71) shows how increase in weight during these years is, viewed absolutely, greater than ever before, and this is valid for growth in general. By the age of fifteen to sixteen years girls have practically stopped growing, while boys continue growing until they are about twenty. Rapid growth in height is often accompanied by lankiness, and control over the limbs and body is usually markedly impaired. The so-called 'body schema', which gives us a conception of the position of the body and limbs, and on the basis of which we judge our position in relation to surrounding objects, is partially lost. It is characteristic of a growing person during puberty to stumble and knock things over. It is, as it were, difficult to remember where the different parts of the body are.

Changes in sexual characteristics

Rapid physical growth and changing physical proportions are important features of development. But we must add to this changes in the primary sex characters (by which are meant the sex organs) and the development of the secondary sex characters – the other physical features that differentiate men from women.

Up to the age of ten years, the testicles have usually grown to only about 10 per cent of their final size and weight. A rapid growth occurs during puberty. The penis increases in length in time with the growth of the testicles. The girls' ovaries grow more regularly.

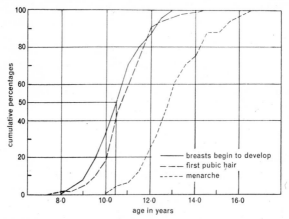

Fig. XIII.1. Time of appearance of certain feminine sex characters, and their percentile distribution in the population. If a horizontal line is drawn from 50 per cent until it meets the curve (as above with reference to development of breasts) and from there a vertical line to the base line, the age at which 50 per cent of the individuals (median age) have the characteristic in question is obtained.

At twelve years of age they are about 40 per cent of their full weight; growth is rapid up to sixteen and seventeen years, after which it proceeds more slowly and stops around the age of 20 years (see Fig. V.10, p. 76).

Pubic hair begins to grow on boys around their fourteenth year. It is fair and downy at first, but a year or so later it becomes denser, and darker in colour. At a later stage, normally around the age of fifteen years, the colour has become still deeper.

The surface of the hitherto soft and almost transparent skin becomes coarser during puberty, and the pores get bigger. The secretion of fat in the skin becomes more abundant due to the increased activity of the sebaceous glands, and this, combined with the functional condition of the hair follicles, commonly causes skin troubles (pimples, blackheads and the like). These may sometimes be very troublesome and often, because consciousness of feeling 'different' is greatly increased, lead to quite serious mental suffering. The sweat glands begin functioning more intensively. This often causes body odour, which necessitates greater hygienic attention.

Skin troubles are, on the whole, the lot of both sexes. Among girls, the hips grow wider and more rounded, and the first secondary sex features become noticeable. The breasts begin developing at about the same time. These changes usually begin during the eleventh year, but most growth in roundness and weight happens during the actual period of puberty.

Figure XIII.1 illustrates in cumulative percentages when the growth of the breasts begins, when pubic hair appears and when the menarche occurs. At the ages of 10;5, 10;7 and 12;8 respectively, these changes have taken place in 50 per cent of all girls.

PUBERTY CRITERIA

There has been a good deal of discussion about puberty criteria in recent years, but it can hardly be said to have invalidated earlier opinions.

Girls

For girls the first menstruation is still regarded as a fundamental sign of puberty, although its appearance is neither the beginning nor the end of the physiological maturation process. The arrival of menarche, therefore, does not necessarily imply a state of fecundity.

The first menstruation is usually followed by a period (varying from six months to more than a year) during which menstruation occurs at irregular intervals, and is of indefinite length. The anxiety which this irregularity often causes among parents and sometimes among the girls themselves, is in most cases quite unfounded.

Menstruation begins before the ovaries are capable of producing mature eggs, and the girl is therefore sterile for some time after the menarche. The duration of this period is usually shorter for girls who reach maturity late. A regular menstruation cycle cannot normally be expected before the fifteenth year, or still later among slower developers. Slight variations in the normal 28-day cycle are also common among adult women.

Boys

If the commencement of puberty in girls is assumed to coincide with the first menstruation, it must be borne in mind that though this does not imply full sexual maturation it is nevertheless an important event in the advance towards maturity.

The puberty criterion most commonly used for boys is similarly limited. This is involuntary seminal emission, or 'pollution' in sleep. 'Pollution' is derived from a Latin word meaning impurity or defilement, which, like so many words describing sexual functions, is fraught with value-judgements.

It is difficult to determine the usual time of the first involuntary emission. Sometimes it is not observed by the boy himself. Nor do such emissions always occur. The frequency of their occurrence may be affected by the practice of masturbation, which is extremely common in the ages when involuntary seminal emission normally begins to take place. Little is known about the frequency relation between masturbation and involuntary emission, but since the latter is a regulating mechanism for too great a flow of semen, it seems likely that masturbation reduces its frequency. Variations between individuals in a number of related factors make precise calculations in this area extremely difficult.

Another, and from the scientific point of view, more interesting method of measuring the progress of puberty is chemical analysis of the urine to determine the presence of gonadotrophic hormonal secretion (Fig. XIII.3). Still another method, of mainly theoretical interest, is X-ray photography of the skeleton. The development of the bones is related in a remarkably uniform way to the ordinary puberty criteria. Thus it is possible, with the help of X-ray analysis, to predict from the degree of ossification of the manual bones the time of the first menstruation (cf. Fig. V.5, p. 68).

STATE OF HEALTH

The rapid physical growth during this period involves many forms of strain. The restlessness and fatigue that appear during puberty are partly due to physical causes. More calories are needed during this period of growth.

An adult male requires an average of 3000 calories a day; a boy aged from thirteen to sixteen years needs about 200 more, and during the later teens the daily need rises to about 3800. The average amount needed by an adult female is 2500, but girls need about 2800 from thirteen to fifteen years of age, after which the amount necessary declines slowly.

It is often the case, however, that eating habits are more irregular during these years than at any other time. Meals are skipped. After lying in bed too long there is only time for a hurried slice of bread before dashing off to school. Girls eager to meet their friends buy a sandwich in place of the dinner that would take too long to eat. Boys coming home after a couple of hours' football are too tired to sit down at table and dine in peace and quiet.

A long list could be made of the reasons given for skipping meals or eating them at irregular intervals. These habits, which are often very difficult for parents to control, and which are frequently combined with late nights, undoubtedly have unfortunate consequences for mental hygiene in many cases. Growing boys and girls seem, it is true, to have remarkable funds of reserve energy, but serious irregularities in eating and sleeping habits during the early teens mean great physical and mental strain on the organism.

Physical health

In spite of the considerable physical strain of growth, and the thoughtlessness with which this strain is often met, the state of health during these years is remarkably good, better than during any other period of life.

Mortality is relatively high during the early years of life, but declines after the eleventh year. It also seems as if frail children with little vitality get a new lease of life during puberty. The only cause of death that takes a greater toll during puberty than at other stages of life is fatal accident. The sickness curve drops steeply after a peak at ten years, and is lowest during puberty. Infectious children's diseases are usually over by the time a child is ten, and new causes of illness have not yet appeared (Fig. XIII.2).

Mental health

The state of mental health at this period is more difficult to estimate. If we counted delinquency, which in both sexes reaches a peak during puberty and early adolescence, as mental disorder, then we should have to assume widespread, serious illness. But it hardly seems reasonable to do so. However, one characteristic of an eleven-year-old is that he anxiously takes notice of his health, wonders if his heart is working as it should, and has generally rather exaggerated ideas about how poorly he is. An experienced Swedish doctor, Bertil Söderling, calls eleven-year-olds hypochondriacs, and like many others he has observed that serious fear of death appears then for the first time. A six-year-old's behaviour is characterized by the fear that

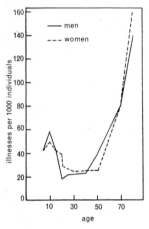

Fig. XIII.2. Number of illnesses per 1000 persons at different ages. A peak is reached at the age of ten years, but the curve (especially for boys) drops steeply towards puberty. (By Cole on the basis of material from Stieglitz.)

his parents will die and leave him alone and unprotected, but five years later he is afraid of dying himself. Stomach troubles and headaches, which are very common during the years prior to puberty, seem to be partly psychogenic.

Quite a number of these symptoms may clearly be described as neurotic, and as such suggest mental illness. But Philip Vernon has drawn up a table showing how the patients referred to English Child Guidance Clinics were classified according to age. The figures show no increase during the years of puberty, rather the contrary, and they are highest in the ages just prior to the eleventh year. Of the total of 212,000 children and young people, 5705 were sent for treatment during a five-year period, according to the following table:

Age (years):	5	6	7	8	9	10
Per cent cases:	9·2	8·6	13·0	13·6	13·3	11·3

Age (years):	11	12	13	14	15	16
Per cent cases:	8·7	7·7	7·1	5·6	6·2	1·7

These figures were collected in the course of an inquiry into the effects upon mental health of a secondary school selection system which obliges British schoolchildren, at the age of 10–11, to prepare for competitive examinations and then leave the primary school and adjust rapidly to new school surroundings. The figures do not provide any evidence that this situation causes increased mental disturbance. Indeed, a tendency in the opposite direction from the eleventh year onwards is clear, and this is borne out by experience. The difficulty of defining mental sickness is clearly responsible for some confusion on this point. If we accept (see p. 204) that puberty implies a conflict situation, the pattern of which is determined by the cultural environment, aggravated by (among other things) the widening of the gap between physical and social maturity, then a possible corollary is that the general neurotic level will rise. However, opinions vary as to what requires care and guidance. Such features of puberty as antagonism, emotional instability due to worry and anxiety, and so on can hardly be described as manifestations of neurotic behaviour in the conventional meaning of the term, but should be considered as normal for that age.

Physical health and social prestige

Good physical health is an important factor in a person's achievement of a position within his own group. There is a positive correlation between physical strength and social prestige. This is very striking if extreme groups are compared. In an investigation the ten subjects with the best physical development had by far the best rating for social prestige and general adjustment in a sociometric test. The ten weakest, on the other hand, were much less popular; they had feelings of inferiority and showed a lack of personal adjustment.

Strength is a highly esteemed quality, but its prestige value tends to fall off in adult society in the west. During the years of growth poor physique and appearance may be handicaps that demand great compensation.

PSYCHOSEXUAL DEVELOPMENT

We have pointed out that the intensified maturation process during the years around puberty must be regarded as fundamental. It affects the whole pattern of behaviour and is of basic importance for emotional development.

The psychoanalytic theory of the development of child sexuality through clearly defined stages is both important and undoubtedly correct in many respects; but after about the eleventh year sexuality, both physiological and psychological, takes on a new meaning. The course of sexual maturation gives rise to strong forces of motivation, which lead behaviour into new channels.

Differences between the sexes

Maturation is manifested in different ways in the two sexes, and Charlotte Bühler's description still seems applicable in its broad outlines. Sexuality arises spontaneously in boys, she wrote, and the drive is specifically sexual right from the beginning, and concentrated in the sex organs. Sexual impulses and fantasies are stronger in boys than in girls. Among other evidence of this is the much greater frequency of masturbation among boys.

In girls, sexuality is latent in character, not only to start with, but also for several years of development, and must, in normal situations at least, be aroused by external influence. It is experienced as a kind of general uneasiness affecting all parts of the organism. No definite relation to the sex organs seems to be present. Puberty in girls is a period of passive expectation.

It is difficult to say which features of behaviour and experience are hereditary and which are due to environment. The Victorians strove to inculcate in daughters an attitude of sweet passivity, an ideal that is hardly in keeping with our own times. Nowadays girls are trained for competition in the labour market. This can lead to greater activity and more initiative, and a marked change in ideas about sexual behaviour.

Scientists who approach this subject in a strictly scientific way can offer only tentative conclusions. Generally speaking, competent workers (Beach in America and others) tend towards the view that as development proceeds, biological factors play a successively less important role in sexual behaviour, while the importance of the social factors increases. This view could probably be extended to cover most aspects of drive-motivated behaviour.

We do not know with any certainty how masculinity and femininity in the psychological sense are connected with physical factors. It has been shown that the equilibrium between the sex hormones is of great importance, but the effects of these hormones are by no

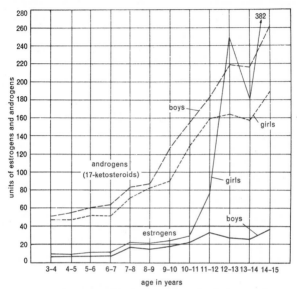

Fig. XIII.3. The excretion of sex hormones determined by urinary assays. Androgens are male and oestrogens are female hormones. Notice how the oestrogen curve flattens out for boys but climbs steeply for girls during puberty, the androgen curve flattens out for girls and climbs steeply for boys, but at a higher level. (After Nathanson *et al.*)

means simple. Both androgen (the male sex hormone) and oestrogen (the female) are present in all individuals (Fig. XIII.3) and they may increase inclination to respond according to either type of behaviour. It is a question of relativity, in so far as the masculine behaviour mechanism is far more sensitive to androgen, and feminine behaviour is more easily instigated by oestrogen.

Experiments with animals show that the masculine behaviour pattern is normally more easily activated than the feminine. This seems to suggest different levels of preparedness in the release mechanisms. From this point of view, too, it seems meaningful to speak of passivity in feminine and activity in masculine sexual behaviour.

Sexual activity patterns

The characteristic patterns of sexual activity vary from time to time. Alfred Kinsey and his co-workers gave us some idea of this variation in their two large works on the sexual behaviour of males and females published in 1948 and 1953. There are great differences between the various social groups, and some results suggest a generally higher level of sexuality now than in the previous generation.

Masturbation is the most usual form of sexual experience during puberty. It is far more common among boys than girls. Formerly the practice was said to be extremely harmful and pernicious, and parents often regarded it as their duty to warn of its dangers. Mental illness and injury to the spinal cord were consequences commonly attributed to the practice.

No one has succeeded in demonstrating such consequences, and all experts are now of the opinion that masturbation is harmless. It is to be hoped that nowadays superstitious opinions about masturbation are expressed only exceptionally. Horrific descriptions of its evils have undoubtedly caused nervous disturbances, characterized by strong feelings of guilt, fear and revulsion. Cause and effect have been confused.

It is important for the physical and mental hygiene of girls to teach them something about menstruation before puberty commences. It will save them much unnecessary worry and helplessness. Boys, too, should be told about what is in store for them. Sex education is *not* 'training for promiscuity' either for the present or for the future; its aim should be to increase the individual's understanding of the biological and social condition of human beings. Feelings of right and wrong which have a restraining influence and are conditioned by responsibility are not harmful, but assets to an individual on his way through life. Man is a biological creature, but this includes also the privilege of becoming, with the help of his reason, a socially creative being.

A tendency to masturbate may be observed even in childhood, although it is then mainly a question of playing with the sex organs. But by the age of twelve years – even before puberty – about 75 per cent of all boys may be assumed to masturbate, and in the period around fifteen and sixteen masturbation is practically universal. The corresponding frequency figure for girls is much lower, about 60 per cent.

In cases where masturbation is carried to excess it must nearly always be regarded as a symptom of emotional disturbance and loneliness. The type of therapy most often recommended is to provide some kind of occupation for the boy. He will then have less time to spend in passive daydreaming and continual wandering into erotic fantasies, and instead be able to direct his attention outwards, away from himself. Excessive masturbation is unlikely to be the cause of emotional disturbance; it is far more probable that emotional disturbance may, in certain circumstances, lead to excessive masturbation.

Still more taboo than masturbation in our society is *pre-marital sexual intercourse*. The widening gap between biological and social sexual maturity has subjected this taboo to greater and greater strain, and investigations by Kinsey and others have shown that heterosexual intercourse is not unusual even in the early teens. According to Kinsey, about 45 per cent of boys in their sixteenth year have attempted to have sexual intercourse, and more than half of the seventeen-year-olds have experienced coition. There are great differences between social groups. In the lower social groups pre-marital coition is many times more common than in higher social groups, where masturbation is more common and is continued until a later age.

Kinsey also showed that the occurrence of *homosexual contacts* between young people during puberty was not uncommon, and that they were particularly frequent in the higher social groups. It must be stressed that this type of homosexuality, which is often the consequence of a diffuse need for occupation or exploration, cannot be compared with the homosexuality in which need-conditioned preference for a person of the same sex is present. It is, however, difficult to give an account of the way in which the different manifestations of sexual behaviour are influenced, and which role the interaction of hormones plays.

Still another common kind of heterosexual behaviour, also mentioned by Kinsey, is *petting*. This was also found more frequently in the higher social groups. By petting is meant manipulations which usually lead to sexual orgasm. Figure XIII.4 shows the occurrence of various forms of sexual behaviour in groups with different educational and age levels.

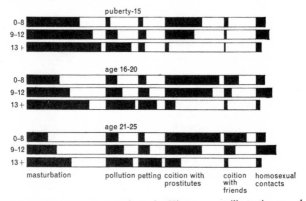

Fig. XIII.4. Some diagrams from the Kinsey report illustrating sexual behaviour in males. The figures to the left indicate the number of years spent at school. At the bottom the type of behaviour is given, and the black parts give the relative scale. The information, particularly that referring to early years, was obtained by interviews with adults.

It is obvious, from available investigations and observations, that the sexual energies which emerge with irresistible force during puberty and reach their maximum capacity in the middle teens, are extremely powerful sources of motivation and cannot easily be fettered.

The community has always endeavoured, by various means and with varying degrees of severity, to keep its members disciplined, clearly with a view to protecting and preserving one of its most important institutions, the family. This must always be a primary social interest, and one shared by the individual. To define detailed objectives and devise workable means for achieving them within a community torn by conflicting values presents enormous problems. Unless psychologists concerned with adolescence are to stand by wide-eyed and helpless, comprehensive investigations are required.

Chapter XIV

PUBERTY AND THE YEARS AROUND
(Continued)

Gesell carried his surveys of development up to the stages indicated by the title of the last of his general surveys: 'Youth: the years from ten to sixteen.' He has based his account on observations of a number of behaviour variables, each of which is extremely complicated in itself.

The data on which it is based comprise detailed interviews and testing of young Americans, repeated year after year. The selection is not a genuinely random sample of American youth, but is, from the socio-economic aspect, slightly above the average. Nor were any cases of grave behavioural disturbances included. It was a sample of young people from reasonably good homes.

Such a survey must contain a great deal of important material, and it will undoubtedly prove of permanent value for future study. But to draw general conclusions from investigations of this type is dangerous for reasons already mentioned. To illustrate and confirm how development is bound to definite sequences, it would have been valuable to have corresponding data from primitive tribes to compare with those from the western world. An approach suggested by Darwin would thereby have been realized (see p. 22).

There is a letter quoted by Åse Gruda Skard which presents the problems in a nutshell, but which also illustrates how difficult it is to collate particular problems with particular ages. The letter is from a mother writing about her daughter.

Gudrun is growing very fast and is terrifically tall, and she is beginning to get a figure, too, her hips are getting rounder and so are her breasts. Two days after her eleventh birthday she had her first menstruation. I thought she was far too young, but the doctor says that girls mature earlier nowadays. She takes the same size in shoes as I. When she is away from home I am told she is kind, well brought up and helpful. But when she is at home she is rude, sour, impudent and quarrelsome. When I ask her to tidy up she just opens the door of the clothes closet and throws everything in pell-mell. Shoes and exercise books are thrown in a drawer together with stockings and handkerchiefs. She often begins howling if she is not allowed to go to the pictures, even if she was there the night before. She is getting on well at school, but could do better if she would work harder. She has begun attending a dancing school and enjoys herself very much, but she says she doesn't like it. . . .

At this age, it is particularly hard to distinguish developmental sequences. We may say that many of the symptoms in the above letter are typical of any girl in our society who reaches puberty early and violently, but it is a different thing to collect features of behaviour for analysis than to form a general theory.

BRIEF SURVEY OF AGES

It is generally recognized by researchers that the way of life of a ten-year-old is normally harmonious and well balanced, and that this well-integrated pattern is broken up in the twelfth year, giving way to uneasiness and anxiety (cf. pp. 62 and 212).

The twelve-year-old usually has a gentler rhythm. His self-know-ledge increases and his social ability improves. An important point is that ability to handle verbal symbols independently of concrete objects now appears definitively (cf. p. 127 ff.). Its further development is one of the most important tasks of the school. A feature of this age is often great enthusiasm, which both home and school can lead into fruitful channels.

With the beginning of puberty during the *fourteenth year* there generally comes a period of uneasiness that is difficult to alleviate; in most cases this is a normal sign of a maturation process leading to deeper self-knowledge. An introverted consciousness and apprehension are stressed by Gesell (in complete agreement with earlier observations by William Stern) as a fundamental feature of maturation in this early stage of youth.

This 'inwardizing' is not confined only to the ego. Events and objects in the external world are eagerly imbibed. 'The interaction of these two modes of awareness constitutes the major key to the psychology of the thirteen-year-old.' Uneasiness at this age is an expression of this interaction and of a need to organize and understand one's experiences for oneself by inner deliberation and self-examination. The individual is beginning to discover himself.

Behaviour is commonly characterized by attitudes of opposition and resistance to authority. The choice of companions is often made more deliberately and is limited to one or a few friends. Difficulties in social contacts are frequently striking.

Typical examples are found in the scout movement and others like it, where members drop out in large numbers around the age of thirteen years.

The shyness and inclination to withdraw into himself that are so typical of the thirteen-year-old are not at all so marked in the *fourteen-year-old*. At this stage a more optimistic and open state of mind usually appears. The fourteen-year-old is generally able to make contacts easily, with both adults and young people of his own age. The circle of companions is frequently very wide. While the age of twelve years is important for the development of thought, that of fourteen shows important changes in the verbal factors – verbal comprehension and verbal fluency – included in intelligence tests (see p. 141 ff.). Thurstone thought it could be shown that these factors reach about four-fifths of adult maturity during this age.

The fourteen-year-old is seeking intensively for a way of life and trying to find practicable ways of getting what he wants. Both these characteristics are present in the fifteen-year-old, but much of the frankness and joy of making friends has been lost again.

The fifteen-year-old is usually in a stage of maturation that presents perhaps even greater problems than those normally faced by the sixteen-year-old. Several of the features of development present in the fourteen-year-old change their direction, and to some extent their character. Frankness turns into reserve, which again causes an increase of inner strain. There is an urgent demand for independence, which makes the individual both vulnerable and somewhat aggressive. Side by side with this, Gesell stresses, goes striking loyalty and the ability to adapt to different groups at home, and school and in society.

The social pressure brought to bear by a number of groups, particularly of young people of the same age, make the fifteen-year-old ready to sacrifice his independence. Then the family group often has to suffer. The intention is not to reject the family; but to act independently of it increases and preserves his prestige among companions of his own age. Rival groups with competing demands give rise to conflicts of loyalty.

At the age of *sixteen years* many of these conflicts have disappeared, and the vulnerable strivings towards independence have turned into a calm feeling of emancipation. There is a more stable outlook towards the future, and definite plans for continued education are often made then. Ideas about marriage and producing children become more tangible and are discussed.

This brief survey makes no reference to the social pressures and problems of adolescence that face the community today. It may be assumed, however, that the features of development mentioned in it reflect what we may designate as sequences. This implies something more fundamental than simple cause and effect on the superficial environmental level. Investigation of social needs and their conditions of development is of particular interest.

SOCIAL BEHAVIOUR

It is obvious, as is stressed by all those working in this field, that the period discussed here implies social initiation and development, which are of fundamental importance if a person is to feel at home in the adult world. This takes place by way of social groups formed by young people of the same age. There is a desire to escape from the pressure applied by parents and the community, which is often great, into an environment where one's views and interests are better appreciated.

During adolescence, membership in groups outside the home reaches a peak. Being accepted in a group is usually regarded as something of the greatest significance. Ability to adjust oneself to the social group at school and in the neighbourhood is often of decisive importance for harmonious development from the age of ten or eleven onwards.

Gangs

Puberty and the years immediately before puberty have sometimes been called the 'gang age'. The gang fulfils most of the criteria for what social psychologists call a primary group. Unlike earlier groups of playmates, which are often only short-lived organizations, the gang is relatively permanent in character. Rules develop within the gang, and they must be obeyed if one is to be accepted. The 'we' feeling of the gang is very strongly marked, and contact between members is intimate and frequent. It is impossible, however, to treat gangs as being all of the same kind.

Thrasher, who wrote a now classic book on the gang during the 1920's, studied 1300 gangs in Chicago. He found that the organization of gangs reaches a peak during the years of puberty, with a marked decline at the beginning of adolescence proper. Then individuals stick more to single companions, and are busy at school or in their vocational training.

There are other workers who consider that the designation 'gang' should be reserved for groups formed by children during the years immediately prior to puberty – the ages eleven and twelve years – and maintain that the introvert and often asocial thirteen-year-olds are not gang types in the usual sense of the term. This is a problem of definition, but it may be said that several purely primary group features are normally lost during puberty.

It is obvious that there is a deep need for solitude during puberty. Retirement is often sudden and violent, from both the family and companions. Everyday occupations at home and school and in the circle of companions often become intolerable, and the individual gets a feeling of repugnance towards them. No new interests appear spontaneously to replace the old ones. As a consequence, he seeks uneasily for something that can satisfy him.

Such uneasiness is also partly due to physical causes based on the rapid and uneven growth of this period, and to a greatly augmented sensitivity about one's own worth. This is what many psychologists call the 'ego crisis'. The individual goes around feeling misunderstood and spiteful towards other people, because they seem happy from his misanthropic point of view. The thirteen-year-old is more than ever in a no-man's-land of conflicts.

When, in the fifteenth year, social contacts are made again, they usually spread to include more than one group. The interests and

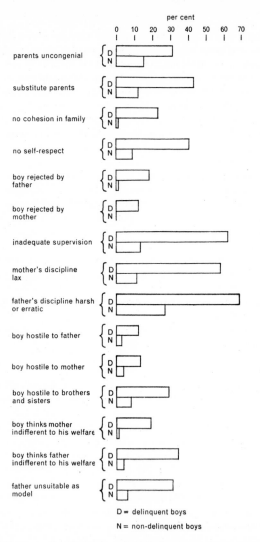

Fig. XIV.1 shows the distribution of criminal and non-criminal boys in relation to certain given home and family variables. (By Cole on the basis of material by the Gluecks.)

experience of this age generally require identification with several groups, which may often differ considerably in character and aims. Of course, intimacy cannot be achieved with several groups at a time. Its strength will depend on how the individual succeeds in his adjustment, and how well the group satisfies his interests. This adjustment to the group is very important, and exclusion from a longed-for companionship may sometimes have a traumatic effect.

Towards the end of puberty, gangs are replaced by what may be called 'coteries', and by definite ties of companionship and friendship. Where the gang survives as a dominant form of social companionship, with little participation by its members in other groups, it tends easily to come under negative influences. It often consists of boys and girls poorly adjusted at home and school and outside their schoolfellows' coteries. Often they do not take advantage of the leisure activities provided by the community, but spend most of their spare time loitering about the streets.

Some of these groups develop into criminal gangs. Others devote themselves to less grave asocial behaviour, consisting of acts of retaliation provoked by those who refuse to accept them, or destructive actions (breaking street lamps, destroying flower-beds and benches in parks) against the community in general. The attitude of the leader, who is often all-powerful, plays a decisive role in deciding what direction the gang's activities will take.

Criminal gangs of young people

Among the many who have studied these problems, the Gluecks in the United States must be mentioned. Typical criminal gangs differ in several respects from ordinary social youth organizations. The members of this type of primary group are below average intelligence, and are clearly retarded and misdirected in their upbringing. They are antagonistic to school and its work, and are dissatisfied with the forms of emotional expression that other young people find adequate and acceptable. Their often deep frustration frequently puts them in heavily loaded action situations, which usually leads them to show enmity and antagonism towards their surroundings. Their home situation is usually unsatisfactory, and often characterized by violent emotional strain between members of the family (Fig. XIV.1.) Environmental factors are of prime importance. Slum districts in large towns are often hotbeds for this type of gang.

Why is juvenile delinquency increasing?

Enormous social problems lie behind the increase in juvenile delinquency. There is no doubt that the factors mentioned above are very relevant. Durkheim, the famous French sociologist, propounded a theory that is still often cited. He claimed that greater mobility encourages criminality.

Formerly the members of a community were compelled by strong ties of family and occupation to uniform behaviour with little scope for asocial activities. Social development has brought about the drift to large towns and hence has broken family ties. Occupations are largely outside the family circle, and old values have been dissolved without new ones being created. This has meant, for the individual, that he finds himself more and more in a social vacuum unconnected to any one place, occupational group or tradition. The members of the community have become more isolated and anonymous. As a result, social controls have become weaker. It is such a society that Durkheim considers to be a breeding-ground for criminality, and its influence is penetrating into the younger age groups.

An American investigation, made in the 1940s, attempted to determine the causes of the marked growth of juvenile delinquency, which increased in some states between 1941 and 1943 by practically 100 per cent. World War II, then raging, was undoubtedly one cause, but the task was to determine which social changes due to the war were of importance to the problem. It was shown, among other things, that the number of young people aged fourteen to eighteen years working in industry increased from 900,000 in 1940 to about 3,000,000 in 1944. Most of these young people had left school early, attracted by high wages.

The economic situation of these adolescents changed very rapidly, and many of them were able to spend their incomes as they wished, without any social responsibilities. There were many who never mastered this sudden change in their situation. Some of them developed habits that were against law and order. Their economic independence was not backed up by social maturity. In addition to this, they were still regarded by adults, both at home and at work, as children.

As a result of such alterations in economic and social position, these young people experienced great conflicts. The violent break with customary situations and traditions created considerable frustration. It is clear that Durkheim's theory is not an unreasonable one.

The conception of the social role

If we define the gang as a group monopolizing practically all the interest of its members, it is not typical of late puberty and early adolescence. Associates and friends are selected according to other and more varied principles. When companionship begins to include members of the opposite sex, and therefore also completely new interests, the individual often encounters special difficulties.

Of all the changes that take place in social behaviour at this age, the alterations of attitudes in a heterosexual direction are perhaps the most marked. Seven stages of development have been noted:

Infants: Both boys and girls are interested only in themselves
Early childhood: Seek association with other children regardless of sex
About 8: Boys prefer to play with boys, girls with girls
10–12: Sexes antagonistic to each other
13–14: Girls begin to show interest in boys, and try to attract their attention; boys supercilious
14–16: Boys begin taking interest in girls; some begin to pair off
16–17: Pairing off is common

Attempts to gain popularity are very noticeable during the adolescent years. This means that adolescents try, to the best of their ability, to play the part that their environment demands of them. In the same way the individual makes certain demands on the roles played by other people in his environment. As a rule, the roles are relatively conventional and recognized between girls and boys, but there is sometimes great uncertainty as to what is to be regarded as suitable social behaviour towards the opposite sex, particularly in the early years of adolescence. A wait-and-see policy is therefore pursued, until the individual has learned how he must play his part.

A sociometric study by an American, Ausubel, and his co-workers shows in an interesting way how the understanding of one's own social position in a group is developed (Fig. XIV.2). If pupils in a school class are asked to list their classmates in order of preference under a certain heading, for example popularity, and are then required to place themselves in this ranking scale, it is usually found that the badly adjusted pupils overestimate their social reputations, while the well-adjusted pupils tend to place themselves rather too low in the scale. As a rule, however, it may be said that the more generally accepted a person is in a group, the better he is able to judge his position in it.

The correlation coefficients of Fig. XIV.2 reflect the degree of agreement between the rating of a person's position made by himself, and by others. An individual's opinion of how schoolfellows of the same age but of the opposite sex rate him improves steadily during adolescence. This is not so with regard to companions of the same sex.

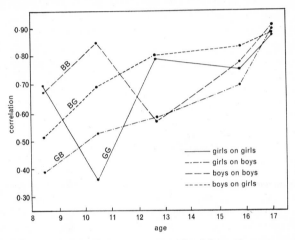

Fig. XIV.2. Agreement between own rating of social status in a group and that made by other members of the group during years of growth. The correlation seems to increase successively as regards the opinion of the opposite sex, but less regularly with reference to the judgements of one's own sex.

The rating made closest to puberty shows relatively poor correspondence between ratings made by the individual himself and by others. Sex differences are particularly interesting.

INFLUENCE OF PARENTS

Clearly the role played by home and parents is of vital importance during the whole period of growth, since the home environment or its equivalent is the seed-bed for the forces that condition the whole socialization process.

Spitz has coined the term 'hospitalism' for different forms of upbringing in children's homes during the early childhood years. In order to be capable of forming satisfactory human relations in later life, a child needs to have experienced a strong emotional bond with some one person – usually the mother – who cares for him in early childhood. A children's home usually provides several mother substitutes (nurses). Spitz maintains that this plurality weakens the important mother-ties and the feelings of security and trust which they generate.

It is during puberty that the first decisive signs appear of how different formative factors have functioned and what fruit they have borne. There is much evidence that the liberating process which takes place during puberty is a test of the strength of the organism as a whole: both of what it has inherited and what it has been given by its environment.

Numerous attempts have been made to classify different kinds of home environment and the ways different parents behave towards their children. Different social climates from home to home may be mentioned, and several categories have been derived from Lewin's theories (see p. 180 ff.). But it is seldom that both parents behave in the same way. In the home environment there are all shades of variation from the situation with the strict father and the mild mother to the complete opposite. This, together with innumerable economic, social, intellectual and emotional factors, all of which contribute to the creation of the home environment, means that any system of classification must involve over-simplification.

Incomplete homes

Everywhere there are homes that are incomplete in one way or another. Though death or divorce may have disastrous effects on a child's development, in other cases the injuries may be insignificant. It is not easy to judge the situation of a child of a 'broken home'. A divorce is often preceded by a long period of deep dissension, which inevitably means emotional strain and discord. The child cannot, as a rule, be protected from this or kept in ignorance of it. A divorce cannot be said, *ipso facto*, to cause a deterioration in the situation.

It is obvious, however, that on an average, an incomplete home situation has injurious effects. This has been shown by a number of investigations. An American study made in 1947 of 211 young soldiers hospitalized on account of grave neuroses, showed that 36 per cent were from incomplete homes. This figure is more than three times as great as the average of the total population. There seems reason to suppose that dissension in a home increases the risk of neurosis and reduces resistance to stress.

Attitudes towards children

One investigation has tried to determine the differences in attitude between mothers of well and badly adjusted American college girls. It is difficult to say how far cause and effect have been confused, but the descriptions of attitudes are not without interest. Mothers of badly adjusted daughters tended to be neurotically attached to their daughters; they either controlled them very strictly or allowed them complete freedom. These mothers showed signs of being unhappy in their home lives; they were unable to talk their daughters into better behaviour, owing either to a demand that they be regarded as infallible or to a general inability to intervene. The mothers often suffered from guilty feelings of having contributed to their daughters' lack of adjustment.

The mothers of the well-adjusted girls were happy to observe every sign of maturity in their daughters; they had many interests outside their homes, they accepted their daughters' failures and emotional idiosyncrasies without agitation, and they could keep in touch with their girls freely and without constraint. The upbringing given by these mothers had been fairly strict but consistent, and was based on understanding and consideration.

It is especially difficult to determine the importance of the father in upbringing. His occupation makes him absent from home during the daytime, and thus he usually has less contact with the actual problems of child-rearing. It is interesting to note how the attitudes of mothers appear again in descriptions of good and bad teachers. The 'infallible' teacher, who can never admit a mistake, is seldom successful. The importance for teachers of hobbies and interests outside their school work is often stressed. To be able to maintain free and unconstrained contact with the pupils and at the same time act with firmness and consistency are among the positive characteristics of teachers. General inability to intervene and keep order, often due to personal uncertainty, frequently causes great difficulty with discipline.

THE CONCEPT OF DEMOCRATIC AUTHORITY

It is interesting to connect some ideas advanced by a psychoanalyst, Erich Fromm, with the above account. Fromm has taken part in the discussion of modern child-rearing, and has also attempted to define the concept of democratic authority. To be productive, says Fromm, is to realize one's potentialities. It is a use of power. But power may mean two quite different things – *power to*, which is the same as ability, and *power over*, which means domination, and which, according to Fromm, is a perversion of *power to*.

It is also possible to distinguish irrational and rational authority. The former is based on power over people. It is maintained by fear, and every criticism of authority is prohibited. Rational authority, which a democratic society has to develop, is, on the other hand, based on recognition of the greater competence and efficiency of one group in a special sphere. Further, it recognizes the principle of equality between the groups.

Fromm propounds a theory of what he calls 'humanist ethics', according to which goodness is 'to live a full life, to develop one's gifts as a human being. Virtue consists of feeling responsibility for one's own existence. Evil is to destroy man's opportunities.' The most important goal of productivity is man himself. Fromm attempts to show how important this is for teachers and parents by an analysis of the nature of selfishness. He maintains that a selfish person does not love himself too much, but too little; in fact, he really hates himself.

The eager solicitude for others that we observe in an exaggeratedly anxious and domineering mother, for example, can help us to understand what Fromm means. While, consciously, she believes that she has an unusually strong feeling of love for her children, she really harbours a deep, subconscious hate of the object of her solicitude. She worries far too much, not because she loves her children too much, but because she must get compensation for her inability to love at all.

Fromm claims that psychoanalysts' experience of neurotic unselfishness confirms this theory. Unselfishness is more than a symptom of disorder, it is frequently the only virtue such people pride themselves on. Behind it there often lies inability to love and experience joy over something, and a veiled but no less intense egocentricity. In opposition to this, Fromm places self-love in humanist ethics, which implies personal improvement and concern for one's own development: 'If one observes the influence that a mother with genuine self-love has on her children, it will be found that there is nothing that contributes towards teaching children what love, joy and happiness are than being loved by a mother who loves herself.'

Of course, Fromm's discussion is not scientific in the experimental meaning of the term, but it is none the less based on valuable knowledge of some essential conditions of human communion. It is a protest against the often unproductive activity of modern people – including teachers and parents – who restlessly demand action, against a *besserwisser* mentality, everlastingly ticking over, giving only the semblance of competence. Fromm advocates a positive attitude to the surrounding world and to oneself.

In the last analysis it is the individual's own ability to realize himself that is on trial. Fromm is concerned with essentials of great importance for the creation of favourable attitudes in adolescents towards grown-ups. Fromm's discussion is a continuation of the ideas, put forward by John Dewey and others, met with in the contemporary debate on education in general and the objectives of the school.

Chapter XV

CHILDREN AT SCHOOL

One of the most important fields of psychological research today is that of educational psychology which is concerned with the behaviour – using that term in its very broadest meaning – of the boy or girl at school and also with appropriate methods for influencing that behaviour in desirable directions. It will be immediately obvious that investigations concerned with learning and with motivation must be central to this field of research. But the behaviour of a child at school cannot be divorced from his general behaviour, so that the research worker in educational psychology finds that his work has links with every other branch of behavioural science.

Child psychology and educational psychology are both firmly rooted in developmental psychology; indeed the first two terms are occasionally used interchangeably. The school and its significance for the adaptation of the individual to the community have already been touched upon several times in this book, but the book is intended to be a general introduction to the behaviour of human beings, and no attempt has been made so far to deal with the particular problem of the child at school. Yet in view of the steadily increasing importance of the school in society (and therefore also for the individual) the book would be incomplete without an extended reference to the psychological problems of school life.

According to a UNESCO estimate there are at present approximately 550 million children between the ages of five and fourteen in the world. Scarcely half of these have access to any kind of formal education.

THE SCHOOL AND THE GROWING DEMANDS MADE BY SOCIETY

The school is an instrument of society. Its function is to imbue the rising generation methodically with skills, knowledge and understanding which will be important to the young people when they later come to work in society. The more complicated and advanced the society that the school serves, the greater the demands made upon the school. The school is also expected to pass on to its pupils the more important basic values of the society.

There are no schools of this kind in very simple communities where children learn the customs of their group from parents, relatives and the other members of the tribe. The economic life of such societies is closely tied up with that of the family group. Specialized training for particular occupations is rare.

All societies strive to achieve as high a degree of uniformity in behaviour as is consistent with the variety of activities which the common life encompasses. In primitive communities the care of children, the acquisition of food for the family, and the transfer of attitudes and values (the process of socialization) are closely interrelated. But highly developed societies incorporate a wide range of specialized activities so that the school – as one of the most uniform instruments of socialization – has come to play an ever-increasing part in the important process of integration.

Home, school and the economic life of society may all pull, at times, in different directions. The onus for resolving any consequent conflicts falls on the school. This is one reason why the school must be a centre of social training. During their most impressionable years nearly all citizens come together in schools which, compared with the diversity of the homes from which the pupils come and the jobs they will go to later, are very like one another. It is true, of course, that some children will have better teachers than others, and that some school buildings may be old-fashioned and other schools well equipped, and that for some children school may be 'just across the street' while others go away to boarding school; but in spite of such variations as these the schools provide an environment which is, in many fundamental respects, uniform for every type of child. Society, by the training it gives to those who take charge of the pupils, and by the demands it makes upon them, and through legal controls and inspections, protects itself from wide fluctuations in the content of education, at least in directions suspected of being dangerous or harmful.

The school and the economic life

An illustration of the way in which the school can perform its integrating function is provided by the pre-vocational training and vocational guidance now given to many children during their last year at school. In some countries these practices are not widespread, in others they are a well-established part of the educational system. In more primitive societies children become familiar with the world of work by watching the activities of their elders and from an early age participating themselves. In an industrial society most adults' work goes on behind doors that are closed to the young – and indeed to all adults not themselves employed in a particular enterprise. This means that parents are no longer in a position to train their children for their future careers, or even in many cases to advise them upon which career will suit them.

Training for industry and vocational guidance are in themselves specialized fields. Here a related branch of applied psychology, occupational psychology, has made valuable contributions towards improving the techniques used by teachers and guidance officers, and also the methods of selection used by employers for finding the right person for a particular job. In Britain there are vocational guidance officers attached to the Ministry of Labour's Youth Employment Service or employed by local education authorities, who may visit schools to advise children about to leave and take up work. Some of these officers, although unfortunately by no means all, have been through special training courses to acquaint them with the appropriate psychological techniques. Many schools supplement this system by allocating to a member or to members of the teaching staff particular responsibility for helping school-leavers in their choice of a career. Talks on jobs and visits to local firms are often arranged. The success of these projects depends to a considerable extent upon the goodwill and co-operation of employers and trade unionists, and much progress has been made in recent years although there is still room for improvement. Too many school-leavers still take the important step from school into their first jobs on the basis of inadequate or distorted pictures of the possibilities the world has to offer.

Nevertheless the important thing to note is that the school has to a very considerable extent taken over the old parental office of preparing children for their initiation into the responsibilities of adult life in a complex modern society.

School and home

The schools have also taken over a share in another of the parent's traditional duties: the training of character. This should of course be seen as a co-operative enterprise. Without good relations between parents and teachers conflicts and tensions inevitably arise. It is only too easy for the teacher to blame 'the home' for all the defects he finds in the child, and for the parent to feel, if he suspects the school of operating different standards from his own, that his authority has been undermined, leaving him helpless and bewildered.

One way of tackling this problem is through the parent–teachers' association, a type of organization which takes different forms in different countries and, in Britain, differs from one school to another. In some schools, however, parent–teacher contact is limited to prize days and occasional open days, and the rare visit to the Head after something has gone wrong. Many headmasters and headmistresses are resistant to the idea of what they feel to be parental interference; and many parents, even when much effort has been put by teachers into the arranging of meetings, feel inadequate or indifferent and stay away. Even the children, at least at certain ages, sometimes view with deep suspicion the prospect of the coming together of the two separate worlds that they inhabit alternately, and would like their parents to have nothing to do with parent–teacher meetings.

Nevertheless it is important that there should be real and continuous communication between all parties concerned in the socialization of the child, or the child may well come to reflect within himself the conflicts and tensions that can take the place of mutual understanding. It is the responsibility of the adults to overcome their doubts and anxieties and work out appropriate forms for such communication if each individual child's full resources are to be developed in the best possible way – an end which is of course in the interest of society as a whole.

There is another reason, particularly important in the context of this book, for emphasizing the importance of co-operation between school, home and vocational life.

In much of the research now being conducted, the superficially separate fields of developmental, educational and occupational psychology come together in their applications to the individual child. So it is important that all those who have the welfare of the child, and of their own society, at heart should be able in some measure to understand and evaluate the work of the scientists. By their efforts to achieve mutual understanding of their respective roles in the preparation of the child for adult life, parents and teachers are themselves contributing to the unending public debate on the aims and values of society which is an essential ingredient in the intellectual life of any democracy: and they are also providing the kind of background that the scientist needs if he is to feel that his findings will be intelligently and fruitfully applied.

MATURATION AND FORMAL EDUCATION

It will be apparent from all that has gone before that the capacity of a developing organism to learn anything new is closely bound up with the process of maturation. Clearly a child cannot learn to write if his motor control is not sufficiently advanced to enable him to hold and guide a pen. Also some minimum of social maturity (including a certain mastery of language, and the ability to concentrate) must be attained before a child can be considered ready for formal education of any kind.

But the issue is not quite as simple as that. In countries where there is compulsory education for all, an age has to be set by law at which all children must begin their school lives. In Britain this age is five, which is low compared with most other countries. In America most children go to school at six or seven according to which State they happen to live in. Seven is the normal school-commencement age in several European countries, including Sweden. Since there is no reason to suppose that the children in all these countries develop at different rates it will be obvious that the child's level of maturity is not the only consideration that the respective authorities were obliged to have in mind when drafting the laws. It is, however, a matter of great importance for teachers and educational psychologists and all who are directly concerned with the child's early education.

Some aspects of this problem have already been touched on in the survey of development given in Chapter IV. The British five-year-old arriving at school on his first day has quite different needs from those of, say, the Swedish seven-year-old. But for either child the first day itself is a very important event in his life. He has been anticipating it for some time. From various sources and in different tones of voice, he has been told what the school expects of him. Some of this information has disturbed him, some has given him confidence. The knowledge that he is a schoolboy at last may increase his importance in his own eyes for a while; the discovery that he is suddenly only one in a crowd may diminish it sharply. The school must respect the child's problem. The wise teacher welcomes and treats the newest member of her class as an individual, knowing that this first formal contact with authority outside the home may have a deep effect upon the development of his attitudes towards education and towards society as a whole.

The concept of 'readiness' in education

What the schools expect of their new pupils does not of course depend merely upon the chronological age at entry. Throughout this book emphasis has been laid upon the fact that norms are abstractions from statistical data: they can tell us nothing about the individual five- or seven-year-old whom we meet for the first time. Above all, they cannot tell us how he 'should' or 'should not' behave. Even within the normal range children differ greatly both in respect of potential and of rate of development.

All teachers are familiar, if only as an outcome of their experience, with the relationship between maturation and learning capacity: they know that it is useless to attempt to force a child to acquire a skill before he has reached the appropriate stage of development. Teachers in Britain are trained to recognize what they term 'reading readiness' and 'writing readiness' in the individual child by watching for the appearance of the necessary perceptual and motor skills during periods of free and guided activity.

Other factors come into a child's readiness for formal education. Charlotte Bühler investigated problems of school maturity as long ago as the 1920's. She attached great importance to what she called 'maturity for work' (*Werkreife*) by which she meant the ability to concentrate on a task until it is finished. She also mentioned that the child must be conscious of certain rules of behaviour. This presumes among other things that social readiness is developed sufficiently to make adaptation to the group possible. In Britain the child passing into the junior school at the age of seven may well have the advantage over his Scandinavian counterpart entering school for the first time, by reason of the higher level of socialization that his infant-school experience has helped him to attain. Even if he has failed to make much progress in the three R's while an 'infant', he still has this advantage.

Tests of school readiness

The English infant-school teacher usually relies upon her own observation to guide her in deciding which of her pupils are ready for formal instruction in the various school subjects. In countries where children start school later it is important that an early assessment of the child's degree of maturity is made so that no time is wasted in getting the child to work at the appropriate level. Interesting comparison can be made with the Swedish practice where specially designed school readiness tests are commonly given – at least in the densely populated urban districts – to children about to start school. These are held at the normal school-entrance age, but if a parent thinks she has a particularly advanced preschool child she may present him for testing before he has reached the age of seven.

These tests are administered by a school psychologist and have proved particularly useful for the early diagnosis of children who will need special attention within the school. New teaching methods and types of class have been created to satisfy the requirements of such pupils. These include what are known as *school readiness classes* for slow developers (these classes are kept small to allow for plenty of individual attention); *observation classes* for nervous, inattentive or aggressive children, where every effort is made to increase the child's feeling of security while at the same time attempting to discover the causes of his disturbance; and *reading classes* for children who show special difficulty in learning to read and write but who are otherwise normally gifted.

A readiness test taken at the age of seven, as in Sweden, would appear to have many advantages. Together with the routine medical examination it provides a double screen through which all junior school entrants must pass, making it possible to pick out many children, mentally, emotionally or physically handicapped, who may be in need of a course of treatment (with, say, a speech therapist, or a child psychologist) or who might be more suitably educated at a special school. Where *every* child passes through the hands of a trained psychologist, it is much easier to discover any problems in their very early stages, and it also relieves the teacher, to a considerable degree, of the responsibility of picking a child out from the class 'to see the psychologist'. This latter method has obvious dangers: it tends to isolate the child and make the parent anxious or suspicious. Indeed, the teacher herself may find it difficult (not being a trained psychologist) to justify in words to a Head who knows the child less well a 'feeling' that something is wrong. In consequence there are still many schools in Britain where the local education authority's psychologists are rarely or never called in for consultation.

Under no system, of course, can the teacher be entirely free from this responsibility, and we shall discuss later her role in maintaining a good standard of mental hygiene in the school. But the selection of children for clinical treatment or for special school education is a highly specialized job requiring not only the use of tailor-made instruments (in the form of diagnostic tests of various kinds) but also the training and experience to assess each individual case on its own merits. The earlier this assessment can be made the better the prognosis for the child.

The selection of children for schools for the educationally subnormal exemplifies the difficulty of the task. Children occasionally fall behind in class by reason of some hitherto undetected physical defect such as slight deafness or eye trouble, and there are other appropriate special schools for such children. Or the trouble may be due to early brain damage, detectable by special tests, and individual remedial teaching may help. Children suitable for schools for the educationally subnormal are for the most part boys and girls with IQs of below 80 whose educational pace has to be much slower than that of the average child. But no decision to transfer a child to any kind of special school should ever be taken on the results of an intelligence test alone. Many children with IQs well below 80 have other personality traits such as ambition and persistence which enable them to hold their own in an ordinary class, while children who produce much higher scores in tests may, either temporarily or permanently, benefit from education in a school where classes are small and emphasis is laid upon acquiring social skills, and where more formal education is taken at a pace to suit the child.

'Streaming' and selection for secondary education
In recent years there has been considerable controversy in educational circles about the practice of dividing children into different 'streams', according to ability, for separate tuition in junior schools, and

(in Britain) the later redistribution of children on the basis of an examination (the 'eleven-plus') into different types of secondary school. Fundamentally the issue is one of weighing the social advantage of educating all children together (both short-term in the form of the aid and stimulation the more advanced children can give to the backward, and long-term through the inculcation at an early age of a sense of mutual responsibility and community) against the possibility of more rapid advance at all levels offered by more homogeneous groups of pupils.

It would be out of place here to enter this discussion at the policy level, but in the past some of the antagonism felt by the opponents of streaming and the eleven-plus has occasionally been redirected on to a scapegoat – the intelligence test which is often used as part of the selection procedure. This is of course as absurd as it would be for a pacifist to condemn tape-measures because they are used in determining whether or not a volunteer is tall enough to join the army.

The predictive value of tests

The theory of intelligence testing has been discussed in Chapter IX, where it was pointed out that elaborate techniques have been devised for standardizing tests and ensuring that they are both reliable and valid (within certain limits). When using a test the important thing (as when using any scientific instrument) is to be sure that we know what questions we expect the test to answer. A test used during a school selection procedure in Britain is designed to answer one question and one only: given three types of school A, B and C with a limited number of places in each, which of the children presenting themselves for testing are likely to do better at school A, which at B and which at C? And if A is a school with a highly academic curriculum the question should mean: which children show most promise in academic subjects? (It should be emphasized here that no psychologist would claim that a test made for this purpose should be used alone to predict, say, technical or mechanical aptitude.) The test is therefore designed to sample the different kinds of mental activity that, in the past, have been shown to correlate well with academic success, and in so far as it succeeds in this it is likely to be a better predictor than even past performance in academic subjects. Extensive research by P. E. Vernon and others tends to support the view that well-designed tests are on the whole successful in this limited objective. Nowadays, where intelligence tests are used in school selection, their results are almost invariably considered in conjunction with reports from teachers upon past performance and/or with straightforward tests in basic school subjects. What neither kind of test can predict is the social effect of differentiated education.

The vast amount of research stimulated by the application of intelligence testing to school selection has spotlighted a number of new problems of direct interest to educationists, which in their turn have been tackled by other research workers. An interesting example of this is provided by the work of Basil Bernstein, a worker in the field of linguistics at the University of London. Bernstein noticed that children from the poorer working-class homes often showed large intra-individual differences in the scores they obtained in different types of intelligence test. Their IQs calculated from tests containing a high proportion of verbal material, might be as much as 20 points below non-verbal test results. It has long been realized that questions phrased in words must be carefully constructed to take account of differences in vocabulary between various social classes (cf. above, Chapter VIII, p. 115 ff).

Bernstein's study investigated social differences in the use of language much more closely than before, and on the basis of detailed analyses of many samples of tape-recorded speech he drew attention to differences in structure and syntax related to the differing uses to which language is put in various types of home. In the poorer homes it is used primarily to increase the social cohesiveness of the family by *references* to common interests; the questioning of parents is discouraged as a challenge to authority. In middle-class homes, questions and speculation are encouraged as a means to assisting the child to differentiate himself from others and individualize his thinking, with the result that he learns to use much more complex sentences which he has to plan in advance (*formal* language). Bernstein's research, by extending our knowledge of the relation between language and intelligence, in turn offers a new challenge to the research worker in educational psychology, whose aim must always be the discovery of educational methods which help to ensure that the resources of every child can be developed to their fullest extent and that, whenever possible, faulty development will be corrected – aims which can only be realized in full when scientist, school and home can communicate and co-operate with each other.

MENTAL HYGIENE IN SCHOOL

Mental health may be defined as the ability to adjust oneself satis-factorily to the changes and problems met with in life. By mental hygiene we mean all measures taken to maintain and foster good mental health. After the home, the school is probably the most im-portant institution in our society from the point of view of mental hygiene.

There are two aspects to mental hygiene, a promotional and a pre-ventive aspect. A healthy school community where high standards are expected, and a sympathetic but watchful attitude maintained towards the deviant, provides the appropriate atmosphere for the promotion of healthy attitudes in all.

A world-wide movement for mental hygiene has developed from the increasing awareness that mental illness is one of the most serious problems of our times. About half of the beds in hospitals have to be reserved for the treatment of the mentally ill. A large proportion of patients in medical and surgical wards also are suffer-ing from one or other of the so-called psychosomatic disorders, of which the physical symptoms are due in part to mental or emotional stress. To these must be added the many people who are so lacking in mental equilibrium that it is extremely difficult for them to live full and happy lives with their fellow creatures but who nevertheless manage to exist, often at a heavy emotional cost to themselves and to their immediate families, outside an institution. The second goal of mental hygiene is to reduce the numbers finding their way into these groups.

TEACHER PERSONALITY

It is hardly conceivable that mental hygiene can be effectively applied in school or anywhere else unless it is in the hands of adequately trained people. (There are, however, teachers who by their very per-sonality have a therapeutic influence, and this is also true of some parents.) One of the functions of a good training college is to devote time to the study and discussion of the development of the person-ality of the teacher. Obviously the ability to learn new attitudes differs very much from one individual to another. It would not be easy to determine how much of a good teacher's personality is the result of general maturation on the one hand, and on the other the result of training.

We must also reckon with widely varying conditions for the difficult work of the teacher. But the possibility of increasing the fitness of a teacher in respect not only of his level of knowledge and teaching skill but also of his ability to appreciate the situation of his pupils, must receive attention as well. It cannot be denied that such things – which are perhaps largely a matter of the individual's general outlook on life – are much more difficult to acquire than knowledge.

Difficulties of judging the suitability of teachers

In most countries endeavours have been made to construct tests to determine a person's fitness for the profession of a teacher, but with little success. C. M. Fleming in her book *Teaching: a Psychological Analysis*, published in 1958, summarizes the most important British and American investigations up to that date and concludes that 'there is no reason to suppose that any one type of personality pattern has a monopoly of the claim to be regarded as that of the potentially successful teacher'. Pupils themselves have very divergent views, that also vary with age, as to the characteristics that go to make up an ideal teacher's personality. A teacher may be eminently successful with pupils of one age but find it difficult to manage an older or younger class.

It is also difficult to predict how a particular training college student will be able to endure the strain of the everyday work of a school. It is one thing to give interesting and even inspiring demonstration lessons during teaching practice and quite another to meet the same class hour after hour, day after day, and keep it at a reasonable level of motivation. Sten Henrysson at the Stockholm School of Education and Eric Linder of the Institute of Education at Uppsala University, have shown that the mark given for teaching proficiency, which used to be taken very seriously by employing authorities, is not in fact a very good criterion of suitability for the teaching profession.

Features of personality appreciated by pupils

Several investigations have been made with a view to discovering what personality traits make a teacher popular with pupils. One such study, made by Witty in the United States, was based on letters on the subject of 'The teacher who has helped me most'. There were 12,000 letters written by schoolchildren from grade 2 upwards to American college level. The letters were analysed to find the characteristic features mentioned most frequently. It does not follow, naturally, that these features are the most important ones for a good teacher. But the letters reflect opinions that it is worth the teacher's while to know, and that he would be wise to take into careful consideration. The following twelve characteristics proved to be the most appreciated: (1) Co-operative, democratic attitude, (2) kindliness and consideration for the individual, (3) patience, (4) wide interests, (5) pleasing manner and appearance, (6) fairness and impartiality, (7) sense of humour, (8) even temperament and firmness, (9) interest in pupils' problems, (10) flexibility, (11) willingness to encourage and praise, and (12) unusual proficiency in teaching a particular subject.

The last-named characteristic is by no means the least important. It is ranked very high in other investigations. Pupils are quite well able to appreciate a high level of knowledge in a teacher.

Mental hygiene and the training of teachers

A teacher in training, then, must be encouraged not to attempt a re-moulding of his personality in imitation of some purely hypothetical ideal but rather to develop the skills which enable him to make the best use of his own most positive personality traits. It has been said that 'teaching cannot be taught' and there may be some truth in this. A training college lecturer is generally a highly experienced and skilful teacher himself and has many ideas and hints to give a prospective teacher. The student would be stupid not to listen to them, but it may well be that the student's relationship with his future pupils will be influenced more deeply by the lecturer's attitude to his own students than by anything he tells them in formal lectures. In no sphere of training is an attitude of 'do as I say, don't do as I do' less likely to be successful.

The student must feel free to experiment boldly with various methods of teaching. Like an artist (and teaching is an art) he has to find for himself his own individual style. The young student in particular sometimes thinks of the people who train him as a race apart, people who 'think they know it all', unable to appreciate the problems of the beginner. A relaxed and sympathetic relationship between student and tutor, within which the student feels himself able to expand and develop and also find understanding support when he needs it, is fundamental to good teacher-training.

The teaching profession is one that makes very great demands, mentally and emotionally, upon those who practise it. Failure may mean personal tragedy. Not only the pupils', but also the teacher's progress through school may become a *via dolorosa*, and for the teacher this path is with his life-work. More insight into the problems of the psychology of personality should – even if one has only moderate faith in what training can do here – reduce the number of teachers suffering this fate. This in itself would be an important achievement not only for the teacher, but for pupils and schools in general.

A teacher must endeavour to become a fully alive human being who never ceases to work for his own further development. The teacher who can feel that his pupils stimulate his own improvement, and who sees in teaching something meaningful – which, of course, it is – has acquired some of the fundamental requirements for success in his work. And he must be helped to reach this goal during his training.

The preventive aspect of mental hygiene

A distinction between the preventive and the promotional aspects of mental hygiene is made here only for practical reasons. Obviously, if good mental health is promoted, ill-health is prevented. But the seeds of serious maladjustment and even delinquency are usually sown before the child begins his school life and one of the functions of the school must be to prevent, if possible, the flowering. Within a healthy school environment the unstable child sometimes finds, with help, his own adjustment. In other cases small symptoms, if overlooked, become progressively graver and the child may need specialist psychiatric attention.

It is therefore important, particularly in a country like Britain where the psychologist is not a member of the school staff but must be called in for consultation when problems arise, that the teacher should know how to recognize the danger signals.

Grave and less grave symptoms

Some insight into this problem can be obtained from two American studies in which a comparison was made between the opinions of teachers and of child psychiatrists on the relative importance of different symptoms of maladjustment in schoolchildren. Fifty symptoms of nervous disorder were placed in rank order, and marked differences appeared between the two groups of raters.

The first investigation, which was made at the end of the 1920's (Wickman), showed greater divergences than the one made in the early 1950's (Stouffer). This suggests that the teachers in the later investigation had come nearer to adopting the mental hygiene viewpoint towards different symptoms of maladjustment. Not surprisingly teachers are inclined to assign greater importance to symptoms that disturb school work. Among the symptoms deemed the ten most serious, both groups of raters included asocial, retiring behaviour; unhappiness and depression; cruelty and arrogance; stealing and pilfering. But anxiety, suspicion, shyness, bed-wetting, touchiness and sensitivity, which were ranked high by the psychiatrists, were rather low on the teachers' lists. Unreliability, mendacity, playing truant, recalcitrance, defiance and cheating were found among the ten most serious symptoms in the teachers' ratings, but were regarded by the other raters as less grave.

Symptoms ranked low by both groups were inattention, slipshod dress, laziness, disobedience and lack of order in class. This may suggest that the teachers were rather advanced in their attitudes. Teachers with less insight into the principles of mental hygiene might well have made quite different ratings. It must be borne in mind, however, that there is no unanimity among specialists in mental hygiene regarding the order of gravity of the different symptoms.

Some general conclusions may be drawn from the results of these investigations. Most important, perhaps, is the emphasis laid on social relations. It seems probable that some of the most troublesome types of behaviour are at bottom attempts to win attention, and so may be said to have their roots in an inability to make social contacts.

The means employed by a person to escape from underlying tensions have been dealt with in some detail in the chapter on emotional development. In addition to the section on defence mechanisms (p. 150 ff.), the account of the cue function of the organism (p. 166 ff.) is very relevant. From the chapter on emotion (Chapter X) onwards, nearly every question discussed has some bearing upon mental hygiene.

Help for the deviant

In the undoubtedly difficult situation that is sometimes the teacher's lot in the school of today, it may seem ridiculous to demand that he make efforts to develop his own personality. He might answer that he has too many problems connected with the behaviour of his pupils to pay much attention to his own. And, of course, successful teaching requires goodwill on both sides. Demands must be made on the pupils too: it is one of the most important functions of a school to make these demands felt in its very atmosphere.

'Goodwill' in the sense in which the term is being used here implies that a person is inclined to direct his behaviour towards goals generally accepted by his society, so long as these do not violate his individual sense of justice. Such an attitude must be strong enough to prevent impulsive actions in directions opposed to these goals. An upbringing that has been indifferent to, or has ignored, socially approved goals must hamper the development of this kind of goodwill.

The circumstances described by Durkheim (see p. 226 ff.) in his theory of delinquency may be responsible in some degree for this type of maladjustment. Where positive social controls are lacking, or are only erratically applied, the sort of social learning necessary for the development of goodwill cannot take place: there must be opportunities to practise it. It is customary to blame the home when things go wrong, but it must be realized that the chain of causes goes very deep and has many origins.

Instead of looking round for someone to blame, it seems more urgent in these cases to try to re-direct the motivation behind the deviant action impulses into more favourable activities. This is not easy. Attitudes, and methods of meeting life's various demands, may have set into very firm patterns by the time the young deviant reaches the hands of the psychologist. It is important, of course, to distinguish between misbehaviour which is the result of the age the child has reached (Fig. XV.5) and fundamentally wrong personality development.

For the really difficult case individual treatment, perhaps at a child guidance clinic, by a child psychiatrist or psychotherapist may be the only solution. Methods have been developed for the elucidation of such disturbances, which may often help to relieve the young patient of his more troublesome symptoms.

THE EDUCATIONAL PSYCHOLOGIST

Enough has been said in the course of this chapter to give some idea of the role of the educational psychologist. His exact duties vary from place to place, but he is always somewhere near the centre of the battle to prevent mental illness. In some countries his function is that of a kind of watchdog within the school, remaining on guard for any signs of danger during the years of development. In others he plays a considerable part in therapy. He is usually a teacher who has taken a degree in psychology and received a further specialized training in the problems of childhood and adolescence.

In Britain he usually works as a member of a child guidance team in close collaboration with a psychiatrist (who treats or supervises the treatment of young patients) and a psychiatric social worker whose particular concern is with the patient's home. The psychologist is the member of the team who first sees the child, tests him, and prepares the report on his condition which forms the basis of the first conference.

In some cases, he takes part in the treatment of the child, or he may give remedial teaching to children with special educational difficulties. For this reason it is important that he should be able to win the confidence of troubled children quickly and set them at their ease in a situation which for them may be heavy with anxiety. He must have a good knowledge of the techniques of testing and of the tests available, but he must also be able to interpret the results in the light of his own observations and judgement.

Because he is the member of the team in direct contact with the school it is also his responsibility to establish and maintain good relations with teachers and particularly with head teachers. He may find it necessary in some cases to break down old prejudices. 'Psychology' is still a witch-word in some quarters. Above all he must avoid giving the impression that he is 'interfering', and he must feel as well as show a proper appreciation of the efforts and difficulties of the teachers and administrators in the school.

THE PSYCHIATRIC SOCIAL WORKER

Behind nearly every disturbed child there is a troubled home. Even where the child's maladjustment cannot be directly ascribed to home difficulties, it may well be causing them. More and more we are coming to see mental ill-health as a product of social conditions and the cure often entails the alleviation of some problem in the patient's background. The preparation of a family case history is a job best performed by a trained social worker.

Sometimes the difficulties may have been caused by material conditions, such as overcrowding; sometimes a parent is found to be in need of advice and support, which the social worker can give, or of psychiatric treatment which the sufferer must be persuaded to accept. In Britain, the Family Service Units have done invaluable work in the rehabilitation of problem families where, through ill-health, low intelligence or inadequacy of personality, the family situation has got completely out of hand. The members of these units are not necessarily trained psychiatric social workers. They may be called in to assist the family, and will sometimes make it their first job to set about cleaning and redecorating the house with the help of the mother who in this way is given encouragement and trained in the duties of a housewife at one and the same time. In all this work the emphasis is upon getting the family functioning as a satisfactory social unit and so providing an environment conducive to a better standard of physical and mental health.

In this chapter on children and school the word 'co-operation' has appeared on page after page. In its important task of socialization the school cannot work in a vacuum. Among the schoolteacher's collaborators we have had occasion to mention the pupils themselves, the parents, the wider community as represented by employers and trade unionists, and such specialists as the vocational guidance officer, the educational psychologist, the psychiatrist and the social worker, as well as the scientific research workers in various disciplines, who are supplying the practitioners with the knowledge and the tools they need for their work. The interdependence of all its members is one of the most striking features of a complex modern society and nowhere is this interdependence more marked than in the field of mental hygiene.

SUGGESTIONS FOR
FURTHER READING

CHARLOTTE BÜHLER: *From Birth to Maturity. The Child and his Family*. Routledge, 1935

L. CARMICHAEL (ed.): *Manual of Child Psychology*. Chapman & Hall, 1954

J. H. FLAVELL: *The Developmental Psychology of Jean Piaget*. Van Nostrand, 1963

B. M. FOSS (ed.): *Determinants of Infant Behaviour*. Vol. I–II Methuen, 1961, 1963

A. GESELL and C. S. AMATRUDA: *The Embryology of Behaviour*. Hamish Hamilton, 1945

A. GESELL, FRANCES L. ILG and LOUISE B. AMES: *Youth: the Years from Ten to Sixteen*. Hamish Hamilton, 1956

J. A. HADFIELD: *Childhood and Adolescence*. Penguin Books, 1962

J. HEMMING: *Problems of Adolescent Girls*. Heinemann, 1960

HILDE HIMMELWEIT, A. N. OPPENHEIM and PAMELA VINCE: *Television and the Child*. Oxford University Press, 1958

SUSAN ISAACS: *Intellectual Growth in Young Children*. Routledge, 1930. *The Nursery Years*. Routledge, 1932

MARGARET MEAD and M. WOLFENSTEIN: *Childhood in Contemporary Cultures*. Cambridge University Press, 1956

P. H. MUSSEN, J. J. CONGER and J. KAGAN: *Child Development and Personality*. Harper & Row, 1963 (2nd Ed.)

E. A. PEEL: *The Psychological Basis of Education*. Oliver & Boyd, 1956

J. PIAGET: *The Language and Thought of the Child*. Routledge, 1948

J. PIAGET and BÄRBEL INHELDER: *The Early Growth of Logic*. New York: Harper & Row, 1964

ROSS STAGNER: *Personality*. McGraw-Hill, 1961

R. THOMSON: *The Psychology of Thinking*. Penguin Books, 1959

L. P. THORPE: *Child Psychology and Development*. New York: The Ronald Press Co., 1955

C. W. VALENTINE: *The Normal Child and some of his Abnormalities*. Penguin Books, 1956

THELMA VENESS: *School Leavers*. Methuen, 1962

P. E. VERNON: *Intelligence and Attainment Tests*. University of London Press, 1960

ACKNOWLEDGMENTS

We are grateful to the following for permission to reproduce illustrations of which they are the copyright owners. The illustrations are referred to by the numbers of the pages on which they occur.

Arne Arnqvist, 194, 196

Davenport Hooker, 32

Life Magazine, 124

Lennart Olson, 48

Anna Riwkin, 54, 62

Sune Spångberg, 18, 38, 50, 104, 120, 125

T. W. Todd and the C. V. Mosby Company, St Louis, 67

INDEX OF NAMES

INDEX OF SUBJECTS